Still
Standing
X

Still Standing x

Kerry Katona

THE AUTOBIOGRAPHY

This edition first published in Great Britain in 2012 by
Orion Books
an imprint of the Orion Publishing Group Ltd
Orion House, 5 Upper St Martin's Lane,
London WC2H 9EA

An Hachette UK Company

1 3 5 7 9 10 8 6 4 2

A CIP catalogue record for this book is available
from the British Library.

HB ISBN: 978 1 4091 2740 6
ETPB: 978 1 4091 2745 1

Printed in Great Britain by
CPI Group (UK) Ltd, Croydon CR0 4YY

The Orion Publishing Group's policy is to use papers that are natural,
renewable and recyclable and made from wood grown in sustainable
forests. The logging and manufacturing processes are expected to
conform to the environmental regulations of the country of origin.

Every effort has been made to fulfil requirements with regard to
reproducing copyright material. The author and publisher will
be glad to rectify any omissions at the earliest opportunity.

www.orionbooks.co.uk

For Molly, Lilly, Heidi and Max.

I've done a lot of things wrong in my life
but when I look at you I know I've done some things right!

Contents

Acknowledgements

Wow, I feel like I've been through a ton of therapy writing this book – it's great to get so much off my chest – good and bad, it's all part of my journey and I hope you enjoy reading it. I've been to a lot of dark places in the 7 years this book covers but I am still standing and have come through it all. I'd particularly like to thank everyone who still supports me after all this time and through the tough times, especially my mum and Nana Betty, Danielle Brown, Cheryl and Milica, Mag and Fred, Martin, Kate and all the Bold team, Nik and Eva Speakman, Peter Andre, Gaz and Karen, Sharon Smith, Chrissie, Lisa and everyone at *OK*, the lovely Lorraine McCulloch, Daniel Whiston, Lynsey, Paul and Ian Armstrong for welcoming me into their family; Amy Weston, Emma Fowers, Emma Donnan, Amanda and everyone at Orion (thanks for bearing with me)! And last but not least a big thank you to both of my ex-husbands for giving me my four fantastic children who are the best thing that has ever happened to me.

So Alone

I slumped back against the bathroom wall and slid to the floor, crying my heart out. I was completely destroyed and heartbroken, and felt like my life was over.

I was only 25 years old, but was sure I'd failed as a woman, as a mother, and as a wife. My husband, the singer Brian McFadden, had left me for another woman. It was now 17 months since he had uttered the words that had ended my world: 'I don't love you any more'. But I couldn't get over him. Instead, despite sessions in rehab, I was sliding into another downward spiral and I couldn't find a way out. I was also starting to date a guy called Mark Croft, and I knew, deep down, he was bad news.

Why didn't Brian want me? Why couldn't he still love me? I had gone over and over and over those questions so many times in the past months, never finding an answer.

All I had ever wanted was to get married and have a dad for my kids, with us all under the same roof. It was something I never had growing up and was the thing I had always promised myself I would get right with my own family. And the fact that I hadn't, on top of the feelings of rejection, was destroying me.

As I sat on the floor that night, I looked out the bathroom door at the hotel room I was staying in, and cried even harder. Because

I was staying in The Conrad Hotel in Chelsea Harbour in London – now called The Wyndham Grand – the same hotel where so much of my life with Brian had been played out.

We had been together from the age of 19 till I was 24 – it was the longest relationship I have ever had – and so many of our nights together happened in that hotel. But in particular, it was where both our babies had been conceived. Our two beautiful girls, Molly and Lilly, both now growing up without their dad around.

And I kept thinking, 'Who is going to hold me at night for the rest of my life? Who will give me that supportive hug when I need it?' Not that Brian was there that often in our marriage, between touring and recording commitments, while I was home alone in our house in Ireland with the kids. But at least I had believed he would always come back.

I knew I was getting myself into a mess, and a night spent crying over the state of my life was not helping things. Then a little thought popped up in my mind: 'What if Brian is thinking the same thing? Maybe a bit of him regrets not giving our marriage and life with the kids another go?'

It had all ended so suddenly, back in 2004. At the time I had known in my heart, whether he would admit it to himself or not, that the main reason he wanted out was how close he was getting to Delta Goodrem. He had been doing a duet with the Australian singer, and I remember him asking if I would go and meet her with him. I was doing the *Loose Women* TV show that day, so I said I couldn't.

He went on his own, and when he came back he kept saying, 'She's a massive fan of yours, Kerry. She can't wait to meet you, she's beautiful.' He just kept going on and on and on about her.

Eventually, I asked straight out, 'Do you fancy her?' But he said no.

Well, I've watched documentaries on his life since, which have shown footage of him and Delta in the studio at the time we were still together. She is so tall and slim, and classy, compared to a small, curvy and gobby northern lass like me. No wonder he had fancied her. And the sexual tension between them was right obvious. Even I, who really didn't want to see that, couldn't deny it. I was gobsmacked, but it was obvious there was absolutely nothing I could have done to have stopped the pair of them ending up together.

But that night in the hotel, I kept thinking, 'What if he had rushed into things with her too quickly? What if the early days of romance and sexual chemistry had worn off and he was sitting there wishing he could get back with me and have our family back together again?' And although I knew it was only a tiny chance, I decided to ring him.

So I called his mobile, and he answered, and I started crying all over again. I could hardly get myself together enough to get the words out, but finally I did.

'Brian, we need to get back together.' I sniffed. 'Please, can't we have some kind of counselling? We can make this work.'

He sighed. 'Kerry, it's too late. You'll be alright.'

I was desperate. 'Please, Brian! The girls need you, I need you! Give us another chance. We have to make this work, we've got kids together. We should be a family.'

'Kerry, it's too late, I've moved on, I'm with Delta now. I don't love you. Goodbye.'

I slid down onto the bathroom floor crying, broken, and hysterical. I had never felt so alone or so, so low. For me, that had been the last-ditch phone call, my final appeal for help and a chance to get my life back on track – and it had failed. So that was it. Game over.

Me mum Sue was in the next-door room, but I couldn't even turn to her for help. I was down in London because I had interviews to do, and she had come with me and brought a friend. But the three of us had gone out on a bender, and ended up having a huge row when she tried to warn me off dating Mark. So I had booked a separate hotel room from her, and we had gone to bed not talking.

So I sat there for the next few hours sobbing on my own. I don't think I have ever felt so miserable and lost in my life. How had everything, that had seemed so right, gone so horribly wrong?

And I'll admit, as well as my pain over being left by the man I loved, there was an element of ego. No one wants their marriage to be a failure, but I think because of where I had grown up in Warrington in Cheshire, I had an even stronger wish for it to succeed. No one else I had been friends with from the town was going on to do anything. But there was me, off as an international pop star, and with the perfect pop star husband to top it off! With my position in the limelight, it felt like I had more to lose, and even more to prove. So my embarrassment when I failed was worse because of it. I felt myself spiralling back to the old Kerry, away from my glamorous lifestyle, and I was desperate to stop it.

When I had met Brian, I had been in the girl band Atomic Kitten. Getting into the group had been great – it had taken me away from Warrington and from the unsettled, and often traumatic childhood I had gone through. But mentally I had felt like I was still attached to the past, and all the negative thoughts and way of life that come with it – until I met Brian, that is.

He had been in Westlife, a bunch of five Irish lads managed by Louis Walsh, who were on the same TV Hits tour as Atomic Kitten. Brian was just five months older than me, and we instantly got on as friends, but as I got to know him more, I started falling for him and we began dating. It wasn't easy for us – band members at that time were always supposed to be single, as fans didn't like to see you paired up.

But I couldn't help myself. He was like my knight in shining armour. He understood me. He listened when I told him about my childhood – my lack of a father, my difficult relationship with me mum, and my years spent in care homes and with foster parents. So when he proposed to me on my first trip to Ireland with him, he gave me a new hope of creating a real family unit. One that would make my dysfunctional upbringing a thing of the past.

But my dream of creating a life together had failed. And now I knew that what I was getting into with my new boyfriend Mark was bad. It felt like we were on a destructive spiral and the ending was not going to be good news. But I didn't know how to stop it, and I wanted someone else to take responsibility and stop me. I wanted Brian to stop me. I thought being back with him could fix things, and I wanted him to be my knight in shining armour all over again. But he had knocked back the role and that destroyed me.

I knew Brian could be cold – he didn't seem to think about it twice when he split with his last girlfriend, S Club 7's Hannah Spearritt, after meeting me – but I didn't feel like I knew the new Brian. How could he cut me, his wife, not to mention his daughters, out of his life in the way he had done?

I thought of my babies, tucked up in bed, back home in Warrington with the nanny, and it broke my heart to think of them growing up without their dad around. Molly was four at the time, and Lilly was two, and I tried to protect them from our split, by pretending that Brian and I were still the best of friends. They were so young I think they just accepted that, but it was hard. I had never imagined I would be bringing them up alone, I had always thought it was something Brian and I would be doing together. The four of us there for each other, a proper family.

I cried through the night, as I tortured myself going over and over everything that had gone wrong in my life. Finally at one point I made my way to the bed. There I fell in and out of sleep, waking up to think it had all been a bad dream – before I found out life really was as bad as I remembered, and crying until I drifted off again.

The next day, Mark came down to London on the train. He had actually been due to drive us all down the day before, but I hadn't seen him for the two days before because he had gone on a drinking binge. So when he turned up that morning all ready to drive, I was furious and upset. He had known I was relying on him, so I felt really let down by him – there was no way he was in any fit state to drive. And I wasn't sure I wanted to be with someone who would just disappear like that for a couple of days, without getting in touch. So we had rowed, I got a different driver and paid for him, and Mark had stayed behind.

He wasn't happy about it, and he'd been kicking off and screaming down the phone all day. But I was just ignoring him and trying to get on with the day.

It had been our first serious argument, but I felt damn sure I had been in the right.

The next day, maybe he felt bad over his behaviour, maybe he thought he was missing out, or maybe he already had his mind on a bigger master plan that I was oblivious to. Whatever it was, while I was still lying in bed, he turned up at the hotel.

I wasn't in any mood to see him – I was still upset from the night before and knew my eyes were swollen and my head hurt. I'd pretty much cried all night, and I hadn't really forgiven Mark for his behaviour. When he came in, I told him I wasn't feeling very well to explain my appearance and he was being extra nice to me, giving me cuddles and looking after me.

But I kept looking at him and going over my thoughts from the night before, and I just knew he wasn't Brian. While I didn't mind dating him to distract myself, I definitely didn't see a future with him. We had fun and that, but he was hardly husband material.

But even as all these thoughts were going through my head, he pulled out a ring and went,

'Do you want this, then?'

I stared at it, not understanding. Then I realised it was a big diamond on a gold band – this was no apology present. It could only be an engagement ring.

Suddenly it was like a light bulb pinged in my head, and I thought, 'I need to fill this hole in my life that Brian has left. This could work.' And for some stupid, stupid reason, that I will never be able to explain, in that instant I thought I could I replace the relationship I had with Brian, with Mark. Despite all the doubts about Mark and about our relationship, which I had been going over literally seconds before, and despite the fact he had been my boyfriend for only six weeks, I just thought, 'Sod it, I have nothing to lose.'

So I made one of the biggest mistakes of my life, and took the ring.

Life After Rehab

I remember clearly when I first met Mark. It was September 2005, and I was back home in Warrington after a six-week stay in rehab in Arizona. I had gone there to be treated for depression, as well as for drug- and alcohol-related problems. The drug bit related to cocaine, which was a drug I had dabbled in over the years, but since my split from Brian I had felt myself starting to rely on it too heavily and wanted to stop. I had been taking it back in Warrington with me mum and friends, and it was becoming too regular. Add that to the epic drinking benders I had been going on, and bouts of depression where I felt like I couldn't cope with life, and it had definitely seemed like something needed to be done. So off to the Cottonwood de Tucson rehab centre in America I had gone.

It felt like it had done me the world of good, and I had come back to the UK with a positive attitude and clean of drugs. But I was very nervous of being back in my hometown, and especially near my friends and Mum.

Walking off the aeroplane, making the journey back to Warrington, I felt tense and twisted up inside. I really, really wanted to stay clean, and I thought I could do it. I knew it wasn't going to be easy, though, and as I got closer and closer to home, the more nervous I got. I was dying to see my children, but I was scared too.

When you are in that rehab centre, it is basically like you are in a cage, but one that makes you feel protected and really safe.

Then, when you come out of rehab, it is like you are coming into a world that's unsafe. All the temptations from your old way of life are suddenly in front of you, and you can't be sure you won't give in to them, so yes, coming home was scary.

And once I was back at my house in Winwick Park, I didn't know what to do with myself. I really wanted to stay clean, and the day I left rehab I was determined I was going to stick to it. But back home in Warrington, it was so hard because I felt so alone. It didn't help that my house, which I had moved into after splitting from Brian, had five bedrooms, so it felt big and empty when I wandered round it on my own.

It was a lovely house, though. It was on a private estate, and had a big garden that backed onto a park with a playground, which was great for the kids. I didn't want to give it up and move away – and I couldn't move house to anywhere else anyway, as I didn't know people elsewhere. Brian had been my escape route, and when we had gone to Ireland I had escaped my old life. But now he was gone, I didn't know where to go except back to Warrington. I had already uprooted the kids from Ireland back to England; I didn't want to do it again to somewhere new.

But a lot of my friends back there, the friends I had had for years before I was even famous, were not the kind that were going to encourage me to escape drugs. Because they had no escape either, so they really didn't know how to get out of that world. You have to remember, I was brought up in a pretty awful area, with some of the worst kinds of people – the cokeheads, the smackheads, the thieves, the backstabbers and the slappers… that was all I knew. Luckily enough I've never been a slapper, I've never been a smackhead, and I've never been a backstabber, so I've avoided three of those pitfalls. But I took coke and that was my life.

So for six lonely weeks back in Warrington, I fought a daily battle to stay away from my old friends and my old life. I would think about giving in, but I would resist, and I tried to keep myself busy by focusing on my future plans.

I had joined the band Atomic Kitten as a founding member when I was 18, alongside Natasha Hamilton and Liz McClarnon. We had four Top 20 singles and toured all over the world, before I left in 2001, when I was pregnant with Molly – ironically, just as the fifth single 'Whole Again' hit Number One. Then I had turned my hand to TV presenting, appearing on and presenting a whole host of shows. The most memorable was *I'm A Celebrity... Get Me Out of Here!* in 2005. That was a crazy few weeks, but I survived life in the jungle and came out as the eventual winner. After surviving a snake under my bed, panic attacks and being trapped in a tank with leeches, eels and spiders – to mention just a few of the nightmares I endured – I was crowned Queen of the Jungle by the public, a real high point for me. After that I had turned my hand to acting – I got a part in an Irish drama called *Showbands*, and although I was very nervous because acting was new to me, I loved it! It was a big hit in Ireland and kind of cemented the brilliant relationship I have with the people of Ireland to this day.

So it was now a case of trying to focus on what I wanted to do next with my career, and then really going for it, to make that happen.

At the same time, I was also spending as much time with Molly and Lilly as possible. I would take them down to the park, and play on the swings and the slide. Or Lilly would tell me to 'Play music!' back in the house, and I'd put on a CD and we'd dance around like crazy girls! Even back when they were so young, those two loved performing, and at the first sound of music, they would be wiggling around and getting me to spin them round and round. Other times we would just curl up in bed, the three of us together, and watch cartoons, or sometimes I even showed them old videos of me from my days back in Atomic Kitten. Obviously they didn't understand what job I had done, they just about realised it was 'Mummy' on the screen, but they found that funny enough in itself!

I was also kept busy for a few days with my new job. While I had been in Arizona, I had received a call from my management: 'Supermarket chain Iceland want you to be their "Face of Iceland".'

I was over the moon about that, and it had given my confidence a real lift – people still had faith in me, and wanted to see me on their television screens! I was worried that Brian leaving me, and then ending up in rehab, might have made people turn on me, so my confidence in myself and my career was very low, but this was a proper boost. I felt real hope again.

Going to film the first advert, I was so excited! I have always really enjoyed acting, and found that it comes quite naturally to me. So that day I went to Manchester, where Iceland had a shop in their headquarters, which we used for filming. They had rented out a house to be my house for the purposes of the advert. From the minute I walked on set, I loved it. Sitting having my makeup done, and talking with the crew, we were making each other laugh. They were great fun. I also had my stylist Lorraine McCullough on set with me, which was brilliant. She's a great friend, who has always been there for me. She knows what I'm going through on quite a few levels, having divorced a very famous pop star herself.

The idea for the advert was that I was a celeb mum getting food delivered, and it was cheap, great food. And of course I had to say at the end, 'That's why mums go to Iceland!' Ah, that famous saying. I love it! Ever since it was first aired, people have said it to me in the street, and I have never got tired of it.

It was an exhausting first day – I think we were there filming for about 14 hours in the end, and the next couple of days were about the same. But then it was all done and wrapped up, which was a satisfying feeling.

Then there was a big gap until I would be filming again. Iceland said they would bring me in to record adverts a couple of times a year, depending on promotions and things, and then I would do voiceovers and radio chats for them too as needed.

Once this first lot of filming was done, it was back to Warrington life again. Obviously I was still a working mum and I wanted to give the girls the best support I could, so I had a wonderful live-in nanny called Cheryl, an older American woman. Having her there gave me freedom to work, without worrying about childcare, and she was really good with them in day-to-day life as well. I couldn't make up for the fact their daddy wasn't there, but she was great at helping me bring the girls up in the best way possible. Not that her being there could fill the loneliness of being a single mum.

My best friend at this time was a girl called Lisa Rhodes, who was living with her boyfriend David and son Callum, and they moved in with me temporarily to give me support, which was great of them.

Lisa's mum and my mum lived together as roommates when Lisa and I were babies, so I literally have known her my whole life. She was only six months older than me, and was in the year above me at school, but that didn't stop us hanging out together all the time. We were especially close during our teen years, and she taught me things most girls learn from their mums. But my Mum wasn't a normal mum, which is where Lisa had come in. She taught me plenty of life basics – even things like how to put in a tampon! She was always very protective of me, and as I got famous she was proud of me and would come to photo shoots and every TV show with me – we had so many great times together. So it was typical of her that she moved in to help me after rehab.

But obviously I couldn't make her sit home with me and live a healthy lifestyle, just because that is what I was trying to do at the time. And I remember one night there was a whole group going on a night out, and I said I would give it a miss, and stay home and babysit everyone's children. So I stayed home on my own with the kids. But as soon as they were in bed, and I was sat on the sofa on my own, I started thinking. I began wondering what was happening to my life. Here I was, in this lovely house with my two beautiful kids, but there was no man with me, nobody to share it. And being clean didn't seem to help. In fact, being clean seemed to make it worse somehow – it suddenly felt like the reason I was stuck in all alone. All sorts of thoughts were going through my head, and I felt so left out and lonely, that I really started doubting I could keep this up. I was starting to convince myself that maybe the real me was destined to dabble in drink and drugs for the rest of my life, but as long as I kept it under control, it wouldn't be a problem. It is amazing how persuasive your mind can be at times like that.

They all came back to the house at the end of the night, all drunk, and when they woke up hungover the next day, I needed to escape the house.

I'd decided I couldn't isolate myself away from everyone forever. So, since my kids were with the nanny that day, I went round to Mum's house, around the corner from mine, to see her. She lived in a terraced house on Dickinson Street – imagine Coronation Street, and you've got it!

'Y'alright, our Kez?' she said, answering the door and giving me a kiss hello. She's a big lady, is Mum: years of an unhealthy lifestyle and medical problems have taken their toll, and she has huge boobs, so a welcome hug from her always kind of buries me in there!

We went through the front room, which takes you straight into the living room, and we sat on the sofa to catch up. It was a familiar place for me, as I'd spent many a day sat in that immaculate room – Mum is pretty OCD when it comes to cleaning – but the link to the past was not at all good. I realised as soon as I sat down that I was daft to go round her house when I was trying to stay clean. One of the things you learn in rehab is about association: who and what do you associate with drugs? Well, me mum and her house are definitely two of the strongest associations I have with cocaine, as soon as I walk through her front door.

We had always comforted each other with it. Mum would regularly ring up, 'I'm feeling depressed', and I'd think, 'Right, I'll take her a bag of coke. That will cheer her up.' And when I did try and get clean any time, say by going to Arizona, she was never supportive. I remember ringing her from out there to see how she was getting on, and she told me she was doing a line of coke. I know that is her humour, but I was like: 'Thanks, Mum, very helpful!'

So I hadn't been there long, when I really started itching for that feeling. The last six weeks of being a hermit, feeling like I was missing out on a life everyone else was enjoying, were taking their toll. And after the night before, staying in as babysitter while everyone else partied, I was feeling rebellious. I kept trying to push it to the back of my mind, reminding myself of everything I had gone through in Arizona, and how much I wanted to be clean. But it seemed a distant memory back in Warrington, where the reality of life was right in front of me. And the urge kept getting stronger and stronger until eventually I said, 'Ugh, I know I'll regret this. But let's order some coke.'

At that moment, despite all the good work I had done in rehab, I just couldn't imagine my life without coke in it. Mum has had various addictions over the years, be it certain bad men, alcohol, coke or whatever, and as a role model she is hardly the best. It was Mum who introduced me to drugs when I tried speed in a pub toilet with her and her then girlfriend Tina. (Yes, she decided she was a lesbian at one point.) I was only 14 years old at the time, and it was like it opened a door to another world for me, which I had never fully managed to shut again.

And nor had Mum, not that I think she had even tried much. It never occurred to me to take her to rehab when I went – I don't think she would have gone anyway, and I always used to think, if I am being brutal, that she was just too far gone to be saved by it.

Our relationship has always been a bit different to the usual mother-daughter relationship. In fact, Mum didn't really take on that role at all. As I grew up, she was too busy to be my role model, lurching from one bad relationship to another, partying, arguing, and taking drugs. Sometimes I was living with her, sometimes with other family or close friends, and at other times in refuges or with different sets of foster parents.

It was hardly traditional, and has caused me a lot of pain and heartache over the years, but Mum and I have got by in our own way. I would be there for her the dozens of times she slit her wrists – whether suffering from depression, and believing she wasn't good enough for this world, or just as a cry for help. We are more like friends – or more often than not, I'm like the mother protecting her, and she is the daughter. We have had incredible falling-outs over the years, but at the end of the day she is my family. Pretty much the only family I have got.

As for my friends, they had all become really close to Mum while I had been living in Ireland. It was like she kind of took everybody off me, which annoyed me, as I thought, 'Why can't she make her own friends?' So by the time I was back, my friends were actually spending more time with her than me.

She was putting so much pressure on me to get my career back on track so there was money coming in, it was horrendous. And she had thought I should still be with Brian – the split shocked and upset her almost as much as me – so she was making me feel like without him I wasn't good enough. I remember when it happened, going round her house and just sitting silent and numb in the corner. I was in shock. But Mum was wailing and panicking as though it was her marriage that had ended. She kept saying, 'Look at all the paps outside. How am I going to cope? My life is totally fucked!' And everyone was gathering round her, comforting her.

She was playing so many games with my head at that time, and I was not in a good place to handle it. Our relationship was a really hard one. She would sit and have a go at me sometimes, just out of the blue: 'You're just as bad a mum as I am.' And I would be like: 'Look, I know I'm not perfect. But I've never slit my wrists in front of my kids, my kids have never even seen me drunk, let alone touch drugs. I'd never let my kids do it.'

Not that you can ever make the decision for someone, but I will do everything in my power to convince my kids it is the wrong choice. You will certainly never see me giving it to them.

But to be fair, despite the bad stuff, Mum and I had our good times too, we still had a laugh and fun together. I could talk to her about a lot of things, and she knew me inside out.

And on this particular day, she was also my drugs partner.

By this time, none of Mum's usual dealers would go round her house anymore, because of the stories about me in the newspapers. There had been some articles about me doing cocaine, and they didn't want to be caught up in it and found out.

But then Mum said, 'I've started using this other guy, he'll sort us out.'

I told her, 'Don't let him see me here. I don't want him thinking I'm doing it. I'm clean now.'

'Don't worry about it. This guy Mark, he's sound. I can ring him at daft 'o clock and he'll be here, so he's a good 'un.'

So a bit later I was sat in the room in front of the fire and this guy came through Mum's back gate and walked in before I could move. He had a baseball cap on, and these dirty clothes, and was one of the ugliest people I've ever seen in my life. I swear to God, he looked like a proper little scally.

'Oh God,' I thought, and just went 'Hiya' and tried to keep myself separate from the whole thing.

'Alright there?' he nodded, and carried on with this arrogant attitude, as though he reckoned he was the big I Am.

I suddenly realised I knew him – or, at least, knew about him. Everything fell into place. I had a friend called Michelle Hunter and she had a friend called Louise Oortwyn. I had known her since I was about 14, but I wasn't friends with her. She wanted to look like Pamela Anderson and was obsessed by her looks and by boys – she just wasn't my sort of a girl.

While I was expecting our Molly in 2001, she was also pregnant with a daughter, Keeley. Michelle used to complain to me all the time about Louise's boyfriend – Keeley's dad, a cab driver called Mark Croft. I remember I said to her, 'He sounds like a right knobhead.' From everything she told me about how he treated Louise, he always sounded like a terrible boyfriend.

Even worse, when I was pregnant, she told me: 'I had this massive row with Mark and Louise about you. Mark tried to say you are only having this baby because of the money, Brian's money.' It really upset me at the time, and that night I actually started bleeding and had a scare. I can't say it was all down to those comments at all – I was already under a lot of pressure. I'd just left my band Atomic Kitten, because I wanted to focus on my baby and my family, and since it was my first child I was especially nervous and wanted to do my best. I had also received a nasty anonymous letter through my door giving me all sorts of abuse and telling me that the baby should be aborted. I was really stressed and upset by all that, so Mark and Louise's comments were just adding to it. But I thought, 'I've never met this guy Mark, who does he think he is? Little piece of shit.' I really blacklisted him in my mind.

And something in me knew straightaway, when he swaggered into Mum's front room four years later, that this was the same Mark. So as soon as he had dropped the stuff off for me mum, and left, I followed her into the kitchen and said, 'Mum, I don't like him, I've heard about him. I really can't stand him, so don't have him round this house.'

She shrugged, busy getting a tray out of the oven. This wasn't any old tray, though: it was Mum's coke tray. She always kept her coke on a tray in the oven. It meant it was hidden if people came around unexpectedly, and it was a good surface for chopping up the coke. That day she was dividing two lines out for us with a razor blade. She mostly used a razor blade, or if she couldn't find one, sometimes a credit card.

I looked at the neat white lines, and told myself, 'This is your last chance to say no.' But I knew I wouldn't. I had got this far, I was going to go through with it. So I had a line with her. And as soon as the familiar numbness started at the back of my throat, and the kind of bitter taste started in my mouth, I felt as though I could relax and put my problems on hold.

I think my weakness was caused by flashbacks of all the good times I had had on it, and I went for it. I had just been feeling so lonely and isolated that I wanted to join in with the people close to me. And I wanted something that could give me a boost and cheer me up, however temporary.

I wish more than anything I had resisted, I wish I could go back in time and snatch it from under my face, and tell myself to be stronger. Tell myself that a life of drugs is only ever going to lead to bad things. But I didn't, I gave in to the temptation.

I can't blame Mum, 'cause I was an adult, and it was my choice, but Mum definitely didn't help. It did feel like she had got her claws into me now that I was back home in Warrington. I was her partner in crime all over again. And from then onwards, partly 'cause of drugs and partly 'cause of friends, I was round me mum's a lot. I was doing bits of telly work here and there, and I was still spending lots of time with the kids, but outside of that, when I wanted to relax, I didn't know what else to do. I tried to convince myself that I was happy, curled up in bed alone watching television or films, or that Lisa and I sitting in with a take-away was all I needed to unwind. But it never worked, and more often than not I ended up cracking and going to Mum's. I didn't really know where to turn to get out of it. It was like I could see myself spiralling back into my old life, the one I had tried to climb out of with my trip to rehab. But it felt like all I could do was watch as coke started to creep back into my life, and there was nothing I could do to stop it.

And after a while I didn't even try to stay off the drugs. I just accepted my life was going the wrong way, and thought, 'That's it, I'm back where I was, where I didn't want to be.'

Mark

From this point I began to find myself living almost a double life. A large part of my life was normal – or, at least, as normal as my life ever gets! First and foremost I was a mum, playing with my girls and watching them grow. Then sometimes I would be Kerry Katona the celebrity, filming my adverts and doing photo shoots. It was glamorous and fun and I'd always be the professional, turning up on time and doing my thing, and doing it well. But during the downtime from my kids and my job, there was a whole hidden side, where I'd go to Mum's and things would be very different. It was very separate from the rest of my life, and I wanted to keep it that way. We would be on coke, and sat on the Xbox for hours, gurning and aimlessly chewing the air – a side effect of the drugs. Or we'd be playing solitaire on Sky, and Mark would come round and join us. And for some reason I still don't fully understand, I started to think he wasn't so bad.

As far as I was concerned, I was functioning normally. I guess I fooled myself into thinking it was just like other people having a beer in the evening, and carrying on with everything else as normal. Only, of course, it wasn't.

Then, as my coke use grew, I started taking it when I wasn't just at Mum's house, so Mark basically became my dealer too. Obviously I would never take drugs in front of Molly and Lilly, or any time when I knew I would be looking after them, but sometimes I would leave them with Cheryl, or they would be staying with friends. Or they would be off in Ireland visiting their grandparents – Brian's parents Mairead and Brendan – as they did for Christmas that year.

Christmas was a real tough one because it means so much to me. I have always loved everything about Christmas and always do everything I can to make it really exciting and fun for the kids. The year before, the kids had been in Ireland as well – the first time I had spent Christmas without them since they were born. And it had been awful: I spent the whole day just moping around.

I had got on with Mairead at times when I was with her son, but I thought she was a very overbearing mother, who thought he could do no wrong – and went into denial when he did. So as my relationship soured with Brian, it soured with her and we no longer saw eye to eye. But I could never fault her as a grandmother. She loved Molly and Lilly to bits, and they loved her, and she was still keen to be as involved as ever in their lives. So I was more than happy to keep that going with regular visits for the kids to Ireland.

But I did feel terrible watching them go as they headed off for Christmas. I knew I was going to miss them like mad – their cheeky smiles in the morning, and the unprompted hugs they would run and give me during the day. The only way I could cheer myself up a bit was by focusing on the freedom it gave me for the other side of my life. I could let my hair down a bit, without worrying about it affecting Molly and Lilly. And so I ended up taking more cocaine, and spending more time with Mark.

There were times when I'd go round Mark's flat to buy a bag of coke. It was just around the corner from mine, and I'd end up staying and talking, and he'd give me some more drugs. It was a nice flat and I felt at home there. It was clean and tidy, and had this massive fish tank for which he had paid £8000 – and which was full of fish that were his kids, he said!

He had split from Louise by then, so it would just be him and me, and coke basically makes you chat and chat and chat, without always knowing what you are saying. I'd be sat there talking about my problems, and he'd be sat there listening. And I was thinking it was great, because it seemed like actually I had been wrong about Mark, and this guy really understood me.

The first time I stayed to talk properly, I told him, 'I don't know what to do about me mum. It's doing my head in that she keeps asking me for money.'

And he said, 'Yeah, I can see that, that's bang out of order, that.'

It felt like he was on my side and that he got me, so I continued. 'And she's always nitpicking at me, and having a go when I have done nothing wrong. It's really getting me down.'

He nodded and gave me a sympathetic look, and I ended up telling him all about my past and how years of moving round different foster parents, when Mum had been unable to cope with me, had left me feeling lonely and lost. How I didn't know who my real dad was, and how it had always eaten away at me, and left an empty hole inside me, when I had imagined what life could have been like if he had stayed on the scene.

Other times I told him all about Brian, and what had gone wrong in my marriage. How I had tried my best to be a good wife and mother, but how Brian had slipped away from me, and was now in the arms of a slim beautiful woman, leaving me feeling worthless and fat. I told him the problems I was having with Mum and how I wasn't sure what to do next with my career, and what my hopes and dreams were, as well as my fears and insecurities. How I still didn't feel like I knew who I was, or what my future held.

And I'll be honest, it was all 'me me me.' He sat there and listened, rarely giving anything away about himself. He mentioned once that he had been in the navy when he was younger, but I didn't get him to tell me anything more because I wasn't that interested in his life. He was still just my dealer, who happened to be a good listener, and it was nice to spend time with him. I felt better after I had been round to see him – I would joke it was like expensive therapy!

It is only looking back that I see those conversations in a different light. I can see me sitting there lonely and with no one to talk to, offloading to this guy, who knew the more I was there, the more drugs I would buy off him. And when you are on coke you think you are having the best conversations, but often you aren't. So maybe, with the amount I talked, the guy had no choice but to listen! Or maybe – and this possibility really hurts to think about – he was gathering information from me to use in the future. Taking advantage of me at my lowest and most vulnerable to find out my weaknesses. I still feel sick saying that and thinking about it now, but sadly, it really was a possibility.

At the time, it felt like I was starting to get to know him. Bit by bit, my perception of him as this arrogant rude idiot was being replaced by the thought that he was a good listener, a kind person and, most of all, funny. Mark had a witty and quick sense of humour, and that is always the most attractive thing to me in a man.

I don't like to be serious all the time. I need to have some fun and banter. And Mark really was witty and quick. I'm very sharp – a lot sharper than people think – and I enjoy having a laugh with it. Brian is really funny as well, and that was one of the reasons we had clicked. So to be attractive to me, a guy has to be quicker and faster than me with humour, or at least be able to keep up. And Mark could. And I think he liked my humour. When I was joking around, I could see him kind of stop, and think, 'Ooh, that's different and interesting'.

Slowly it dawned on me that I was starting to think of Mark as more than a friend. I was becoming attracted to him in a fancying kind of way. And that did horrify me, because I knew deep down he would be a bad choice of partner and I still thought he wasn't good-looking. But I couldn't help what I was starting to feel.

I remember saying to Mum, 'Don't take this the wrong way, but I think I've got a weird crush on Mark.'

She shrieked, 'You what?!'

And I said, 'I don't fancy him, but he's funny, he's quick-witted. I don't know, there's just a bit of something.'

And of course, Mum being me mum, she wasn't happy. It didn't help that she had thought Brian was the absolute best catch ever, so no one was ever going to compete. She ended up telling Mark what I had said, but in her true style she added, 'You fucking touch her, I'll kill you.'

She told me, 'Mark shows me videos of him shagging girls, I swear it is like a different one every week, and I don't want my daughter to become one of those girls. Stay away from him!' Surely hearing that should have made every alarm bell ring?

I'm not sure if she was warning us off each other to protect me, or if it was more a case that she just didn't want us together in case we left her out. She would always tell me, 'Mark was my friend before yours', and let me know when he would be spending time with her. So say I was out and about, or at home with the kids, she'd let me know:

'Oh Mark's around, we're just having something to eat.'

It didn't bother me, so I'd say, 'Alright, then, enjoy it.'

But it soon got that it was Mark and I who were hanging out all the time.

Then, one night in February, I had Mark's daughter Keeley, who was four by then, to stay when he needed someone to look after her at the last minute. The next day he asked, 'Can I take you out for dinner as a thank you?'

I was surprised, as it was just a favour, but still thought he meant as mates, so I said, 'Yeah, sure, no worries'.

We went out for a meal and got stuck into the drink, and before I knew it, I ended up back at his and fell into bed with him. I can't even remember the night properly, but I remember waking up the next day naked in his bed, and thinking, 'Shit.' My main worry was Mum finding out. I thought, 'Oh God, she will go absolutely ballistic when she find out about this.'

Mum didn't like me having relationships – she never has done – because she loses me then. She is no longer my priority, which is something she has always hated. So I knew she would put up a fight against Mark and me.

But despite my initial panic the morning after, Mark and I as a couple made sense to me at the time. He had been growing on me more week by week, and although I didn't think we would actually end up as a proper couple, we had a laugh together. It gave me a confidence boost – and, to be honest, he took my mind off Brian. Plus there was a bit of me that liked us having it as a secret. It was a way of getting away from me mum's attempts to control me. I was like a teenager having a rebellious moment. So without discussing it, we kind of fell into a relationship, and I kept it quiet for a few weeks and we were just sneaking around. It was fun, and amusing, and he still kept me laughing. Basically, he laughed the knickers off me!

I liked making him laugh too. I remember at the time I was going to see a psychiatrist once a week, following on from my treatment the year before. And he sent me a text to see how I was going. I texted back, 'I'm sexy as hell, but off me tree!', which amused him.

Of course, I did end up telling Mum about Mark and me. 'Cause as frustrated as I got with her, she was still my best friend, and you always end up telling your best friend these things. So, two weeks later, I just blurted out, 'Mum, I slept with Mark.'

'You what?!' As I had expected her to, she went ballistic. 'What the hell did you do that for? Do you realise you will just be yet another girl to him? God knows, there is probably a video of you going around right now! You stupid idiot!'

But then she calmed down, and even admitted, 'I've seen you growing closer and I'll give you it, you do seem to have fun together.' Then she said something really bizarre, 'You know what, no one will ever look after you better than what he will.'

And she seemed to accept the relationship, so for the next few weeks we all got on well. That was a result!

So well, in fact, that before I knew it, Mark had moved into mine, and went and got my name tattooed on his back! I couldn't believe he had done that. I had had boyfriends' names tattooed on me before, but not after a few weeks of dating. Things were definitely moving fast. But there was, of course, a dark side to this: drugs. Take drugs out of the equation, and I guarantee 100 per cent Mark and I would never have ended up together. It was definitely the glue that tied us together. But date a dealer, and I guess it is inevitable that you get sucked into their world.

As for Molly and Lilly, they didn't spend that much time with him in the beginning. I liked to keep them for myself, and time with Mark was separate. But once he was living in the house, they got on well. He wasn't the type to actually play games with them, but they would tease each other, and they thought he was funny. Just the fact there was even a dad-type figure in their life was, I thought, a good start. So I was really happy that someone who was good with them had come into their lives, and they liked him. It wasn't just me anymore, and that felt like it might be a good thing for them. Perhaps, looking back, I didn't examine the situation carefully enough about my own motives. Because although my kids have always come first, and always will, I think at the same time there was a bit of me thinking that, because I had married Brian so young, I deserved to be a bit selfish and enjoy my life. I had given up five years of my life to Brian and being a mum, at an age when most other girls were out partying and having fun. I didn't at all regret my marriage – after all, my two baby girls came out of it – but there was a small part of me that felt like I did have some catching up to do, that I was entitled to it.

Then out of the blue, after six weeks, came that proposal in The Conrad, and suddenly our relationship was all about the long term. I mentioned Mark's proposal at the end of my book *Too Much Too Young*, and I made it sound ever so romantic. But it wasn't. I was just trying to convince myself at the time that I was doing the right thing. Deep down, I was very confused. The first days of being engaged are exciting, and different, and there were loads of 'up' moments, but really I had a horrible suspicion I was getting myself into a proper mess, that there was a dark side to our relationship. I kept pushing the feeling aside, telling myself nerves were normal after what had happened with my first marriage. And there were plenty of fun moments to celebrate.

One of the first things we did after we were engaged was a shoot with *OK!* magazine to discuss our news. I have done a lot of work with the magazine over the years, and love working with them. I have a weekly column with them, in which I get to put forward my views on the world and let people know what I am doing. And I have done literally hundreds of photo shoots with them. The shoots are always a lot of fun, and can happen anywhere in the world, with all sorts of dressing up involved.

My favourite shoots are the ones with the kids, as I love having beautiful professional photos with them to keep. But this time it was Mark and I. Mark took to it well – so long as you aren't a shy person, it's not too hard to stand there and pose – and when we were interviewed, I didn't try and tell Mark what to say. I just let him answer what he genuinely thought, and I think he took to it well.

While we were enjoying the early days of being engaged, though, my friends and family were less impressed by my decision. They made a few noises about how quickly we were going into things, and the press were pretty dismissive about it too. But I didn't care. I was still feeling rebellious and had set my mind on the idea that distracting myself with someone who was the complete opposite of Brian was the way forward – and you couldn't have got more different than Mark and Brian!

It was Brian who was the one person who was quite vocal about his disapproval of the engagement. We had a strange kind of awkward peace at that point. We weren't friends, but we weren't enemies. We were on friendly terms for the girls' sake, and that was it. Apart from when he got drunken upset calls from me, that is! But all bets were off once I got engaged. He completely turned and said he was worried about the kids and there was no way he was having them live with Mark. He had heard Mark was a drug dealer and that was not what he wanted around Molly and Lilly. Looking back, I can see why he was concerned and I understand where he was coming from; I wish I had been able to listen to him. But I couldn't get past the fact that the criticism was coming from him. I just thought, 'Don't give me this from the other side of the world. If you really care, come and actually see your kids. It's all well and good saying you care. Well, then, show it.'

It always upsets me to think about it. I know the girls have got me, but it was hard being a single mum after Brian left. I really did try but I can't give them everything that you would get from two parents – they needed their dad.

I remember one heated conversation when he told me, 'My career is in Australia, so I can't do anything about it.'

I said, 'As far as I'm concerned, you made your career in Australia long after the kids were born, and your career should be where your children are.'

So I put his concerns about Mark to the back of my mind and turned back to life with my fiancé. But the problem was, drugs were part of the relationship, and one of the problems with cocaine was that it stopped me from admitting the effects it was having on me.

Let me tell you how far into denial I had got. One afternoon I was sat on the floor at Mum's house, I think two of her friends were in the room, and we were doing coke. Apparently I just fell backwards and started fitting. I was having an epileptic fit. I don't remember it, though. I just remember coming back round and pushing this woman off me, and getting up and trying to do another line. What drew my attention to it was Mum yelling at me, 'Erm, Kerry, do you know what just happened there?'

'No, Mum.'

'You just had a fit of some sort. That was bloody scary, that was!'

I didn't even really believe them – or care. I just shrugged, and was like, 'Whatever, you liars!'

But me mum was really shaken by it, and wouldn't let me take any more coke. Instead she called Mark to come and get me.

It wasn't rocket science, though. I was doing coke, hardly sleeping, and not eating properly: of course a fit might happen. And awful though it sounds now, I just accepted that as a side effect of doing drugs. The reality is, I think, that I was just hitting the self-destruct button.

I didn't even see it as a warning alarm about Mark. What kind of a guy watches his fiancée have an epileptic fit caused by drugs, then happily carries on supplying her with it? A proper boyfriend would have gone, 'You know what, enough is enough. We've had fun, but this is going too far. Let's calm this down now, because I really don't want to see you harming yourself like this.'

But he didn't.

And after that first argument we had had, the day before we got engaged, we started to have more. Not that many, but just occasional ones over silly things, and I did see another side to Mark. He had a side that made me pretty uncomfortable, where he would suddenly lose it and go off on one, calling me all sorts of names.

Say I forgot something I was picking up at the shops, nine times out of ten he'd think nothing of it, but suddenly one time he'd be, 'Are you fucking stupid? Can you get nothing right, you silly cow?' And he'd be so mad, he'd be red and practically spitting.

But it was such a flash of temper, and would then disappear so fast, that I almost wondered if I had imagined it. And one thing I will say is, he never abused me physically in any way. It was all about the mind with Mark.

But still, there were some good times, and I was no longer on my own, without Brian. I had someone now. And awful as it sounds, I think I wanted someone who was not going to leave me, and I thought that Mark never would, because really, deep down, I reckoned I was better than him. He was a skint, unattractive drug dealer, and I was a reasonable-looking, rich celebrity. And although my self-confidence was pretty much at an all-time low at that point, even I had the sense to see he was probably punching above his weight.

So he could never leave me, could he?

Finding Old Family

Don't get me wrong, though: coke was pretty central to our lives, but it wasn't there every day. I couldn't have functioned as a mum for a start if that had been the case.

We would go on benders, but there would be a gap before the next one. So there was plenty of time for other things in our lives.

We would go back to being just like any other family. I'd get up with the kids in the morning, and get them cereal for their breakfasts, laughing and joking round in the kitchen with them. The kids have always been the kind who get out of bed and are full of energy straightaway. So breakfast time was lively, to say the least, in our house. Then it was time for the school run, which I did, unless I was working, when Cheryl would go. Then I'd pick them up again at the end of the day, and they'd play for an hour or so before tea. Sometimes I would cook, sometimes it was Cheryl, and sometimes me mum would come round and help out. Or I'd take them out. We've always liked eating out, so we'd go somewhere for food – if the kids had any say in it, it was always Pizza Hut. They loved it there! Then, once we were home, it was bath and bed.

Maybe it was because of the changes I had been going through with the men in my life, but one thing I spent a lot of time doing in the spring of 2006 was thinking about me dad, Arnie Ferrier. He was my stepdad really, but I always called him Dad, as that is what he was to me really. I feel uncomfortable calling him Arnie.

He had married Mum when I was three years old. He was 30 years older than her. Sadly, I don't think Mum ever loved him. I think she just hoped he would provide a stable life and some security for us, because even she had realised our life moving from house to house was not a good one.

And while me dad did provide that on some level – we had a nice place to live, and lots of his family around us, who wanted the best for us – the relationship was so volatile, and they argued so much, that they split after three years.

Then for three further years, until I was nine, I spent my time bouncing back and forth between their houses as well as other family and friends, while they fought for custody.

Dad took me on as part of the package that came with me mum, I guess. But it wasn't like I was just there as someone he had to put up with, he really did take me on. All his own kids had grown up, and other than a bit of truck-driving at one point, he wasn't really working, so he had a lot of time for me. Mum, meantime, spent the day working as a machinist, and then the evenings out partying – mostly with friends and men other than her husband. So it was Dad and I at home together.

When I wrote my first book, it reminded me of all the things he had done for me. There were times when he really did bring me up on his own. And although I'm not going to paint him as a model dad, because he wasn't perfect – he gave me a good hiding every now and then and he drank a lot – I realised that if it wasn't for him, I wouldn't have had a roof over my head at times during my childhood.

He had really tried his best, brushing my hair, making sure I got a decent meal, teaching me to tell the time. He even wanted to adopt me, but Mum wouldn't have any of it.

We had stayed in touch throughout my teen years, and when Brian and I married in 2002 in Ireland, I had wanted Dad at the wedding. I had even thought about getting him to give me away. But Mum had said that if he came to the wedding, she wouldn't. She forced me to choose between them, and I chose her. So me dad and his family fell out with me, and none of them were at the wedding, which left me gutted. But I didn't feel like I couldn't have me mum there either, so I was in a horrible position.

And now, years later, I just kept having this dream, no word of a lie, that me dad was going to die. I started thinking, 'If he dies and I never get a chance to say thank you for everything he done for me as a kid, I'll never forgive myself.' And I thought I wouldn't get a chance to go to the funeral because all the family hates me for not speaking to him. That strange train of thought kept going through my head.

Well. I went for a Chinese one night with Lisa, and the restaurant was over the road from The Stocks pub, in the Padgate area of Warrington, and Dad's flat was behind the pub. I was sat there, looking over at me dad's local, when a delivery guy walked in and went, 'Hiya, Kerry!' I said, 'Hiya, love', and he said, 'Oh, you here for your dad? For your dad's party tomorrow?'

So I just played dumb, and without letting on that we hadn't spoken in years said, 'No, what's that, then?'

'Oh, he's emigrating to America in a few weeks, didn't you know?'

Well, I thought, how weird is that? It was too much of a coincidence that I was thinking about getting back in touch with me dad, and this guy walks in and tells me he's leaving. It was definitely a sign for me to do something about it.

So I got straight in my car and went round and rang his doorbell. Lisa came with me but stayed in the car. She used some excuse about looking after her cat, which was in a cage in the car because we had picked him up from the vet earlier. But really I knew she was just giving me time alone with Dad.

I went to the door of these flats, and there was an intercom system. So I pressed the buzzer with my hand shaking, and after a few seconds this gruff voice said, 'Hello?'

I was so scared, but I was determined to go through with it. I went, 'Hiya, Dad, it's Kerry.'

He didn't answer and there was silence for what seemed like ages but was probably only about five seconds. Then the buzzer went, and I went up the stairs to his flat and he opened the front door.

'Bloody hell, what do you want?' was the first thing he said. Clearly he was as straight talking as ever!

I went in and sat at his bar with him – he had a breakfast bar that divided the kitchen and living room, and he had always sat there, in his favourite swivel chair. It hardly looked like the place had changed much since I had lived there as a kid, apart from the fact me dad was now living there alone. He had his slippers on and his shirt hanging out with his vest on underneath and he was wearing his glasses, and he was all concentrated on making himself a roll-up cigarette.

I looked at him and almost thought it was like old times. Except, I thought, God, he looks old. He had proper aged since I'd last seen him. His white hair was thinning, and his blue eyes weren't as sharp and bright as they had been. He was an old man, he was 70-odd, but I hadn't really realised it until that moment. In my head he hadn't aged since the man looking after me as a little 'un. That was the picture I still had in my mind.

'So,' he said. 'What do you want?'

I could tell my visit had thrown him, but he was trying not to show it. 'I hear you're off to America,' I said. 'I just wanted to come and say hiya first.'

He seemed to relax a bit then, and told me how he was moving to Texas. That had always been his dream. He loved the whole country and western thing, and every year he would save up and go out there for a holiday. A whole bunch of men would go each time, all into the same music and lifestyle. He always used to say that he would emigrate there one day to live out the rest of his life, and now he had enough money, so he was doing it. I was so pleased for him, getting to make a reality of what he had dreamed of, but at the same time I was sad. There we were, finally making up, and he was about to disappear.

Then he opened up his cupboard and he had these pictures of me in there that he'd kept, and it really upset me. I was sure after we fell out that he would have forgotten about me, but he had kept these treasured memories, as well as following my career in the papers.

But me dad's not one to get upset and emotional. He's a very proud man, so he continued on, talking all factual. Then he said, 'I'm not leaving for a few weeks, but I'm having a leaving party tomorrow at Smithys Pub, in Harpers Road.'

'Would it be alright if I came?' I asked tentatively.

'I'd love you to be there,' he grinned back.

I was worried about the rest of the family, as I hadn't talked with them either, but he said, 'They'll be fine about it if I'm fine about it, and I am!' Then he started filling me in on the gossip.

He had been divorced before he met Mum, and had five children from his previous marriage, all older than her. I knew them all well when I lived with him, although his daughter Pat Ferrier had been my favourite. She had been a body builder, and had really looked out for me, like an older sister, or a second mother. She had still been living at home, and she used to spend lots of time playing with me, and looking after me. But we had lost touch as well, so I was excited but nervous about seeing her again too.

Then I left, promising to be at his leaving do the next day, and went back to the car to tell Lisa all about it. I had been gone so long she knew things had gone well, and she was excited to hear all about it. We had been so close for so long she knew everyone in my family and all my history, and what this meant to me.

I woke up that morning, and wrote a cheque for £1000, and put it in my pocket. Then I headed to Smithys, bringing Lisa along again for moral support. I thought I was running late, and I'd got myself in a right panic that we might miss it. When we got there, I threw the door of the pub open and went sprinting in – and all the Ferriers were sat there, looking at me. There was nobody else in there, and everybody just went silent.

Well, that wasn't half awkward! They all just sat looking at me and I walked over going 'Hiya!' and trying to act like it was all perfectly normal. But me dad came over, said, 'So glad you could make it', and gave me a hug – and that was the hardest part over. After that, everybody was great and they were all fine with me as though no time had passed since we had last hung out together. With Pat especially, it was as though nothing had ever come between us – we both apologised for everything that had happened in the past, and that was it, we were back chatting away like old, bonding like sisters again straightaway. It was amazing.

Then Dad did a speech about how he was off, and said, 'I'm obviously sad to go and I'm gonna miss everyone, but I've gotta follow through with this dream of mine, and I'm just really made up you are all supporting me. And if anyone ever wants to visit, I'd be very happy!'

And somehow, it felt like he was giving the speech to me. Like it was me that he wanted to hear what he had to say that day.

At one point he took me to one side and sat me down, and we were chatting and having a few drinks, and he got really upset. He's not one to cry, not at all – normally he'd be the one going, 'Stop it, you daft bugger' and brushing it off, making light of a situation. But he said to me, 'You know I've always looked at you as a daughter' and got tearful. It was so lovely to hear that, and I knew he had been my proper dad. I was just sorry we had missed all those years together.

I apologised for not always having been there for him, and gave him the cheque, saying, 'Here you go, here's some spends for you.' Then we both had a bit of a cry. And actually for once it was me who was the stronger one, and I pulled myself together and I said to him, 'Stop it, you soppy old bastard!', which made him laugh.

It was such a lovely day. And I realised that I had always been so concerned about never getting to meet my real dad, I forgot that Arnie was a true dad to me. He was the one dad I should have been most worried about and thankful to.

After that, for the next few weeks, until he had to leave, I saw him all the time. We really rebuilt our relationship, and made up for the years we had lost. I brought Molly and Lilly round to visit him, and just spent time relaxing and talking, catching up on all our missed years. Molly and Lilly took to him straightaway – he had a real way with them and would tease them and play around with them, and let them sit on his knee. I could see the caring part of him that must have drawn me to him as a child as well.

On the day he left, I took him to the airport and said goodbye to him, sad to see him go, but really happy he was finally off to lead the life he had talked about so much when I was a kid. And I used to ring him up all the time when he was out there and swap all our news and stories.

I rebuilt my relationship with the rest of the Ferriers too. Pat and I got close again, and it felt like I was a kid back with them. And no one stayed mad at me for what had happened because they knew what my mum was like, so no one blamed me. I'll be forever grateful to that chatty delivery guy!

Expecting Again

Mark had been really supportive of me getting back in touch with Dad, which was very important to me. I had talked about him through our months together, so he knew that there was a gap there for me that needed filling, and having that contact again really helped. Mark did it by taking a back seat and not telling me what to do, but just listening, and encouraging me to spend time with him, and giving me hugs when I needed. He also met Dad a couple of times and they had a laugh together. So in that way Mark was great.

I also liked the fact that Mark was a very tactile boyfriend – we were always touchy-feely with each other, and he was always kissing and hugging me, and telling me he loved me, which made me feel good and start thinking that we were actually quite good together.

We were certainly good in bed! We had a great sex life, if I'm honest, and it was definitely one of the things keeping us together. We had sex pretty much every day – and that goes for the whole way through our relationship. I think subconsciously I made a special effort with sex, though. It was always in the back of my mind that one of the grounds for Brian divorcing me was a lack of sex, so I suppose I needed to prove something, if only to myself. The fact that the lack of sex had mostly been due to the fact Brian was never there, was something I knew, but it didn't stop me being hurt and insulted by it anyway.

Towards the end of our marriage, Lilly used to sleep in our bedroom in a cot, and Brian would come back from tour and want sex. But I didn't like having sex when my kids were in the same room. It was weird and it freaked me out, so I would refuse. I have memories of lying in bed on my own late at night as a kid, and listening to me mum having sex with some man or another, or other times walking in on them by mistake, and it used to really upset me. That is not something a child should have to hear or see. So that is the bad memory I've got of that, a scarred memory. And I didn't want to repeat that for my daughter, even though she was only a baby at the time. But Brian never seemed to understand.

But seeing it on paper, in black and white, really struck a nerve: 'divorcing for lack of sex'. So with Mark, it was as if I needed to know that someone could want me often, and that I was good at that side of things.

I had a coil inserted as contraception at the time, but in the spring it was causing me trouble, so I took it out, and in theory Mark and I were using condoms.

A few months later – in July, I think it was – we went on holiday to Marbella with Max Clifford, who did my PR, and his partner Jo. As well as working with Max, he had become a close friend, and as an older man, he was also another father figure. Because I haven't had my real dad there throughout my life, I have found over the years I tend to take on other older men for that role. Although it is never completely the same, it does help. And Max was very good in that way.

While we were on holiday, I felt all bloated and horrible and was convinced I was constipated. So I sent Mark out to get me some laxatives. I took so many of them, honest to God, before finally it dawned on me that I might be pregnant again. So I sent

Mark back out – this time for pregnancy tests! I did eight tests before I accepted it was true.

I was absolutely made up. I love being a mum, and it felt like this was just what I needed to well and truly move on with my life. It gave me a real purpose again. And I knew Molly and Lilly would be really excited about having a new brother or sister.

Mark was over the moon as well. And I did imagine that he would be a good dad. Because one thing that I was appreciating about Mark was that, even though Molly and Lilly weren't his, he was treating them as though they were. He would play silly games with them, and he never touched them or smacked them, or shouted at them when he shouldn't. And he came to school plays, sports days and parents' evenings with me, and would tell the girls how well they had done, and listen to what teachers had to say about them. I can't fault him on that, I really can't. And I would always compare him in my mind to Brian in that way, and he would always come out better, just for the basic reason that, for a start, he was actually present in their lives.

The night we found out I was expecting, we went out for dinner to celebrate. I didn't drink. I take that side of pregnancy really seriously. Once you are carrying a life inside you, you have to respect that life and stop anything that could harm the baby.

Despite wild accusations in the papers throughout my pregnancies, I have always been like that. I might have the odd drink while pregnant, and that is it. I also stopped doing coke, of course. It was the one thing that motivated me the best to stop coke – the damage I could do my baby. So as soon as I had done the test, bang, that was it: over. No more drugs. And that is the God's honest truth.

The only thing I will say I still do when pregnant is smoke occasionally, but I hugely cut that down. I can't say I am proud of it, but I went to the doctor's when I was pregnant and told him, 'I'm trying to stop, but am really struggling. I'm finding it really hard, and I keep getting worked up. How can I do it? I need some help.' And he told me, 'Stress is worse for an unborn baby than having the odd puff, so if it is making you that anxious, and you are really struggling, don't try and stop, just try and keep it to a minimum.' So I had the odd puff. I have taken a lot of criticism for it over the years, and I know it is not ideal.

Meantime, though, I was more concerned about other medication I was putting into my body.

Just before I went to rehab in Arizona, a doctor had diagnosed me as being bipolar. I wasn't that surprised, as Mum suffers the same. In a weird way, I was relieved because it explained a lot of the feelings and emotions I was going through. It is a genetic illness, so more than likely I inherited it from Mum.

Bipolar disorder – also called manic depression – is like a total exaggeration of the ups and downs that normal people feel in life. Sometimes you are so ecstatic and giddy and kind of crazily happy without really knowing why, and other times you are down and feel like life is hopeless, and you are going through really miserable dark times, for no reason. It can be really severe, and take over your whole life, and lots of people don't understand it, so they just write you off as a bit crazy.

The medication I was given by doctors theoretically worked by keeping my mood somewhere in the middle, with the idea that the highs and the lows would not be so extreme. I can't remember what I was put on in the beginning, but I came off it when I was pregnant, as I was advised that taking the medication while pregnant wasn't a good idea. And my baby being healthy and well was my priority over the state of my mind.

Coke-Free Troubles

Once medication and coke was taken out of the equation, though, I was shocked at the change in our relationship. Suddenly Mark and I were fighting like cat and dog. We'd row over anything, and I cannot tell you how many times I would break off the engagement. I'd take my ring off or he'd take it back, or I'd kick him out. It was never over anything major, but just small fights that would escalate, and become huge before I knew it.

One night I said to him, 'Mark, get us a kebab would you? I'm starving!' He was always really good at doing things like that for me, especially when I was pregnant. I'd say, 'Mark, get us a cup of tea' or 'Mark, do you mind running to the shops?' and he'd be straight off to do it. But this one night he went out and was gone for about three hours getting a kebab for me. He got home about 2 a.m. and straightaway I said, 'Where have you been? How did getting a kebab take you that long?'

He said, 'Don't be daft, you're being ridiculous. I haven't been that long. You are paranoid. It's coming off the coke and the medication at the same time is making your mind go funny. Give it a rest!'

And I did wonder if I was making a big deal out of nothing. He was so good at arguing, it was very hard not to lose track of my original point and whether I was right or wrong. But without coke at the centre of our relationship, we weren't so sure what was holding us together, or how to have a good time as a couple without it. I could see our whole relationship had been stuck together by it. At times, I started getting scared that I didn't actually know him, that he was effectively my live-in dealer and that by giving me drugs so often, he had been controlling my relationship with him. So without it, he was a bit lost.

The public perception of Mark was not good, and it seemed that most articles written about us would use any opportunity to have a dig at him, which made life hard for the team looking after my career. Max Clifford had taken over my management just before the holiday when I got pregnant. Before that I was with James Grant for management, and Max did my PR. But the team at James Grant didn't like Mark, and made it very clear they thought he was bad for me, which I didn't like to hear.

Mark also kept getting involved in my management and criticising it, which obviously the lot at James Grant hated. So one day when I was on the phone to one of them arguing about something, the guy just said. 'You know what, why don't you just get Mark to manage you, then.'

Well, I thought that was out of order. I put the phone down and that was the end of that, they were no longer doing my management. I was gutted really, because we had got on so well before I met Mark and they had really looked out for me through thick and thin. But I felt like I had no other choice. In my mind, it was no one else's place to criticise my partner.

It is only looking back that I can see why they were frustrated – what I saw as Mark helping out, I now see as the power going to his head. He was getting in the way of their job. It was clear that Mark loved the idea of fame and being married to Kerry Katona. He was starting to get above himself and think that he was the big man. It was as if someone had given a parking attendant a badge and a bit of power and he had started bossing everyone around and driving the Ferraris around as though they were his. He was kind of like that – the power went to his head quickly.

But I didn't see that at the time, and thought the people at James Grant were in the wrong, so we went our separate ways and Max took over my management as well as my PR.

Deep down, though, there was always a bit of me doubting that Mark really wanted me. In my low moments, I wondered if he was just with me for the money and the fame. I hated that I was starting to have such thoughts in these drug-free months, when there was little holding us together. I tried to bury them and ignore them. But I was forever faced with it from me Mum, friends, and even people in the street. There were comments shouted out at me, or people attempting to give friendly warnings: 'Kerry, keep an eye on your cash, You know Mark would be happy to get his hands on it!' or 'Careful, our Kez, make sure Mark isn't using you for money and fame.' All those kinds of things. I ignored most of it – let's face it, most men would have been worse off than me, so it was an inevitable assumption that my money would be part of my attraction.

But sometimes I'd ask him questions to try and reassure myself. One time, we were lying curled up in bed in Winwick Park, and people's comments were playing around in my mind. So I said to him, 'This ain't a setup this, is it? Are you with me for me money? Have you got me pregnant to make sure you get me?'

And he looked all shocked and was just like: 'You what?!'

'All this,' I said. 'Why are you with me?'

'Don't be daft! I'm with you 'cause I want to be with you! You're right insecure, you. Stop those thoughts.' And he gave me a cuddle and changed the subject.

But whenever I was feeling low, I really started to have moments where I did think that he was there for my money. And that the whole relationship was maybe a plan to get it. But to acknowledge that to myself would have been incredibly painful, so I always pushed any niggling doubts aside. My heart and my ego were both so damaged from the split with Brian, I don't know if they could have handled it.

Plus, there was always the fact that maybe it wasn't about that for him. And I would tell myself I was being paranoid. I knew I was an insecure and messed-up person, so I'd tell myself my doubts were just a symptom of that.

Besides all this, I was pregnant. And one thing I have never had is an abortion, so I was going to go through with having his baby, no matter what I thought Mark's intentions were, and I didn't want to do that alone. No way was I going to have two of my babies' daddies leave me!

Despite all my own growing doubts about Mark, I was not prepared to hear them from anyone else. I didn't feel like it was anyone else's place to judge him.

And that age-old thing started happening – the more people tell you not to do something, the more you rebel and do it. So the more people criticised Mark, the more it pushed me towards him. How dare people say he was only with me for my cash – what did they think that said about me? That I wasn't good enough for him, that he must have an ulterior motive to be with me?

I couldn't hear a bad word against him from anyone, least of all me mum.

But one day I went round her house, and she said, 'You know Mark isn't behaving himself? I've been told by a friend of his that he is still messing round with other girls.'

'Mum, I don't want to hear it. Stop stirring!'

'It's true. He has been with other girls since meeting you, and it breaks my heart, Kerry. You shouldn't be with him.'

'Mum, you introduced me to him and told me what a great guy he was, and now you are saying all this shit? Don't even go there!'

For her to be telling me I shouldn't be with him... well, it just made me mad. And I think she realised she had pushed it, so she stopped, but from time to time she would make little comments.

I know she says it was one thing for him to be a dealer and a friend to her, but she never in a million years saw him as someone for her daughter. The problem is, once you put two people together, you can't always control what they will feel for each other.

And from Mark's side too, once we were together, he didn't get on as well with her. He had been her friend initially, but once their roles changed, he didn't like her being around. His attitude was very much: 'We don't need her around, she's a pain and a problem. You are doing too much for her and she is sponging off you. She has built up a coke bill with me yet again, and said you'd pay it off for her. Do you really think that is okay?'

At the same time, my friends were siding with me mum, making me feel even more isolated. They would all sit around her flat, and because I wasn't there with them any more – Mark and I would be off doing our own thing – they would sit and bitch about me, and I wasn't there to defend myself.

Before I knew it, Lisa was best friends with me mum instead of me, and I became the outsider then. From that moment onwards, Lisa, who had always been my closest ally and friend, just drifted away from me. And it makes me so sad, but we have never got back what we had.

Over the years we'd had so much fun – as well as getting into so much trouble together! I remember one time taking her car when she had only a provisional licence, and we had to push it up the hill before we could start the engine so we didn't get caught. We were always there for each other. She would listen when I was upset or angry after another falling-out with Mum. And I even missed my Nan's funeral to be there for her because she had broken up with a boyfriend and was really upset. I would have fought to the death for her friendship, but it felt like she walked away from me and wasn't strong enough to defend me when that was needed.

I'm not going to entirely blame her; it is partly my fault as well. But sometimes I will drive past a certain place or remember a good time we had, and it does hurt. It saddens me that I will never have that friendship again, as no one will ever replace her. I'm devastated I have lost that, and the link she gave me to my childhood.

There were signs that there was more to Mark than I was seeing. Every now and then I would see flashes of temper, and realise it went deeper than just a bit of anger during our rows. I knew he had to be a bit of a hard man. In his neighbourhood, and in the life he was leading, you can't show any weakness. And while it scared me, in a weird way I also thought he was someone who could protect us all. It was a stupid way of thinking, and I was mistaking tough behaviour for real strength.

But there was no way I wanted to be around someone really violent. And in some ways I think that he wasn't as hard as all that. It was a role he was playing, and I think he was getting tired of it, because he started suggesting we move out of Warrington. So we began looking around.

Betrayal

One thing Mark did, which upset me horribly, was to sack our nanny Cheryl behind my back. It was terrible. Cheryl was a complete rock to me at that time and really helped me to keep the house in order and the kids in line, but she didn't like Mark. She is strong-minded, and says what she thinks. She told me she could see right through Mark and that he wasn't right for me, and Mark knew she thought that. So I guess he saw her as a threat and wanted to get rid of her.

It came to a head one time over a silly row, when Keeley was staying and Cheryl had given Molly and Lilly their breakfasts and forgot about Keeley.

Things really kicked off. But I thought Cheryl was great, and when he wanted to sack her I told him she wasn't going anywhere.

Soon afterwards, I had to go to hospital for a minor operation, and he sacked her while I was gone. She was devastated and went around to Mum's crying. It is one of my regrets in life that I didn't fight Mark about it when I got out of hospital. But it felt like the damage had been done and I couldn't really reverse it. Besides, I didn't have the energy for another battle that I was just going to lose. Looking back, this was one of the first major episodes where I can now see that being on all that medication made me weak, and unable to do the right thing. The very thought of losing Cheryl would normally have brought me out fighting hard, because of her importance to Molly and Lilly. But I didn't. I just let the situation ride me along. Then according to me mum – not that she told me until years later – Mark told a mutual friend, 'I've got rid of Cheryl, now I've just got to get rid of her mum.'

Whether he did say that or not, it was actually me mum who made the final move that killed our relationship. She got rid of herself from my life all by herself, without Mark even having to lift a finger.

I knew Mum had always sold stories about me to the papers. It didn't bother me too much when it was harmless stuff, or information about where I would be. I can't say I loved it, but at least she was making some money – saved me having to give it to her! And it was never anything too bad – until one Sunday in the autumn.

At the time, Mum was skint. I helped her out when I could, but she was on benefits, and so much of her money went on drugs because she was really badly into the coke at that time. The week before, we had had an argument over money – something to do with a payment she was getting for helping me on my first book. It was in the process of getting sorted.

And then a reporter from the *News of The World* knocked on her door. It was someone who had worked there for years. He said he had cash for Mum if she was willing to do a story on me. He also promised her more when the story was published.

Now, I will come back to my mum's part of it in a minute, but I want to say something here about the coverage of me in newspapers, particularly the *News of the World*, and the way that it was done.

It wasn't a first to offer money in exchange for a story, either. There were several reporters who regularly went around to my mum's in the hopes of her doing some coke and spill a story while they were there. They did the same with other so-called friends of mine. And sometimes they got some truth out of them, and sometimes they got some rambled rubbish, which they turned into a story anyway. Because people will say anything when they are off their heads and make all kinds of shit up if they think they are getting money for it.

And as far as the stories they were writing... well, sometimes they were true and sometimes they weren't, but they were pretty much, without exception, majorly slanted against me. I have a file of all the stories the *News of the World* have written about me over the years. And seeing them all in there together makes shocking reading. You can follow through quite a clear bullying campaign. I get really upset looking at it. They made me famous for all the wrong reasons.

As for the coverage of my drug-taking... well, imagine having a problem and it being bad enough for you that just your friends and family know. The *News of the World* made damn sure it was the whole world who knew, and the whole world judging me on every step I took. And it was written from such a biased angle, with no hint of sympathy or suggestions on how I might want to get help. It's the same old thing of newspapers just wanting to pull you down, 'cause shit sells. And the fact that so many of the journalists did coke themselves made it even more hypocritical!

There were times when the *News of the World* pushed me to the point when I nearly topped myself. They had a real vendetta against me, and I honestly felt they would have been happy if I had killed myself. It felt like they were pushing and pushing in the hope that I would die. I guarantee they had a front page all written up and ready to go: 'Kerry Katona Found Dead!'

Well, you know what? I'm still here, and the *News of the World* isn't!

But back to this one time with me mum. This reporter was at her house discussing the deal, when I went round to pick up something for Molly. I was immediately suspicious because me mum left me standing on the doorstep and locked the door behind her when she went to look for the bag. And she had white powder on her nose from doing coke. At the time I didn't realise there was anyone there – I found out afterwards he had been hiding in the kitchen. Then he took her off to a hotel in Liverpool, where he and another female journalist interviewed her, and kept her hidden there until the paper hit the shelves.

And that was the first I knew of it – when I saw the papers on 22 October 2006.

The headline across the front of the *News of the World* was: 'My Daughter The Cokehead'.

I went into complete shock.

Of all the people who have let me down over the years in the newspapers, I really didn't think Mum would do that to me. Don't get me wrong, she has let me down plenty of other times over other issues, but to sell me out like that on the front of the *News of the World*... I was so angry, hurt, betrayed and upset. Even thinking about how I felt that day, I can feel the anger still welling up in me. I don't think anyone has ever betrayed me on a bigger scale.

Mum has since told me that she had talked to the paper out of desperation to get through to me about Mark, and that she had told them she wanted the article to be about him, not about me. She also said she had never said the words that they put in the headline. In fact, when she rang up the female reporter afterwards and went mad, the reporter admitted me mum hadn't said them – a conversation me mum taped.

I do believe her. I know how words can be twisted by the media, and I am sure she did mean well but got out of her depth. But even with the tape, none of that makes what she did forgivable.

She tried to explain herself at the time, but then and there I decided I never wanted anything to do with her ever again. It made me sad, but the hurt and anger completely outweighed my love for her. Not only that, but I didn't want her near my children. If she put money over family, she was not an influence I wanted in their lives.

The Wedding

The call came out of the blue one day when I was sat eating in TGI Friday's with Mark. I couldn't hear my solicitor on the phone very well because of the noise in the restaurant, but I could just make out that my divorce from Brian had come through. The date – 18 December 2006 – is still clear in my brain. I was six months pregnant at the time, and although I was secretly devastated and felt like crying, I acted dead normal.

Brian had filed for divorce just two weeks after telling me he didn't love me. At the time I was absolutely destroyed, and still couldn't believe it was happening. But Brian pushed ahead despite my pleas. It took a fair bit of time, though. He wanted to divorce me in Ireland because the footballer Ray Parlour had recently divorced, and his wife had got a higher payout than usual and a share of his future earnings. Brian thought that meant I might do the same to him if we divorced in the UK.

I said to him, 'Brian, I don't want your money, I'm not going to fight for anything like that, I just want me kids. That's all I want.'

Well, he accepted that. So the divorce went ahead, and I got the kids, but financially I didn't do great. We split the house fifty-fifty, I took the jukebox that had been my pride and joy, and his mum took all the rest of the furniture, which I had carefully chosen to make our house a home. It broke my heart seeing that all taken away so soon after I had chosen it with a happy heart, thinking of our future together with the kids. Brian kept another penthouse apartment that we owned in Ireland.

The agreement was that his contribution to the children would be to pay the mortgage for the kids and myself on a new £400,000 house back in Warrington. He paid the initial deposit, but several months into us living there, I got a letter saying I was in the red and none of the mortgage payments were arriving. I just cleared the debt and picked it up from there.

We went to court and it was decided that instead he would pay £2500 a month towards the children, which he paid for a matter of months – and then stopped. Since then, he has made the odd contribution to school fees, but that is it. I never fought Brian for the rest of that money, but looking back, I sometimes think I was a mug. Of course he should have been paying something towards the upkeep of his kids. But at the same time I think I have always accepted that they are my children, so I am never going to begrudge paying every penny for them myself. I suppose it is more the principle with Brian, in terms of how it makes me feel about the respect he has for the kids and myself.

But at that moment, when I got the call, all the details and the wrangling seemed very far away. All I could think was that that was it. That was the end of what had seemed at the start a fairy tale. Though I had known the marriage was over, it felt strange to hear it was official.

Perhaps because of the divorce, and it being so final, I knew I had to focus on the future. I decided to make Christmas 2006 an extra-special day. I invited Mark's ex, Louise, and their daughter Keeley for Christmas. I never got on with Louise, but I like to think I am the bigger person, and the fact that I love Keeley to bits made me put my dislike to one side. I thought it would be nice for Mark to have his daughter there at Christmas, and for Keeley to have her mum and dad there. Maybe I was trying to do something for her that I wanted for my own kids. Or something that I wish I had had myself growing up. So Louise came to stay with Keeley, as well as her two sons by a previous boyfriend to Mark.

We had everything planned out and went to bed leaving everyone's presents wrapped up under the tree. I had bought her boys an Xbox and I put a rope round the door and a sign saying, 'Santa says don't open until Mum and Dad are up'. But we woke up the next morning to find the kids had been up and opened the whole lot of them before we were even awake on Christmas morning – and not just their presents but all of ours too! I was so mad, I grounded all the kids all day long – it was the worst Christmas Day ever. My kids would never dream of doing anything like that normally, they really wouldn't. Christmas is important to me, so I was really upset.

Throughout this time there were always rumours that something was still going on between Louise and Mark. They probably were just rumours, and if I am really honest, there were moments when I didn't care if he was cheating. I sometimes think I even wanted to catch him misbehaving with her, hoping that it would give me an excuse to go, 'Right, it's over.' Because ultimately, despite some of the good times we had, I still knew it was crazy that we were engaged. Mark was never going to be the love of my life. I just couldn't see how to deal with it, though, so discovering him cheating would have made the decision for me. I know that sounds weak, but sometimes it is easier to put things in the hands of fate. Nothing happened.

*

Of course, I was also busy focusing on my pregnancy, which was pretty tough.

One day I woke up in agony, crying. I simply couldn't move. It hurt to go to the loo, to walk, to do anything. It turned out my pelvis had broken in the night. Apparently it is quite common for pregnant women, especially after a few kids, and there was nothing they could do other than strap me up and put me on crutches for a while. I was more frustrated than upset, because I had already begun to feel less capable of doing things thanks to my big pregnant belly. Now I was totally helpless. I sat on the sofa all day long, bored and watching telly, not able to do a thing for myself while it healed.

So, however excited I was about becoming a mum again, by the end of January, when I was seven months pregnant, I was feeling anything but blooming. My pelvis had started to heal, and I was off the crutches, but I still wasn't on top form when I came down to London and was staying again at The Conrad Hotel. Yep, I was there a lot, I practically lived there! Every time I had to go to London for work, it was the place I chose to stay.

So there we were, relaxing in The Conrad that evening, when I noticed that Mark was acting all strange, and kind of nervous. He seemed like he couldn't sit still, and kept getting up and walking around, and wasn't really listening to anything I was saying. Finally, after we had got into bed, he said to me, 'I need to say something to you, before you read it in the paper.'

Straightaway, I went, 'Who is she?' That probably shows better than anything the way I thought about him, and the state of our relationship.

But he brushed me off. 'Oh, it's nothing like that, don't be daft. We're getting married in two weeks, on Valentine's Day.'

Valentine's Day! I'd previously asked Mark what we were

doing for Valentine's Day, and he'd said, 'We'll go to Scotland and get a little log cabin.' That had sounded nice and romantic. And also thoughtful, because it meant he had listened to me when I'd told him that I'd always liked the idea of going to a log cabin in the winter and curling up in a big woolly jumper with a log fire.

'You what?' I said, stunned.

I didn't know what to say. I know we were engaged, but I had no plans to get married to Mark. I felt awful and fat and tired. I was just two months away from giving birth. A wedding was the last thing on my mind. But Mark was determined we should get married before the baby was born.

'We're getting married in Gretna Green. It's all planned. The banns have been read out, which is what you have to do two weeks before you get married, but now it's done, the press have found out and are about to run the story tomorrow, so I had to tell you. Sorry to ruin the surprise, but I'd rather I told you about it than you read it in the papers. Max knows all about it. He's looked after the publicity and sorted *OK!* magazine to come and cover it. I've invited my mum, and my step-dad and two of my friends and that's it – we can keep it small and personal.'

'What about Molly and Lilly, though, Mark?' I asked. 'They won't be back from Australia in time!' The girls were in Australia with their dad and Mairead. It was the one and only time they have ever been out there to visit him.

'It's fine,' he reassured me. 'This is really just for you and me, we can celebrate with the girls later in the year. It will be an excuse for another wedding!'

'But Mark, I feel too huge and pregnant, and not like a bride!'

'Babe, it will be fine. I will sort us a blessing abroad later in the year. That can be like our real wedding. We can have our honeymoon then as well. But for now, our real wedding at Gretna is going to be great!'

Well, how do you get out of something like that? Don't get me wrong, not all my thoughts were negative or panicked. Part of me thought it was quite romantic, and I was impressed at the effort he had taken. It's not every day that a guy plans out a whole wedding to surprise you. Mark also told me that he wanted to sign a prenup, to prove to me and other people that he wasn't with me for me money, which was reassuring.

But beyond all this, in the back of my head I felt I was being controlled. I had been offered no choices or say in the matter. So my thoughts were swinging between 'How sweet' and 'How the fuck do I get out of this one?'

It didn't help that over the next few days the newspapers printed the news that we were getting married: when it was there in black and white, it was as though it was hard fact, something that was definitely happening. The whole country now knew, so the pressure to go through with it was even stronger.

The worst thing was, I didn't feel like I had anyone to talk to at the time. Mum and I still weren't talking, and nor were Lisa and I. I had become so dependent on Mark for company that, sad though it sounds, there was only person I could talk things through with: him. So I just went into autopilot and pushed ahead and organised my dress – the one thing Mark hadn't been able to sort. My stylist Lorraine McCullough arranged for Philip Armstrong to design a pale pink, babydoll-inspired, chiffon dress that went to my calves, and which had blue ribbon trim. Most importantly, it worked well around my huge bump! I planned to wear it with diamanté stilettos, and to curl my hair.

*

The two weeks passed in a flash. The time was taken up with getting the dress and sorting myself out, and I also had to call the kids and tell them the news. I knew they wouldn't properly understand, but I still wanted to tell them.

I got them both on the phone at the same time and said: 'Hi, baby girls! Mummy has some very exciting news. Mark and I are getting married!'

They were silent for a moment, then full of chatter. 'Yay! Can we come?' 'Will we be bridesmaids?' 'Do we get princess dresses?' All the important questions!

'This is a little one now, then later in the year we are going to do a big wedding, and yes, then you will be bridesmaids in beautiful dresses!'

Their excitement helped keep my thoughts off my swirling emotions. But the night before the big day I just had a sinking feeling in my stomach. You know when your gut instinct is telling you that you are doing the wrong thing? Well, I was getting that, and kept thinking that I needed to get out of it. Yes, I cared for Mark, I had feelings, but I didn't want to marry him; I just knew deep inside me that it wasn't right. I said to him, 'I don't feel well, I can't go, we'll have to cancel it to another time.'

Don't they say Gretna Green is traditionally where people run away to, when they want to get married but people don't approve? Well, I was probably the first bride that felt like running away from there! Not that I was short of people who disapproved. At times, it felt like the whole country thought I was making the biggest mistake of my life.

But Mark laughed my doubts off as nerves, convinced me we would be alright, and the next day we drove to The Mill Forge at Gretna Green, where we were holding the ceremony and reception.

As we approached the venue, I saw the whole area around it was thick with press and paparazzi. As we got out of the car they were yelling my name, and pushing each other to get a shot of me. That's when even the little bit of me that kept thinking, 'I can still pull out', faded. I'd come this far, and there was no way I could do that when there was so much attention. I just had to go with the flow.

It was just Mark, myself, and his four guests for the ceremony, which began at 8 p.m. Oh, and *OK!* magazine and all their security with ear pieces in, holding umbrellas and anything else they could think of to block the view of the 50-odd waiting paparazzi! *OK!* had paid for an exclusive and obviously didn't want it ruined. But there was definitely more security than guests. A bit depressing, that.

The Mill Forge was a cute, old set of buildings that felt like a step back in time to an old country village. There was a mill wheel and a rose garden, and a chapel in the grounds, which were filled with lanterns, lilies and roses – it felt quite romantic. As I waddled to the bottom of the aisle – remember that as well as being hugely preggers, I was still all strapped up for my broken pelvis under my dress – I said to Mark's stepdad Alan, 'Will you walk me down please?' It's kind of sad that, isn't it? I didn't have any bridesmaids, anyone from my family there to watch this happen, let alone a dad to walk me down the aisle. Even Max Clifford had had the sense to stay away.

And it was just a really boring, horrible service. It lasted all of about ten minutes and I remember looking at Mark as we were saying our vows, thinking, 'Oh my God, what am I doing?' It was like I had lost control of my own life, and was just going through the motions. But I said, 'I do' – and that was it. There was no getting out of it. Exactly a year after I'd horrified myself by falling into bed with Mark, he was my husband.

*

The reception was a medieval-style meal, including haggis and champagne! But even that didn't go well. Right in the middle of the meal, Max rang up and said there was a video doing the rounds of a girl sat on the edge of a bath with a towel on her head, fingering herself – and everyone thought it was me. The papers were looking into it, and the thinking was that Mark had sold the video. Can you imagine getting that call at your wedding reception? It was awful – I was sat there trying not to cry.

Max sent me a visual of the video to my phone – I was actually eating my wedding dinner while I was looking at it – and I nearly spat out my food. I am not joking, I was like, 'What am I doing?!' Because it really did look like me! It wasn't me, just a damn good lookalike! She had the biggest bust you have ever seen in your life, bigger than mine, and there were other subtle differences I could see. But I can't blame people who thought it was me. It really did look like me. Did I need to have that conversation and see that clip at my own wedding, while seven months pregnant? Probably not!

The bridal suite was a cute room with an old, four-poster bed. Being the wedding night and all that, it should have been romantic and special. But it wasn't. I guess I was uptight and thinking, 'What the hell have I done?' and Mark was drunk and gunning for a row. I don't know why – it used to happen sometimes once he had had a few drinks. He kicked off at me over the video, and we ended up having the biggest row ever. I went and stayed in a different room. It was a horrible end to a horrible day. I really don't have a single good memory of my wedding day to Mark, at all.

Of course, even us sleeping in separate rooms managed to leak to the press, God knows how, and they put in a call to Max to try and get to the bottom of it. He managed to just make a joke of it. He said that Mark had been farting all night long, and I had moved to escape the smell! Hardly the most romantic story, but probably better than the reality. I've never told anyone until now what really happened that night because I was so embarrassed. Who the hell starts married life like that? I was trying to escape the shame of my marriage to Brian failing – but a lot of the time it seemed like I was walking into something else even more embarrassing.

We didn't go on honeymoon, because I was ready to burst with my pregnancy. But we'd agreed that later in the year we would have a blessing abroad – more like what our wedding might have been had I not been pregnant – and then a honeymoon.

Something to look forward to, I suppose!

Early Arrival

Six days later, and six weeks before my due date, my waters broke.

Mark was asleep in bed next to me in Winwick Park. I woke him up, and he took me to Macclesfield General Hospital. I was reasonably calm – having done it twice before, I knew what was happening, and what each feeling and contraction meant. But my baby girl was breech, and refused to turn around, so I had to have a Caesarean in the end.

She came out on 20 February, and she was dead tiny, weighing just 4lb 9oz. But she was healthy, and we both cried. It was a lovely moment. It is so strange, but so beautiful, the first time you meet this little person who is so important in your life. You have carried them for so long, but this is the first time you get to set eyes on them.

When I first held her, I thought how tiny she was, and how much she looked like Mark. I had a picture taken of her in my arms, and Mark was really emotional. If I ever had cynical moments about his motives for getting me pregnant, this was not one of them. He was genuinely moved by it all.

He collected our Molly and Lilly from school the day she was born and brought them in to visit, and they had no idea what was waiting for them! They were so excited to have a new little sister, it was lovely to watch. They had known she was coming, obviously

– they had seen me getting fatter, and I had also explained to them there was a baby in my belly. And when the midwife had come to visit while I was pregnant, they had listened to her heartbeat through the stethoscope.

Although they knew Mark was her dad, while their dad was Brian, it made no difference to them. I had been very sure to tell them while I was pregnant that this baby was their sister, and they treated her with the same love and care they showed each other. Molly was 5 by then, and Lilly was 4, but they were like two little mums! 'Can we hold her?' 'She is so little!' 'Does she need food?' All kinds of questions came out of those two!

While I was in hospital, I was in that lovely state, that lovely feeling that all that matters is you and the baby. But there was the odd dark cloud. Mum called the hospital to see how me and the baby were doing, but I still didn't want to know. As far as I was concerned, I had said I wanted nothing more to do with her for the rest of my life – and I had meant it. It was hard having to do that, but I had to focus on my baby.

After I had been in hospital for three nights, I left at 1 a.m. on the Saturday morning. Mark came and got me and we did a runner. We had bought a new house, and he was taking me straight there in the middle of the night, as we didn't want any of the press to know where we were moving. It was kind of crazy, really, smuggling our new baby and me out the doors and to the car! And that first night we arrived, we hardly had any furniture, so we had to sleep on mattresses on the floor, with all the baby stuff scattered around us. It sounds extreme, but we wanted to have a bit of peace just for a little bit in our new house. We didn't want any photographers to follow us, so we hadn't wanted to draw attention with big delivery trucks.

The house we had settled on was a five-bedroom house in Wilmslow, a town in Cheshire. It was called Hartree House and I fell completely in love with it. Inside, there was lots of room – four floors with a cinema in the basement – and it was modern and clean, with loads of light, and a gorgeous, open kitchen. Plus it was in a really nice area with good schools for the kids, and celebrity neighbours including Wayne Rooney. And it was not too far from our family and the world we knew.

We settled in really quickly. I was busy looking after the baby, who was good as gold, and Mark sorted most of the arrangements for the house, getting it decorated, and new furniture. Not that I was impressed by the job he did – I remember going into the cinema room when he had got a new couch for there, and it was orange and green and gave me a migraine to look at it! But at least he was trying.

For the life of me, I still couldn't think of a name for my new little girl, though. Nothing seemed quite right, no matter how many names we suggested to each other. But then, two nights after we moved into our new house, Mark woke me up in the middle of the night and said, 'What about the name "Heidi"?'

And 'cause he had picked it, and he was her dad, I thought, 'Yeah, I'll go with that.'

I always get these images of what life will be like down the line, and I imagined Mark and I still together, and me telling Heidi, 'You know, your dad picked your name', and her being pleased about that. Not that my images always turn out to be true, but I can only dream.

Mark was very hands-on with Heidi, he really was. He got involved in nappy-changing, the lot, and I can't ever fault him for how he was as a dad. He was brilliant with my other kids too, fully involved in looking after them. They liked him too, and were bonding well with Heidi. Molly especially became like a second mum to her, and always wanted to feed and change her. She has always had a caring nature, looking out for others, and Heidi brought it out in her even more. It was very sweet, and it really started to feel like we were becoming a proper family.

We had tried a few new nannies since Cheryl had left, but it was only around this time that we found one we were happy with – a young girl called Gemma Story, who was about 20 at the time. She got on well with the kids and I liked her as a person.

She moved in with us and had her own area of the house, where she lived with her boyfriend. They had been together for years, and he was really good-looking and lovely, so it was nice to have them there with us.

A new baby, a new house, it was like a new start. I decided I was going to put myself into this marriage 100 per cent, and put all my doubts aside – and I hoped we could be happy.

So many things were going right for me, but not everything was rosy. As always, what looked great on the surface had cracks underneath. For a start, I was still getting a hard time in the press at this point, and it made me want to withdraw even more from public life. I hardly ever went out unless I was going out for work, to film for Iceland or do shoots. When I wasn't with the kids, I would be on the Internet, playing games or chatting on Facebook. I was becoming a bit of a recluse, and Mark encouraged it. He would point out to me how bad the outside world was, while reassuring me that he was there for me and protecting me. At the time I appreciated it, and started to lean on him more and more.

Practically the minute we settled into our new home, Mark was offering me cocaine again. At first, I made attempts to knock it back – I had lasted the whole of my pregnancy, and told myself it would be good to carry on free of it. But having given birth, I no longer had the motivation of being responsible for a life inside me, to make me say no. And when Mark was sat doing it so blatantly in front of me, it felt daft to be the one sitting there without. So I cracked, and started having sessions of it again.

It seemed the only people we were hanging out with were Mark's friends. All of mine had drifted away, or had been cut out by Mark. Instead, all his friends would come round, and all they ever wanted to do was drugs. It felt like I was moving in a real low-life circle. All these scuzzy kind of people would be round, the kind that wouldn't have been given the time of day by the Kerry before Mark. Yes, you could say a lot of my old friends did drugs, but they were still a classier kind of person. Some of my old friends have never ever sold a story on me to the press, they have resisted that temptation, whereas most of Mark's friends were financing their lives by doing exactly that.

It wasn't just about drugs, either – I was having trouble with my bipolar. Sometimes the disorder – or the medication I was taking for it – literally made it impossible for me to get out of bed, and I'd be curled up under the duvet by myself, lost in my own world. I'd feel like I couldn't move or function, and I knew it was getting worse.

I loved spending as much time as possible with the girls and going through the daily routine with them: getting their breakfast in the morning, having dinner or a take-away with them at night, and all curling up on the sofa to watch TV. But I was very aware when I wasn't in a fit state, and I never wanted them to see me like that, and that is when Gemma took over. I would be in my room with the door locked so the kids couldn't come in. It was the same when I took a line – I would do that in the bathroom off the shelf with the door locked as well, to be doubly sure they would never walk in on me.

Gemma was really good at looking after the girls, and keeping them out of the way when she knew we were having a drugs session, or on days when I was having trouble with my bipolar. I would hide myself away and deal with that. Gemma was good about this, either telling them I was ill or working. Not ideal I know, but it was the best way I knew to deal with it at the time, and it was better than them having to witness the truth.

The other thing that changed around now was the way the finances worked in the house. I was very conscious that Mark should not feel like I was earning all the money and providing for him, because I didn't think things should feel so uneven for my husband. So I was always trying to get him involved in my work, and got him to act as my driver for a lot of my events and jobs. Then, whenever we did any joint shoots, I was always clear with him that half the money was his, even if the magazine or paper had asked us there because of me.

Because he was my husband, I also thought I should give him a bit of control over the money, so little by little I gave him more power over my accounts and the money coming in from work. I tried not to question too much about what he was doing with every penny, as I wanted him to feel like the man of the house. Looking back, if I had been in a more conscious frame of mind, I wouldn't have been surrendering financial control. But I just wanted to trust my husband and be left alone to deal with my mood swings.

At the time, my main incomes were from my deal as face of Iceland, my column for *OK!* magazine, and general photo shoots and interviews. I reckon that my annual income was a bit over £1 million a year, and slowly but surely Mark was taking control of all of that, and of how it was spent and where it went. One of the ways he started spending it was on cars for himself. He was always a huge fan of cars, and this was the start of a period where brand new sports cars and motorbikes started appearing on our driveway, with Mark casually mentioning he had bought them.

I didn't mind. If it kept him happy and was a hobby of his, it wasn't a problem. Having enough money hadn't been an issue for me since becoming famous, so I didn't worry about that side of it. More fool me!

Trip to the United States

Dad had always said he would love to show us his life in the US, and I had said when he left that I would go out and see him. But I don't think he ever thought I would. One day in the spring, though, I got a call. It was me dad, and he had bad news.

'I've got something called DVT – deep vein thrombosis,' he said. Immediately I panicked. 'I need an operation and have to get some of my toes removed. I want to come back to the UK to have it.'

'I'll come out and bring you back. Then I will finally be doing that visit I promised!'

I was joking with him, but really I couldn't bear thinking about him making the trip alone. And I knew this was my chance to pay him back for all the times he had been there for me.

I booked a week-long trip for me and a friend, Claire – we had met through Mark. The idea was we would stay with him, then he would fly back to England with us afterwards. Heidi was three or four months old, and I wasn't that happy to leave her behind, but I knew she would be in safe hands with Gemma and her dad, and it was better for her than bringing her along to America.

Oh, he was over the moon to see us, me dad, he really was. And we turned up to his new home, and he lived on this proper stereotype of a white, trailer-trash park. He lived in a mobile home with two rooms, and it was a mess.

But he loved it. And as soon as I walked in I saw he had a picture of me from my days in Atomic Kitten on his wall. I had signed it: 'To my dad, love you always, Kerry'.

It was just nice spending proper time with him. My friend and I had one bedroom and he used to sleep in a bunk in the other room, and we just hung out during the day.

Dad was sleeping only about four hours a night 'cause of the pain. And you could see he was so tired. He was still smoking his roll-ups, but he was always falling asleep with a roll-up in his hand, so there were burns all over the carpet, and orange marks on the table from where they had fallen.

I'd say, 'Dad, get in bed, you need some rest.' But he'd refuse, 'cause he knew he couldn't sleep. I had some sort of Valium with me for the plane from when I'd flown out there, so one night I gave him two of them, and he went to bed.

Well, me dad was always up before me, but the next morning I wake up and what about Dad? He wasn't up. So I'm knocking on his door, and calling his name, and there's no answer, and he's a really light sleeper. I remembered the Valium and I was petrified: 'Shit, I think I've killed me dad!'

Finally he woke up and came out stretching. 'Oh, best night's sleep I've ever had that, Kez. Thanks!'

What a relief!

He took me to the War Veterans Club, and he was shuffling along because he was old and in pain. But there were some much worse sights in there – there was one old man sat in there with a bloomin' oxygen tank keeping him alive, and at the same time he was smoking a cigarette! And he was still as cheerful as can be, all like: 'Howdy, how ya doing!' and all of that. It was total madness!

Dad was as lively as ever, and we were knocking back the beers and the shots, and he was telling everyone, 'This is me daughter.' They all had my Atomic Kitten CDs and they knew all about me.

The next day, I was talking to one of his neighbours back in the park, who said, 'Oh, he's always on about you and how you're a great singer and he keeps us up to date on what you're doing and he told us you had written a book.' Apparently Dad had the book in his caravan – he had everything – and he was showing it to everyone.

And it was only then I realised about me dad: that despite us not having talked for all those years, he was really proud of me but had never told me. I honestly didn't realise until that moment, you know, and it felt so good to have that realisation. It made me feel so happy that I had been wrong when I thought he wouldn't be aware of, or care about, the things I had achieved. Knowing I had actually been making him proud all along was so important to me... and to him.

Another day, Mandy, a daughter of one of his friends, came and picked us up and took us into town. We went to all these Irish bars and me dad loved it. He was just made up that someone could come and see where he lived and he could show these places off to us. It makes me well up even thinking of that trip now. I can't explain how glad I am that I did it.

I flew him back first class. His feet were looking terrible, so I wanted to get him back for the operation quickly, and in as much style and comfort as possible. And I put him in his chair and got his leg up and gave him a bottle of champagne.

I'm sat in front of him, and I remember clambering onto my knees and turning round and leaning over the back of the chair, and saying to him: 'You alright, Dad? First class alright for you? You know you've got a proper bed there and your own telly?'

And he just grinned and leaned back, and said, 'It's bloody great, I feel great.'

I was so glad I got to do that for him. I was so, so made up about it, I really was. I smile even now, thinking about it, while I write this.

When we got back to the UK, he had to go into hospital for him to have his operation. Of course he was scared, who wouldn't be? But he tried not to let on, and made up for it by cracking even more jokes than usual.

It was a relief when he was out of surgery, though, and I went straight to visit him. He was sat in bed looking tired, but he said, 'Glad to still be here!'

I used to go and visit him in hospital all the time, and I'd take the kids when I could. Even Mark went down once or twice when I couldn't make it.

When he recovered, he moved back to his old Warrington home and stayed there for a while. He couldn't walk very well at first, and had to rely on a walking stick or, when he was out and about for longer, a wheelchair. But I think he was happy just to be in his old home, out of hospital and with a sense of independence again.

Mark was planning our blessing abroad at this time. Obviously, I was paying for it, but he was planning it all as I surprise, so he wouldn't tell me anything about it! But I did the proper thing, and asked me dad to give me away. I told him I would sort wheelchair access and it would be as easy as anything. But he said, 'No. I don't want to be a burden. I'll be in everyone's way.' I said to him, 'I *want* you there, I want you to give me away. That's a dad's job, and you're my dad.' But he was adamant that he was not going to do it. So instead I tried to get him involved as much as I could beforehand. I told him any little snippets of gossip about it that I could work out in advance, whenever Mark let anything slip. And after I had chosen my wedding dress and he was round Pat's house one time, I came in wearing it. He loved it and started crying. It was so nice to have him as part of that. I felt really emotional, but I told him to stop being a soft git. Me dad was such a hard man, but I managed to make him cry several times!

Violated

One Sunday night, 15 July 2008, Mark and I were at home just chilling out. Molly and Lilly were in Ireland, and we had Heidi with us. Mark's friend had been round earlier in the evening, and now that he had left we were relaxing in the cinema room, which was in the basement.

It was an ordinary evening. Mark was playing on the Xbox, and I was sat behind the double doors into the room on my laptop. I had to sit there 'cause I needed to plug in my laptop. I was playing bingo – yep, you can see all the mates I had, that *that* was the dead exciting way I was spending my evenings at the time!

Heidi was in her car seat in the corner of the room, fast asleep.

A bit after 10 p.m., Mark turned towards the door and went, 'Oh. Hang on a minute now, mate.'

'Cause of where I was sitting, I couldn't see who he was talking to, but what I could see, was this knife, poking round the door – this bloody great carving knife, which I recognised straightaway from my kitchen. Even now, I can't get the image out of my head. The blade looked huge: I couldn't take my eyes off it.

In that moment, I was sent straight back into my childhood, back to being a 13-year-old girl.

I had been living in London with me mum and Dave Wheat, her boyfriend at the time. One night, after an evening in the pub, he had turned violent. Not a one-off – until he pulled out a knife and stabbed Mum right through her thigh. When I tried to help her, he said, 'I'm going to kill the little bitch now.' He chased me up the stairs, swinging the knife, pretending to be Freddy Krueger from *A Nightmare on Elm Street*, and threatening to cut off my feet and hands.

He didn't hurt me in the end, but the mental torture went on most of the night, and the memory of it has haunted me forever.

So to see a knife come around the corner of my room… I felt all the feelings I had kept buried deep inside for the last 15 years rising up again, and I started screaming and shaking. Then three men walked into the room, all with balaclavas and caps on.

One of them was holding that knife, another had a sledge hammer, and the third had a butcher's hook. I was hysterical. I couldn't stop looking over at Heidi in the corner. I desperately wanted to get to her, but they were in the way and I didn't want to draw attention to her. In my head, though, I was thinking, 'Make no mistake: touch her, and I'll kill you.' As I stood there, I couldn't help sobbing, until one of them told me, 'Fucking shut up and keep quiet.'

Mark was the absolute opposite of me. He was dead calm, and quietly said: 'What is it you are after, mate?'

And they said to him, 'We want you on your own. Get her out of the room, we want you.'

'They're going to kill him,' I thought, and I got even more hysterical, shouting to him, 'I love you, I love you, Mark.'

But Mark was still calm, and really in control of himself. He went, 'Just a minute, mate, can you take my daughter out of the room, give her to her mum?'

And, thank God, they let me go over to her.

I picked her car seat up. I was shaking so much I could hardly hold her, but bless her, she was still fast asleep, without a clue what was going on around her. I sat there so scared that I pulled my jumper over my head. I don't really know why, I guess it was just a childlike reaction; I wanted to hide from it all. But I wasn't even allowed to do that – they were convinced I was making a call or something inside my jumper – if only that had been possible! So they made me take my jumper off and I had to sit in a little vest top.

I was that scared, I literally wet myself. I used to think people were joking when they said that, but no, I was so terrified it happened to me. This was true terror, and I was completely powerless.

It soon became obvious the three men wanted our stuff. So I did everything I could to help. I thought if I co-operated, we would have more chance. I told them where the watches were, where to find my credit cards, what the PIN numbers were. They kept discussing it all over our heads, calling each other 'bro'.

They decided to march Mark around the house with them, so they wanted to tie me up. I couldn't believe it. I could hardly speak, but I pointed out that I needed to be able to get to my baby. It was hardly like I was going to run for it, with them and their weapons in the house. So instead one of them stayed with me. I remember he told me, 'If you scream, I swear I will fucking cut you up.'

He was right cocky, a really horrible lad. He kept calling me Kelly, and eventually I got enough strength together to say, 'I'm Kerry, not Kelly.' And he replied. 'Ah yes, you was in that Atomic Kitten band, you was the best one in that, you was. Do you want me to get you a drink?'

It was unreal. I was in a complete state of shock.

Meantime they were clearing out the house. Televisions, jewellery (including my wedding ring and engagement ring), watches – anything worth anything really was taken, and loaded up into the cars outside, including one of our cars. They were marching Mark around with them and getting him to show them where things were, and even help carry stuff out for them.

The longer I sat there, the less afraid I was getting, and the more angry. How dare they come in my house and start taking my things? Things I had worked hard to earn and buy for my family and for me, messing around with the home we had made our own. What would have happened if Molly and Lilly had been home? They would have been affected by this for the rest of their lives. And as I started working myself up, one of them came in with a cheque for a large amount of money made out to me, and said, 'Great, I'm taking this.'

I just answered, 'You thick fucker, it's written out in my name, so good luck with that, you knob.' I could feel myself getting angrier and angrier, but I knew it was nearly over, and I couldn't risk them deciding they might hurt us after all, so I kept it in check.

Eventually, after they had been there for an hour and ten minutes, they put Mark, Heidi and me in the downstairs bathroom. Luckily they hadn't hurt Mark, and they gave me milk, nappies and a blanket for Heidi. I had calmed down a bit by this point and I even found myself being grateful for that small mercy.

But then they blocked the door shut with the pool table. It was horrendous. I thought they were going to burn the house down with us inside it. I kept going back to my childhood in my mind, thinking there was no way someone could survive two awful attacks like that. Everything was going through my head, all the things I had been through and survived, and I was thinking, 'This is it now, I'm going to die.' In my head I was telling Molly and Lilly how much I loved them, and being so thankful they were away.

I don't know how long we were trapped in that room, but after a bit Mark managed to force the door open, and shouted out, 'Me wife needs her medication, mate. Can you help?' There was no reply, so we knew they had gone. We looked out the window and could see the cars with all the stuff inside had gone, so we ran upstairs and called the police.

Can you believe, Heidi was still asleep? My little baby girl had slept through the whole thing and never had a clue what had happened – for that one thing, I am so thankful.

After phoning the police, I found myself doing something unexpected. I called Mum. Although we hadn't spoken since the year before, I knew she would hear it on the news and be worried. My fury at her had thawed a little – just enough that I didn't want her to panic. So I called her quickly and said, 'I'm just phoning to say I'm alright, 'cause I knew you would be worried.'

She burst into tears and said, 'Kerry, don't ever forget I love you and the babies.' It was a hard moment, because a bit of me just wanted to rebuild our relationship and forget everything, but I was still angry, and the sense of betrayal was still too strong. So I hung up, and turned my mind back to the robbery.

I just couldn't believe what had happened. How the hell had they got in? We had a keypad lock on the door, eight CCTV cameras around the outside of the house – and a bulldog sat upstairs in the kitchen, which they had walked straight past. That dog was as soft as shite, and didn't even bark at them or anything. Fat lot of good! Though I don't know how they were so sure of the dog.

And yet they still got in. The CCTV had picked them up, but they were all so well covered up that it didn't lead to anything. There was a door to the garage, and another door to the kitchen from the garage, and apparently neither was locked. Lucky for them, that. As was a random guess on a door, which turned out to be right – especially as the CCTV showed they made a beeline straight for it.

Later on, the police came back with CCTV footage of them using my card at a cash point, but you couldn't see anything more than what you could see on our CCTV.

In the days afterwards, we started trying to get our lives back together, and put in a claim for everything we had lost with the insurance company – it came to over £100k. But the money and the things they took were basically unimportant. It was the fact that it had actually happened that was playing over and over again in my head and driving me mad.

And while I was going through everything and trying to sort it out, something else happened that wrecked my head. I was tidying the house to distract myself, and I can't even believe I am saying this, but I came across a book called *How To Burgle A Home*. I couldn't think why Mark would have something like that in the house so soon after everything that had happened. It was really insensitive. I confronted him and said, 'What is this doing here?' But he shrugged and said, 'I've never seen it before in my life! Maybe it was left by the people before?'

'No way! Are you winding me up? You must know why it is here?'

'Let it go, Kerry, it's nothing.'

Then a million theories started whirling round my mind. He couldn't be linked to it, surely, but was it possible he knew it was going to happen?

I had never really discussed the robbery with Mark – I tried to ignore it – but now I was wondering. Questions, such as how they knew how to get in, came back into my head. My mind was racing. But bad though I thought Mark was at times, I couldn't believe he could put the mother of his child through that, especially with his own baby in the house. Then again, maybe he was linked without realising – an old enemy of his could have targeted us.

In the end, I decided I wouldn't let myself think about it at all. He was as much a victim as me, I decided, and that was that. And it is not something I ever got to the bottom of afterwards. There will always be questions about it in my head, and I guess I will never know the truth.

I moved out of the house and in with me dad, taking Heidi with me. It was nothing to do with my find, but just because I didn't want to be in the house, 'cause I was that scared and it was too full of memories from that night. Mark was fine, he just carried on living at our home. But for me it was a horrific time and I just couldn't handle being there for the time being.

Being back with me dad was kind of reassuring. It was like I was back to being a little girl, with him looking out for me again – except this time I was able to do a lot for him too around the home, to make life easier for him. And he was overjoyed to have me back living there. At that moment it felt like a real sanctuary for me and I found myself able to laugh and share a joke with him when laughing had become impossible at home.

They're My Kids!

Much as I tried to get my head together after the robbery, I just couldn't. I was a jittery mess. Asking myself why that had happened to me, and going over my childhood, and thinking again and again about that knife.

So after four days at me dad's, I went to The Priory. The Priory is a private hospital in Roehampton, south west London, which specialises in mental issues. While you are treated, you stay in what are kind of basic hotel rooms, then you have various sessions, both group and individual, with nurses, therapists and psychiatrists to deal with whatever issues you have. It has become famous over the years for treating various celebrities, but by no means does that make it glamorous – it has a job to do, and it gets on and does it.

Every time I ever go in The Priory, people assume, 'Oh it's drugs, it's alcohol.' It rarely is. In fact, I think I have been there only once for drugs. Most of the time it was about my bipolar medication, to change the dose or the levels.

This time, I had what I know now was basically a breakdown. I had so much on my plate, I just couldn't cope with life. I was being invaded by the press constantly, which I had been just about handling, but then being invaded in my own home was the final straw. And the fact that they had used a knife sent me over the edge.

Before I went in, I rang Brian's mum Mairead in Ireland because she still had the kids with her. Molly was six at the time, and Lilly was four, and I didn't want to confuse their minds with what was happening. I wanted them to think their holiday was just being extended – not something most kids mind! We hadn't told them about the burglary, and we didn't intend to, either. I said to Mairead, 'Please don't panic, but I have to get myself sorted, I'm just really scared, and I'm finding it hard to cope.'

She was lovely, and said, 'Don't worry, I'll look after the kids, I'll get everything sorted, Don't worry, I'll get the kids into a school.'

And I was relieved, and said, 'Thanks so much Mairead, but don't worry about schools. I'm only going to be there for a week at the most, so I will be out before they need schools, so it'll be fine. I'll be out on Tuesday, so they can come home then.'

Heidi was to stay at home with Gemma looking after her, and that was it, I went to The Priory.

The Priory has always worked for me as a break to get away from everything. Remember this was not just something I was dealing with in my head, it was all over the news too. I was such a wreck when I went in, I just couldn't go on. But a week there really helped, and I came out again feeling stronger and ready to face the world.

While I had been in there, Mark had gone on his stag-do to Magaluf. I'd found that pretty stressful because it had been on his stag-do just before our wedding that Brian cheated on me – not that I had found out until after the wedding. Another incident during our marriage also made me suspicious that he had cheated. But at the time Mairead had given me a talking to about how boys will be boys, and I had to put the issue behind me and get on with my life with Brian. So although I didn't want to give him the impression it was acceptable, I had done exactly that.

Even after we split, I would get people telling me about their friends who had slept with him during our marriage. To be fair, I will never know if they were 100 per cent true, and it is so far in the past now that I am really beyond caring.

But when Mark asked me before he went whether he should cancel his stag-do, I really wanted to be sure he didn't get punished for Brian's mistakes. So I told him to go and enjoy himself – but to make sure he behaved.

While I was in The Priory, I kept in close contact with him as well as my kids. I rang them in Ireland every single day, if not twice a day, which is what I always do when they are away, or I am away working. And this time I told them, 'Mummy is away working, but I really miss you, and I can't wait to see you on Tuesday!'

And they completely accepted what I was saying, and would chatter about what they had been up to, and tell me they loved and missed me too. Knowing I was going to be meeting up with them again, and knowing I'd be feeling better after getting help made things bearable.

Tuesday came and I was out of The Priory and moved back in with Dad. While I felt stronger, I wasn't ready to go back to the house yet.

Then I called Mairead. No answer. Strange. So I left voice messages, and tried ringing Brian. Also no answer. While alarm bells were ringing I thought there was probably an easy explanation, but as the night wore on and I left more and more voicemails I was getting really worried. Had something happened?

I knew Mairead was a good grandmother, and she would never let anything happen to my girls. But when she didn't reply the next day I started to really panic. At that moment realisation dawned as I suddenly became aware of what she was doing – trying to keep the kids. I thought maybe the comment she had made about getting them into schools hadn't been a misunderstanding but was actually something she was planning to do.

I kept ringing – and still no answer. Now I could feel the fright and the anger welling up inside me and I felt so helpless. Stuck in the UK, I didn't know whether to fly to Ireland. I didn't know what to do. I didn't want her to have a change of heart and fly them home while I was on my way there. And I still didn't want to believe she would really be trying to take them off me.

But a couple more days passed, and there was still no reply from her or Brian. I was frantic and rang Louis Walsh, and also tried to get hold of Simon Cowell, who had signed Westlife in the first place – any way I could think of to get through to Brian – but without success.

Eventually, after five days, I had had enough. So much for getting my head sorted in The Priory – I was a total mess again by now. I called one last time to Mairead, but no reply, so I left a voice message saying, 'Mairead, I haven't a clue what is going on. I need my children, I haven't spoken to them in a week. You have to let me know what is happening.'

But she didn't. So I called the police and my solicitor. It seemed ridiculous to do that to the girls' grandmother, but I felt she had left me no choice.

I left a voicemail for her, 'Mairead, a solicitor's letter is on its way to you, and the police are coming round. I need to know my children are safe.'

Within a minute she rang me straight back, screaming and swearing. 'These are my grandchildren, you left them last week, you are not getting these kids!'

I yelled back, 'Actually, Mairead, they are my children. I get held hostage in my own house, and unsurprisingly I'm in a state from it, and you are blaming me for that? That's my fault?'

Molly and me – I was still a kid myself at this stage but the rot was already setting in my brain.

Lilly was the image of me at this age. Her accent is now the opposite of mine though!

Coleen Nolan and I remain great mates today.

Still upsets me now seeing this. Realisation that my life was falling apart was starting to dawn on me.

Our Lilly Pops' 9th Birthday. Where does the time go? She's turning into a beautiful young lady.

Me and my mum. We've been through a lot together but we've come out on the other side, stronger than ever.

Don't they look great? We got a ton of sweets that night . . . even a few quid! But don't tell the kids!

Molly and Lilly dressed up for school. I have no idea where they get it from . . .

Me on Halloween, 2011. But don't be fooled, it's what is under the mask that is scary!

Pete is one of my best mates and always will be. Claire and I had our differences (and still do!) but I have a lot of fond memories from the early part of our relationship.

So giddy with Rod. One of my all time heroes and still looking fit as . . . can't believe I actually got him in a headlock!

The Three Musketeers. Molly, me and Lilly on holiday together in Marbella.

Every year Danielle and me take the kids away and do our best to give them an amazing time. Even without dads around!

Me and the gang strawberry picking. I'm so proud of them.

Look how cool my beautiful babies are!

Max and me in the pool having the best time ever. He's such a mummy's boy but I wouldn't have it any other way.

The three of us away on holiday together. I could eat them up on a butty!

As grandmother she had no legal right to them over me, and Brian wasn't there – the police called round and it was just her at home with the children. But while I was waiting for the girls' return, he flew back from Australia. And then – and I 100 per cent believe that Mairead, not Brian, was the force behind what happened next – Brian applied for full custody of the kids.

I felt everything collapsing around me. My kids were my life, there was no way I was giving them up, and I felt a huge force of panic welling up inside me. Yet alongside the panic I recognised my inner determination rising too and I got very angry. So, so angry. This was Brian, who until now had been happy for me to look after the kids so he could get on and live his own life in Australia, who hardly paid anything towards their upkeep, and who did have contact, but not exactly a lot. On average, I would say, he sees them once, maybe twice a year. And then maybe they have three or four phone calls a year with him, while they are with me in England – more, I imagine, when they are in Ireland. And he wanted to take them off me. He actually thought he could do that to them and to me. For him to be all of a sudden making out that they were the most important thing in his life, and that he suddenly had their best interests at heart and was about to start playing dad. And I knew full well it would have been Mairead who ended up looking after them, not him! I was truly raging. But my mind was becoming very clear and I was ready for this, the most important fight of my life. Those rats who had invaded my house in their ridiculous balaclavas faded into insignificance.

I was beside myself. I couldn't bear to go this long without seeing my babies and now it looked as though I was going to have to wait for a court hearing before it could be settled. I threw myself into looking after Heidi – I didn't want her to be left out, while I panicked over the other two. And Mark and Gemma were a great support at the time, just giving me hugs, and keeping everything else running in the house.

Luckily we got a court date quickly, at a court back in England. I went through the back entrance to avoid attention, but Brian went through the front entrance, with his shirt hanging out and a fag in his gob, all cocky as can be.

Brian had a QC and all these big lawyers, and was claiming I wasn't fit enough to look after the kids. Because he had taken me to court, I had to take the stand, and I was asked all these questions. I said, 'Look, my kids know nothing. Yes, I have done wrong, I have done drugs, but ask my children what they have seen, and they will tell you, nothing.'

They sent a Cafcass officer to go and see the kids. Cafcass stands for Children and Family Court Advisory and Support Service, and they look into issues involving children's welfare. I had to go through a similar thing when I was a kid, and the last thing I wanted was for my children to go through it too.

On the one hand I was absolutely mortified, but on the other I thought that the court would see the truth and understand that Molly and Lilly and their little sister Heidi were my world.

Needless to say, the judge ordered the kids to come home, and gave me full custody – the main reason being that Brian and Mairead had broken the rules of custody by keeping the kids in the first place. I was elated. The feeling was indescribable, better than any drug. Now I just had to see their faces and hold them both in my arms.

As soon as I got out of the court I went to a hotel to pick them up and Mairead was there but she wouldn't look at me. I was so angry at her for putting me through that, but looking back now, I suppose I see what she was doing a bit differently and even can understand it in some ways. I imagine she was reading all the exaggerated and spun stories in the papers, stories about drugs, and the burglary. She would only have been hearing the one side, and yes, she probably did panic about the way the kids were being affected. She will have had their best interests at heart, and I guess she genuinely believed they were at risk. But I wish she had called me about it instead and I could have told her the truth. There is no way I would ever have let my babies get harmed. They were – and still are – my life!

As soon as the kids saw me that day, they ran so fast to me, and I was shaking. They were like: 'Mummy, we have missed you! What's been going on?' And I said, 'Mummy has been busy working, darlin's. Nanny has been looking after you for me, but I've missed you so much.'

I never said a word about what had been going on, the court case or anything. I took the blame for them having been in Ireland for so long, to protect them from finding out. Protecting them and keeping their innocence for as long as possible has always been my aim.

Despite the trauma of the whole episode, I didn't stop the girls going over to Ireland to stay with their grandparents. Hard though it was, I knew it was an important relationship to maintain. There was a court order in place, so I felt certain Mairead wouldn't try the same thing again. Deep down I knew it was in the girls' best interests to keep that connection, and I knew they needed the bond they had had with their grandparents from birth. Now that I knew the terms were clear and we understood each other, I felt calm about the situation. Plus, the most important thing of all, I know that she and her husband adore the girls, and more importantly, the girls love them to bits. I would never want Molly and Lilly growing up and thinking I had stopped them seeing their grandparents. So I encouraged them to keep going to Ireland to visit.

Completely out of the blue, not long after they were home, Molly came home and, looking confused, said, 'Mum, was the house burgled while we were away?'

'Who told you that?' I asked, buying some time while I thought of an answer.

'One of my friends went past while we were in Ireland, and saw police at our house, and police tape all around it. She told me about it today and said she heard we were burgled.' As kids do, she gazed at me expectantly, waiting for the answer.

Mark and I looked at each other. We had decided not to tell the kids, 'cause we knew they would be scared about it and it could get them worried at night, or make them afraid of it happening again. We had got everything replaced by the insurance company before they got home, so they had no way of knowing. So we just exchanged very obvious confused looks, and I said: 'They must have got the wrong house, darlin'. If we got burgled, how is all our stuff still here? Don't you think they would have taken all the jewellery and other expensive things?'

I could see her standing there, processing it in her mind. Luckily, she finally accepted that, nodded, and wandered off. We gave a sigh of relief. I have told them since what happened, after we moved out of that house, but they were too young at the time. I felt the need to protect them. The world has enough bad in it, and the longer I can protect them from it, the better. That was definitely one thing I learned from my childhood – learning far too much when I was far too young was no good thing. As any parent knows, white lies are there for the kids' protection.

At their age, I had seen far too much – Mum slitting her wrists in an attempt to kill herself, huge rows between her and Dave, big bust-ups with Dad that meant the police had been called, all of them regularly drunk – and I knew how lasting it can be on your memory. I know it's ingrained forever in mine. It was something I would give anything not to repeat with my own children, so while, yes, I was lying to them, I felt like it was lying for a good reason.

Test of Trust

What I probably could have done with about now was a little less drama, a little less trouble. No chance. I suddenly had a new problem on my hands. Mark, the person I had been leaning on throughout this ordeal and who was my one stability within all this, was about to be accused of cheating on me.

In the few months beforehand, Max Clifford had kept saying to me, 'Kerry, he's cheating, he's doing this and that' – I suppose because he was hearing it from the newspapers and there were a few rumours. But without some definite proof, I refused to believe it. I couldn't think of many times where it was possible, but then again I had been busy, what with work, being robbed and fighting for my girls.

Then it landed. One Sunday morning at the beginning of August, I got a message from a friend asking if I had seen the papers. I went out to get them and the *People* newspaper had a story that Mark had cheated on me. It was an interview with a barmaid called Clare Bonello, who claimed that Mark had cheated on me with her. She was an ex-girlfriend of his, and claimed that she had slept with him just days after he had proposed to me. She also reckoned he had told her he was only with me for the money.

I was gutted. It was like a complete punch to the stomach.

I was round at me Dad's house, and he completely lost it. He'd held a lot back about Mark because of everything that had been going on but that was about to end in no uncertain terms. Since he had been back in the UK, I had been vaguely aware he didn't approve of Mark. They got on well enough when they were face to face, and although I think he was oblivious to us taking drugs, he had heard so many other bad things about him, to do with money and cheating, that he obviously began to think he was bad news. But he had never voiced those negative opinions until that moment.

'I wish you would tell him to fuck off,' he said. 'I can't stand him.' Then, waving his stick around, he said: 'When I see him, I'll bleedin' well belt him!'

He was so angry on my part, bless him. While I might not have been his daughter by blood, I was still his little girl, his youngest as far as he was concerned, who needed protecting. Seeing me hurting was really getting to him. And it didn't matter that he was old – he would be effing and jeffing with the best of them. He had been quite a hard man in his day, had Dad.

I was furious and hurt. The things that Clare said made sense. She said that once, when he was getting a kebab for me while I was pregnant, he had gone round to hers. And I couldn't stop thinking about that night when he had gone out for just that reason and come back several hours later... No one takes three hours to get a kebab in the real world, do they?

I was living at me dad's at this time, but as far as I was concerned the family home was still mine because I had paid for it. So I went round and got mad, and refused to listen to what Mark said, eventually, summoning all of my strength, I kicked him out of the house while I got my head together.

Deep down of course I didn't want to believe that he had cheated at all, but the story kept developing. Clare did a lie detector test with one of the papers, which came back saying she was 100 per cent telling the truth.

Mark was adamant that the Clare story was not true. Once I had calmed down a bit, I agreed he could come round and talk, and he told me she was doing it for the money and the fame, and why would he be interested in her when he had me? He talked and talked at me about it, and really started to win my head around. As he could see me wavering he would start laughing and joking and then out came the coke and I would forget about his apparent cheating, we would have a laugh, and I would wonder what the issue had ever been. Then, when I came down to earth I would torture myself mentally again and bring it up. He'd be like: 'What? We already discussed this. Are you going to go over and over it? Decide to forget it, please, and let's move on!'

This is how it would work. He would start to convince me again, and we went round in that circle a few times. Until finally I decided I would give him the benefit of the doubt and allowed him back into the house.

But Max, who was not a fan of Mark's even if he never out-and-out said it to me, must have seen this as his chance to get rid of Mark and make me see the truth. He very cleverly said to him, 'Do you want to do a lie detector? It's the only way to prove your innocence to Kerry, really, and save your relationship. The fact that Clare has done one and come out apparently telling the truth makes you look bad, and if you've got nothing to hide, well, sure, it won't be a problem.' I suspect, although I'll never know, that on the quiet he told him that they were dead easy to pass, and he could sail through it either way, to encourage him to do it.

Mark refused at first, but then agreed to do one – not for the papers but just for me. And he failed. I remember he called me up to tell me, and he was like: 'It's all bollocks anyway, you know those things don't tell the truth. Clare probably never even did one, it will just be the papers claiming that to make a good story.'

He kept on and on non-stop and finally convinced me that Max was setting him up, and he was the victim in all this. Or maybe he didn't convince me, but I chose to believe it. Because maybe believing that was better than having to face the fact that my husband had cheated on me. The part of me which should have screamed down my ear that I was being stupid just closed itself down. Meanwhile the part of me that wanted an easy life, and wanted the family to stay together no matter what, took over.

After everything I had been through that month with the custody battle for Molly and Lilly, I just wanted life to be simple again. I wanted to get things back to the way they had been at the start of the summer: Mark, the girls and me together as a family. So I closed my mind to any evidence, and I decided to trust my husband. The alternative was just too much to bear.

Celebrations

Straight after the whole Clare Bonello story, Mark did his best to be the perfect husband and make things good with us again. And when he wanted to win me round, he was very good at it. He knew the things to say and do to make me feel good about myself, and he also knew how important us being a family was to me, so he really focused on that. So, for a time, things were good.

I think the fact I had my family back together again made me feel so relieved and happy that I overlooked all my doubts, especially because I appreciated Mark's support in fighting for Molly and Lilly. One thing he was good at was always knowing when to give me a hug and when to sit and listen. That was the thing with our relationship – things would change so quickly, it was hard for me to get a clear perspective. I have to give him credit where it's due, and there were many things he did deserve credit for.

We had a few weeks of things feeling right and on track. For a while drugs became a thing of the past. We weren't always on drugs of course, but it was really rare for us to be both clean and getting on well together at the same time. So it felt like everything was changing for the better. We would spend evenings cuddled up on the couch watching movies, or in bed watching TV. We always watched *NCIS* and *House*, and Mark loved the Comedy Channel.

Sometimes we would stay downstairs and watch TV with the kids – Mark didn't like them coming in the bed with us – and we would watch a kids' movie, or just jump about on the sofa, playing our own silly games, with Mark and I giggling as much as the kids.

Then one day, out of the blue, Mark said to me, 'Let's try for another baby'.

We were so happy at the time, it made sense to me in that moment. I felt thrilled at the idea. And I said, 'Alright, then. But while I love my girls to bits, this time I would love it if I could have a boy!'

Mark said, 'Too bloody right! How do you think I feel being so outnumbered in the house!'

'Ha. Lucky you! Okay, let's do it. Then our family really would be complete.'

So we started trying, and had fun with that until one day Mark came cuddling and kissing me on the sofa with a certain cheeky grin on his face, which I knew meant he had something he was going to ask me. He looked as though he was about to try and win me round on something.

'If I get you pregnant with a boy, will you buy me a Ferrari?'

Kiss, kiss, hug, kiss...

'Please, then it would be two amazing presents in one go!'

'Oh alright, then!' I laughed. He knew how easy it was to get round me.

The natural next step was for us to plan our long overdue wedding blessing. Because we had done everything in such a rush for Gretna Green, and with hardly anyone there, we wanted to make this a better, more memorable day. Mark was organising it all, which I was more than happy about. All I knew was it was going to be abroad and I let him get on with all of the details, just as I had done for our Gretna wedding.

We invited about 50 of our friends and family, and we paid for them all to fly out and stay there. The invites gave an indication that it was in Spain, but it wasn't. Not that I had a clue!

We went to Manchester airport and even all the screens in the airport were turned off. I have no idea how they managed to get them to do that, but it was really romantic, and I was amazed at the effort Mark had made. Then we got on our own private plane.

And the destination was actually Italy, to a place called Piedmont, right by Lake Orta. We stayed in Villa Crespi, an *Arabian Nights*-style castle. The place was out of this world, and so unbelievably romantic.

And we had the whole place to ourselves – it was like being on an amazing four-day holiday with friends and family. Though, of course, one sadness was that my closest family weren't there. Me mum wasn't there because we still weren't talking, and despite all my persuasion, Dad still stuck to his idea that he didn't want to be a burden, so he refused to come. And, of course, a couple of people from *OK!* magazine came along too – I think they have covered just about every major event in my life!

No dramas, no turmoil, no arguments or problems. This time we just had a laugh, and it was really good.

I was clean at the time as well and determined to keep myself that way, especially while we tried for a baby. But I remember one of Mark's guests smuggled drugs over to Italy for the trip and I was fuming when I found out. I really kicked off because I wanted my marriage blessing to be drug-free. It got sorted out quickly, and I can genuinely say I was happy. Everything was beautiful and actually fun!

The only downside was that the day before the blessing, Mark's mum Marilyn and our Pat had a huge fall out. I can't remember what it was over, but I never really liked his mum; she could be a real pain and it felt like she was always moaning. I loved his step-dad, but his mum – no, we never got on. Sometimes when she drank, she would get really drunk and then kick off, and this was one of those times.

It was horrible, and made me nearly not want to go through with the blessing – how dare these people get on like this at our wedding, especially when I had paid for them all to fly out there and stay? It just seemed ungrateful. It was sorted out in the end, and I decided that nothing should ruin our wedding this time.

The ceremony the next day – 5 September – was amazing and romantic, and everything I wanted it to be. Although – I hold my hands up – the poor guests were seated and waiting for me at 3.30 p.m., and I was 45 minutes late… But I wanted to look my best! I was wearing a white, strapless, long Philip Armstrong gown with diamanté detail. And I had my hair up with a white rose holding it, and I generally felt a lot slimmer and prettier than I had at my Scottish wedding. I felt gorgeous, like a bride should!

My three girls, Mark's daughter Keeley and sister Jane, and my friend Claire were my six bridesmaids, all dressed in white too. I don't think Heidi knew what was going on at all, but she looked really cute in her little outfit – and Molly and Lilly were over the moon to get the job. They had been excited for weeks in the run-up to the big day, and the night before had hardly slept at all. My promise made to them before Gretna was coming true, and I was thrilled for them – and for me too.

They did a great job, walking down the aisle in front of me. Max Clifford was giving me away. I was really close to Max at that time: he was someone I worked with, a friend and also an older advisor. So without me dad able to take on the role of father of the bride, he seemed like the next best thing.

We had written our own vows, and not heard each other's until the day. Mark went first. He had this piece of paper. I can't really remember what he said, as it was all a bit of a blur, but knowing Mark, he probably got it off the Internet! It didn't matter though, I was happy.

Then it was my turn. I turned to my bridesmaid and got this huge scroll off her and went whoosh! and unrolled it right down the aisle. That had everyone laughing, it was dead funny. But then I said my vows for real. I said, 'Mark, when we became mates, I treasured our friendship – and the Xbox, of course! I knew you were loyal and you gave me trust. Days turned into weeks, weeks turned into months and before I knew it I was falling into something deep. I turned to you when no one cared.

'At the end of the day, babe, they have tried to shoot us down, but we have stayed strong and you make sure no harm is done to me. All I have ever wanted is someone to look after me always, but – more importantly – you look after our three children and put them above and beyond our relationship. For now and always, I love you, babe.'

And I really did mean what I said. I did feel like I was in love with him. After all the negatives there had been about him by that point in our relationship, I know that must sound crazy, but it was true. He was my husband and had been a real husband at last.

Mark was bawling his eyes out – though he tried to claim his eyeballs were just sweating! Oh it was lovely, it really was great.

After we signed the register, 'Nessun Dorma' was played, and then we had the meal. We had prawns for starter, and steak and chips for main – both Mark's and my favourite. Then it was time for dancing and partying!

Max did a speech about the battles I had been through, and how I now deserved happiness. Mark said some thank yous, and I said a few words – of course I wasn't going to keep quiet! – and thanked those few friends of mine there who had never sold a story on me.

Then we hit the dance floor, starting with our song: 'Don't It Make My Brown Eyes Blue' by Crystal Gayle. My favourite dancers of the evening were Mark's gran Peggy and her two sisters. They were all glammed-up and loving the occasion – so we nicknamed them the Golden Girls!

At midnight, when it changed to 6 September, it was my 27th birthday. So everyone sang Happy Birthday and I got all emotional and teary. It really was what I imagined a wedding to be. Gretna Green hadn't been great – it had been so rushed, and I had been soooo pregnant, and then we had rowed... But this, this was what our wedding should have been.

We had a great time – and it only got better overnight, because when me and Mark went off to bed it was quite a different story to the night in Gretna Green. And, well, that is when I got pregnant again! Of course, I don't know for sure it was that night. Maybe it was before we went to Italy, but I like to think it was on our wedding night. It's a nice idea! I knew straightaway I was pregnant. It's pretty easy to know with me. My boobs get bigger and start getting dead sore and sensitive. So as soon as I got home from Italy, I knew I had a test kit in the house, so I did it. I said to Mark, 'I'm only bloody pregnant!' And he was like, 'Yes!' He was made up, he really was. And Molly and Lilly were happy too – they were still as cute and protective as ever with Heidi, who was six months by now, and were excited they were going to see it happening all over again!

This time, I didn't come off my bipolar medication. I had become quite reliant on it and didn't think it would be a good idea to come right off it. So instead I was put on to Chlorpromazine, a different kind of bipolar medication that was safer for the baby, and which was supposed to be only for the duration of my pregnancy.

Our honeymoon, a few weeks later, was a trip to the Maldives for two weeks. I paid for it and organised it because Mark had organised Italy. It was absolutely beautiful and amazing and romantic, and everything you could wish for from a honeymoon.

You had to get on sea planes to get to the island, and Mark was in pieces 'cause he was petrified of flying! But it was worth it when we landed on this island, and it was just full of honeymooners.

Yes, we missed the kids like mad, but we spent time chilling together and relaxing and just having a laugh, and of course no drugs. There was no way to get them on the island, even if we had wanted to – and, of course, now I was back pregnant it was a definite no-go again anyway.

It really was the perfect honeymoon – definitely better than the one Brian and I had in Mauritius. There were romantic things to do every day. One day we went on a trip on a yacht, another we had a table in the sand in the shape of a heart, with our own personal chef. In the evenings we would eat out and have a slow dance afterwards, and kiss and cuddle. It was the most romantic thing I ever did for Mark, sorting that holiday.

We didn't argue once, we just laughed, talked, had sex, and generally were a normal couple in love and having fun. Honest to God, I think it was the happiest Mark and I ever were. At times, when I am down and question if there were good times with him or if it had all been a mess from start to end, I remember the Maldives, and I know that there were.

If only there had been a few more moments like it.

Finding Me Real Dad

When I was very young, I thought Arnie was my dad. But when I was eight years old, he and Mum were going through a custody battle for me, and me mum's girlfriend Tina blurted out, 'Arnie's not your real dad.' Mum hadn't wanted me to know, but after that she told me the story of what had happened.

She said me dad had been a really nice man, but that he had been married when he met her. They had feelings for each other and ended up having an affair, but he stayed with his family. He visited me when I was eight weeks old, so he did meet me once.

At the time, I couldn't believe it, but I was excited as well. It answered some of the things I had wondered about – like why I did not look like any of my older brothers and sisters. I was the only one with dark eyes and olive skin. So maybe my real dad was the key to that.

Since then, I have always thought about him. I have looked out for someone in the street who could be him, or daydreamed about what life might have been like had he stayed.

I don't know what it was about this exact time that made me decide to find out more about him. Maybe it was because I no longer had a relationship with me mum. Maybe it was having got married twice, and never having been given away by my real dad. Maybe it was my own worry that Molly and Lilly didn't have the kind of relationship with their dad Brian that I wanted them to have.

I don't know, but it really started to eat away at me and I started to think of ways I could do something about it.

All I really had to go on was a name: Ronnie Armstrong. I didn't even know basic facts, like what he looked like. So I finally decided to hire a private investigator. I wasn't about to waltz into my dad's life, but I thought if I learnt a bit more about him, that might satisfy some of the ongoing, gnawing feeling inside me about it. Sitting down with the investigator I felt like I was actually going to get somewhere... and I was right.

Very quickly, the investigator came back and said he had traced him, and had got pictures and a video of him. He lived in Skelmersdale, just north of Liverpool – not even half an hour's drive from where I had grown up in Warrington.

He had brought them round with him and produced a big brown envelope. I was frozen. 'Oh my God, I can't actually look at it. I'm too scared!' Mark was with me, and he encouraged me, and reminded me that this was the moment I had been waiting for all this time. He was supportive of me looking for my dad, and realised what it meant to me.

So I put the DVD on. It was so surreal, one of the strangest experiences I have ever had – like watching a stranger on the screen but knowing that, actually, this was Dad.

In the video the man was walking out his house, his wife was at the door, and he had a little girl with him, and he was taking her to school. It was a really straightforward video. Then there was another one of him pottering about in his garden, on his front lawn, and that was it.

There were some pictures, too, and it was weird to look at them. It sounds strange, but I was surprised that he was such an old man. I think that when I had asked me mum to tell me the story of him again and again, I had created this image of a really handsome, young guy, and that image hadn't aged – even though he, obviously, had. But here was this small guy with a bit of greying hair and glasses, a big nose and dead straight teeth. It was a shock. It was a very weird moment, even though it was one I had dreamt of for so many years.

But at the same time, I could see things that answered some questions for me. Me mum always used to take the mick out of my nose and say I have a big wide boxer's nose. Well, Dad's was the same. And yes, he did have dark eyes.

Then there were other pointers too. My mum is 5' 6" and I am 5' 3" and she always said Dad was smaller than her, and he was. There were even bits of him that I could see in our Lilly – she is the spit of me when I was a kid, tiny with long blonde hair, while Molly is broader and with lovely blue eyes, just like her father.

And as I looked at these pictures which were actually my real dad, I went through so many thoughts. Had he followed my career in the papers? Had he ever been tempted to contact me, or had he tried to forget about me? I started to imagine how things might have turned out if he had been single when Mum met him.

But I took it no further. I knew he had a wife and some sort of family, and I couldn't go knocking at the door. 'Oh hello, do you know your husband had an affair years ago, and I was the product of that?' No. It was hardly something I could do to the poor woman. And how much worse would it be as well that it was me? Oh shit, it's Kerry Katona! It makes it worse, doesn't it?

So instead I kept the video and pictures stored away safely. Of course it would have been nice if I had been able to take things further and to have gone and met him and his family, but I wasn't going to be the person to potentially wreck their happy family, so I put those dreams to one side. Hiring the PI hadn't solved my feelings of missing out on something, but it was still nice to know more about my real dad and to have seen him.

Life in Front of the Camera

Professionally, life was good. I was still the face of Iceland, and doing my column and photo shoots too numerous to mention. But I was frustrated by how there was such a difference between how our lives really were and what the perception in the press was. Everyone had an opinion about us and our relationship, and I felt like I wanted to take control in some way. What I was able to say in my weekly column wasn't enough to set the record straight. Then Max told me we had been offered a reality TV show, with cameras following our everyday lives, and that suddenly felt like a way of putting the real us out there. The us who had such a terrific wedding, such a romantic honeymoon. I wanted to show viewers the fun and the liveliness as well as the normality of our household. That even celebrities living in big grand houses have the same stuff going on as everyone else. And of course I wanted to show them the craziness too, like living with paps on your doorstep and reacting to a big news story about yourself. And I'll be honest, it was well paid, which of course is something we had to consider.

The show was to be called *Kerry Katona: Crazy in Love* and the idea was to show the truth about my life, in particular my relationship with Mark.

We had to think about it hard. It would mean letting the whole world into our lives, and while I have always tried to be open in interviews, this was moving it up to a whole new level. At the same time, you have to remember that with the paparazzi on us all the time, it felt like we were living in a goldfish bowl anyway. And that goldfish bowl was a distorted one, one that offered only one viewpoint. Doing this TV show would be a way to defend ourselves and our family. Besides, it was certainly no secret that I have always loved being in front of the camera and being filmed, so a bit of me was secretly looking forward to it. And Mark, despite all his claims that he was never in our relationship for the fame, got pretty keen on being on the show too! It seemed like being in the spotlight could be a good move for us on many fronts, setting the record straight and solidifying our marriage.

At first we were worried about the kids, but I decided it wouldn't be harmful because they were too young to be affected by being in the limelight. We also said they could be filmed only when they were with us – they weren't to be followed to school or anything. And they are such natural performers that I knew they would play up to the cameras and never be short of things to say to the camera crew – and I was right!

Even me dad managed to get a part on it. I'll never forget him talking to camera about someone who had sold a story on me. He was there with his walking stick and ranting, 'These people get right up my nose, they do!' Very protective was my dad and never afraid to defend me.

The filming really did take some getting used to though. The film crew would turn up at the house at all hours of the day and night, and the deal was they could film us anywhere apart from the bathroom, and doing anything from messing round with the kids to being in bed together. Sometimes we would create a schedule for the day, so that there was something more definite to film, such as taking the kids horse riding, and if we went on holiday the crew came too. There would be two, three or four camera crew, depending on what we were doing, and then other people such as a producer, researcher or runner.

And although we could say no to some bits, I tried not to, as I knew they had a job to do. We had agreed to make the best show we could, and that meant trust all round, and most importantly completely honest access to our lives.

Over time, the crew became like good friends. You couldn't spend that much time with a group of people, and let them see that much of your life, and not get close to them. You have to remember for every hour that appears on television, hours and hours more will have been filmed, so they really got to see my life inside out.

We didn't get to see what was going to go out on air in advance, until it was actually on the television, so there was no editing it from our end! Which was actually quite scary, but I didn't think I could object – I have always prided myself on being real and honest, so I didn't want to start trying to control my image on the show.

And actually, after years of feeling the papers had been creating my image, I was pleased that people could see the real me. So, in a way, it was therapeutic having the crew there. I felt comfortable with the whole process and happy that I was doing the best job I could.

But when the first episode was aired, I wasn't a big fan of it. I didn't like what I saw of myself. Seeing Mark and me together onscreen made me cringe, deep down. And I didn't let the children watch it – it was aired at 10 p.m. and so too late for them, plus I thought they were too young to see it anyway. But

I still hoped the public would take to us. Well, the ratings were brilliant and MTV were happy – and so were we. It is only now, looking back, that I realise what the public was enjoying: not us, perhaps, not a couple in love, but the original definition of car-crash TV.

Changing Family

2008 did not get off to a good start. We had a New Year's Eve party at our house, and invited all our friends and family over, including Mark's mum and stepdad. I was pregnant with Max, and was waddling around, all big, and not drinking, so I was completely sober.

We were downstairs in the bar and cinema room, and everyone else got really drunk. Watching people get drunk when you're sober is an odd experience and this was certainly weird. I don't know what the cause of it was, but Mark's mum Marilyn kicked off on our Pat again for some reason – just as she had the night before our wedding blessing in Italy.

Then she stormed over to me. 'Kerry, word upstairs, now.' I sighed, knowing a rant was inevitable, but I wanted to keep the peace so I followed her up. Once we got to the dining room she started: 'Now let me tell you about your Pat.'

Well, I wasn't in the mood for more arguments over family. I was very tight with Pat at that time, and wasn't prepared to hear Marilyn complaining about her just because she had had one drink too many.

Still determind to keep everything calm, I said, 'Marl', I'm not interested. It's New Year's Eve, let's all just have a good time. I really don't want to know.'

I was trying to make her see sense so we could just get on with the party. But she was raging. She looked at me in disgust and went, 'You're no daughter-in-law of mine.' That comment really annoyed me. How much time and money had I spent trying to keep this woman happy, and I was supposed to take it as it was thrown back in my face? Not this time, I thought. You're in my house and I don't have to take this.

'Well, you know where the door is,' I told her, feeling my temper rising.

And that was it. She completely lost it. 'Fuck off!' she yelled, and slapped me. Remember, I'm sticking right out pregnant, and I fell against the piano. Not that my condition stopped me defending myself: I got straight back up and launched for her.

Now, in my dining room there were glass doors, and across the hall was the living room, where her husband was sitting with her daughter and her other son. I'm not sure if they saw it all, but it didn't take long for people to come running in. And Mark went mad at her: 'How dare you treat my wife like that, especially when she is pregnant. Get out!'

We didn't speak to her for ages. In fact, I've never spoken to her again since.

Surprise, surprise, the next week, she sold a story on me. It never takes people long to get round to doing that, and is always the way you can tell who in your family is loyal – and who your real friends are. Sadly, over the years I have been let down by many people.

Of course, it was the *News of the World* that published the story. And she came out with the most twisted load of nonsense I've ever read. She claimed in it that I had attacked her, that I had slapped her, that I used my kids for fame, that I drank through my pregnancy – and there was more. It was all a complete load of rubbish. Despite being used to seeing constant lies in print this still managed to hurt me deeply, even though it was completely ridiculous.

One of the bits that made me most angry about it, and actually may have explained where some of her resentment towards me came from, was when she accused me of making sick jokes around her mum's deathbed.

What had happened was that in December of the previous year, Mark's gran Peggy – the mother of his stepdad Alan, not Marilyn's mum despite what she said in the papers – had been ill. We didn't go to see her that often, but for some reason, out of the blue one day, I got a feeling that we should go and check on her at her home in Warrington. I said, 'I know it's a daft feeling, but I think we should go and visit her'.

When we got there, she was lying on the couch, and we could see straightaway that she was really poorly, so I said to Mark that we had to get her to hospital. She was 80 years old, and obviously needed proper medical care. We took her straight to Warrington Hospital and got her in, and they put her in a bed and gave her morphine for the pain. They said she didn't have long left, so we called the rest of the family, and they came and were there when she was being given morphine.

I was trying to cheer Peggy up and make her feel relaxed by joking around, and making the situation as fun as it could be. So I was going to her, 'Hey Peggy, you're having morphine there – it's bloody brilliant stuff, that. Can I have some too?' Just being daft like that, typical me style!

Well, Marilyn hated the fact that I was the one who got her to hospital and looked after when she was there. I think she felt it made her look like she had failed in some way, and she resented that. So when she sold the story, she said, 'To stand at the bed of a dying woman and make a joke of having drugs sums her up. She wants to be the centre of attention, no matter what the occasion. The doctor looked at her like he knew she wasn't really joking. My mother died that night and I'll never forget what Kerry said.'

Twisting it like that, and then selling her story, was a seriously evil thing to do. I don't need an award for what we did for Peggy, but not having it turned into something to use against me would have been nice.

On the other hand, I am still in touch with Peggy's sisters – the Golden Girls who had been at my wedding. They are lovely and said they would never forget what I did for their sister.

Mother-in-law woes aside, I was feeling horrendous by this stage with the pregnancy. From about four months onwards, I had looked ready to pop, I was huge. At one point the doctors thought I had pre-eclampsia, which is a condition in pregnant women that could have been life-threatening to both the baby and me. What I really had, it turned out, was very bad water retention. My feet were like elephants' feet – in fact, every bit of me proper swelled up. I don't know what causes it, but I was so big it was ridiculous. It was wrong how massive I was! And I kept feeling weak and faint, and getting a temperature and ending up in hospital. Don't forget I was on the bipolar meds all this time as well, so that probably didn't help.

I cheered up, though, when we found out we were expecting a boy! I was really happy we were going to complete our family with a little son. Mark was over the moon as well – partly 'cause he was getting his wish of a boy, and maybe partly 'cause he knew that the Ferrari of his was now within reach! In fact, he went straight out that weekend and bought a Ferrari Spider and had it delivered to the house. I think it cost about £125k, but I didn't mind. It made him happy, and I knew he loved his cars. There were times when I worked out exactly how many cars he had bought, and when I was feeling down, I did think it was taking the piss a bit. But as far I was concerned we had the money to pay for it, so why not?

I lost track over the time we were together of what cars he bought during our marriage, but I have since read a breakdown in a newspaper. If the article is to be believed, Mark bought a Ferrari, two BMWs, two Range Rovers, a Lamborghini, four Porsches, two Aston Martins, an Audi and two superbikes – which all together the paper says were worth an estimated £1.5 million. Pretty mind-blowing that, really.

And there was a point when I did start to say to him, 'Mark, this is ridiculous, it is getting embarrassing.' Because not only the papers were talking about it, but so were my friends. Even on the set of filming for Iceland, it used to be an ongoing joke. My stylist Lorraine would laugh, 'What car is Mark going to turn up revving the engine of this week, then?!'

I was less worried about the money, as I still thought there was a fairly endless supply, but I just thought it was unnecessary and extravagant. Like he looked like he was showing off. But the Ferrari was the one I couldn't begrudge him… after all, I had my baby boy on the way!

Even though my baby was still inside me, I started thinking of names. I have always preferred really old-fashioned and normal names. I hate the trend for names like Apple and Bluebell. That was how I named my first two girls. I knew I wanted my first girl to be called Molly, even before I was pregnant. When I was excited in the early days of dating Brian, I used to tell me mum, 'If I marry Brian and have a baby, she is going to be Molly McFadden.' I thought it was really Irish and had true star quality.

Lilly's name wasn't so easy. Again I wanted an old-fashioned one, and was thinking of Mary. But I was lying in hospital watching *Friends*, and it was the episode where Rachel and Phoebe go and get tattoos. Rachel got a love heart on her hip, and Phoebe went to get a Lilly after her mum's name. And I sat there thinking, 'Lilly, hmm. Kerry, Molly, Lilly. That has a nice ring to it and sounds like a proper family.'

But as for boy's names, I was a bit stuck, until Max took me out for dinner. We were sitting chatting, and he mentioned that his full name was Maxwell. I'd never heard that before – to me, Maxwell was just a brand of coffee! But I thought, 'Ooh, I like that, Maxwell Mark Croft.' It sounded good. And that it was a tribute to Max Clifford was an added bonus. So then I was all ready for my son's arrival!

On 9 April 2008, I went into labour with my son – five weeks early. It was a tricky labour in some ways because it was so long, but two days later I finally gave birth to him naturally. As for my size, well the minute my waters broke there was so much water, but everything just went, and it was like I shrivelled up. I remember being all excited and going, 'Oh my God, I can see me feet!'

But I had to be rushed into theatre afterwards for a 'scrape' because the placenta wouldn't come out. Literally a man with a big glove scrapes the placenta out of you. Not exactly pleasant, I have to say – but after what you have just gone through, you don't care! Not one of my pregnancies has been easy.

Max was tiny, although not as tiny as Heidi, weighing 5lb 4oz. But he was fine and healthy and lovely and that was all that mattered to me.

I hate being pregnant, but weird though it sounds I love giving birth. It is like you push and forget about everything else other than helping this little life into the world. And then you hold this tiny little stranger, and become like a lioness protecting her cubs, and telling everyone, 'Back away from my baby *now*!'

The different thing about this birth was that it was all caught on camera. I had agreed to let it be filmed as part of my MTV show, *Crazy in Love*. Not the actual bit where Max pops out – that would have been a step too far – more just the lead-up to it, and then straight after he was out. And there's my exhausted but happy face as I'm holding him!

Some people have criticised me for letting a camera crew in, but I don't get why. I watch *One Born Every Minute* and I think it is fascinating and a great thing to have on camera. A lot of people have told me it made them cry to watch, it was so moving. And me doing it is no different to ordinary people, but for some reason I got criticised. Max really does live *The Truman Show*!

I haven't shown him the video yet, but maybe when he is learning about birth and that at school, I will. When the time is right.

Having a boy was such a different experience to my three girls. By then, Molly was 6, Lilly was 5, and Heidi was 1. Again, the older two doted on him, and wanted to help look after him, while Heidi didn't know what to make of him, and would just sit and look at him for ages, studying him with her big eyes!

Max definitely cried a lot more than the other three had. I don't know if that is the case for all boys, or just him, but it did mean it was more tiring. Also, it was really weird, but the first few weeks changing his nappies, I was like: 'Oh my God, his widgy is going to fall off!'

All my kids are loving, but I think Max is especially so, he is very affectionate. There is something different with a mother and a son, he is a real mummy's boy. He is the apple of my eye, and even now I will sit and watch him, and think he is the only man in my life that really truly matters. I could just eat him!

Mark doted on him as well. He was really happy to have his boy, and was always saying that at least he wasn't so outnumbered now! He was also happy that, just as Heidi really looked like him, so too did Max.

Weight and Surgery

One of the effects of my lifestyle, combined with four pregnancies and – I hold my hands up – not the best diet in the world, was that my weight was forever fluctuating. It used to drive my poor stylist Lorraine mad. She would style me one week and I would be a Size 10, and a couple of weeks later she would bring that size to the shoot and I could be a size or two in either direction.

But I'd go through phases of forgetting to eat, and then obviously taking coke makes you lose weight, and then other times I would be living off take-aways – curries and kebabs.

It wasn't good for my mind or my body – especially as it was constantly analysed by the newspapers and, in particular, the magazines. It is like I can never win, and it can really get you down.

And Mark didn't help. He would joke, 'You're chunky, you're my little whale. If you used to be my little sweetshop, now you are my supermarket!'

I'd laugh, but inside, he was grinding me down by making me feel like shit. I didn't always realise that was what was happening. It is the same humour as my mum has, where she finds it funny to put me down. Which is maybe why I was used to it, and thought it was funny, without realising what it was doing.

*

One thing that annoyed me as well were my boobs. They were huge! I was always complaining about them, especially the back-ache they kept giving me. In 2005, I had implants after splitting with Brian. I had lost three stone and was a Size 8 at the time. I had always been proud of my DD boobs because they were a nice pair (if I do say so myself!), but they had disappeared, and I was just left with skin. So I had implants to fill them back out.

But as I had put on weight, they got bigger and bigger. Not only that, after giving birth to Heidi and Max, the implants stayed in place but my actual boobs drooped, which created this weird effect, like I had a double bubble.

But despite all my moaning – and I'm sure I probably did say I wished I could have surgery – I never actually intended to do anything about it.

But the TV producers of *Crazy in Love* were keen for a new storyline now that Max was born, and they wanted me to do something else that they could follow on screen. So one day one of them suggested I have surgery and allow them to film it. I was like: 'No way, I'm not having surgery!' and I straight up refused. But it played on my mind. Were they all trying to say I was fat and ugly by suggesting I get surgery? I had lost two stone since I had given birth to Max, but I still had a fair bit to lose before I could honestly say I was back to my old shape.

And they kept saying, 'Come on, think about it. We could call it 'Whole Again', it would be great!' 'Whole Again' was the title of one of my songs from back in the Atomic Kitten days.

They said I would get the surgery for free, as they would sort it all out, and they offered me lots of money to do it, and I started to warm to the idea.

And once I agreed to getting the implants taken out and a reduction and uplift to my boobs, they casually suggested getting liposuction too. I was so paranoid by then! At first, I was like, no way – but then those media stories criticising my weight started to play on me mind. I knew I didn't look so good after having four kids – who does? – but if I could make myself look better for free, was that so bad? So I went for the surgery and had an incredible four stone of weight taken away, so that I came out weighing just eight stone. Altogether, had I paid for the surgery, it would have cost £15k, which I would never have paid myself. As it was, I was so happy with the results.

After everything had healed and the swelling had gone down... well, I was so thin! It really was a shock to my system in every way possible.

Loss

Dad had decided to go back to America at the start of the summer. Although he was recovered from his operation on his foot, he still wasn't in the best of health, and doctors suspected he had the onset of pneumonia. But he was determined to get back out there. He had moved there with the idea of living out the rest of his life over there, so he wanted to follow that through.

I was just happy I had got to spend more time than I expected with him during his return to the UK, and that all my children had got to know him and him to know them.

But he hadn't been back in America for long – literally a matter of weeks – when he went to hospital because of his chest. And they were checking his pneumonia when they ran a series of tests and realised he was riddled with cancer. There was nothing they could do about it, he was dying.

I was devastated. Straightaway I talked with our Pat, and booked flights for her and me. I got the first ones available, but they were a couple of days away.

He called Pat on the phone. 'Please, hurry up.'

'We'll be there in two days, Dad. Hang in there, don't worry,' she reassured him.

'Just please hurry up and get here.' He must have known the end was near.

The night before we were due to fly out, I was in our bed in

Wilmslow with Mark and the phone rang in the early hours. I jumped up and said to Mark, 'Don't answer the phone, please don't answer it.' I was working myself up and screaming and crying, and had my hands over my ears. I don't know why, but it's always something I do when I'm scared.

'It's me dad, he's dead. The flight's tomorrow and I've not got there in time, I'm sure he's dead.' I just knew it, and I was begging him not to answer, 'cause I was thinking, 'If we don't answer it, it won't be real.' But he did, and of course it was our Pat.

Yes, he had, he'd died. I was devastated. So he had been right when he called us. We were too late. I never really speak about it, as I get upset even thinking about it. I was so upset then, and I still get upset today. I really miss him.

Even though we were too late, we flew out anyway, our Pat and I.

When we got to the morgue, I was in pieces, terrified.

'I can't go in, Pat,' I said. I just thought it would be too much and I wouldn't cope.

She gave me a hug and said, 'You've got to come in or you'll regret it.' So I did 'cause I knew I had to say goodbye. And I saw him for the last time. It was good in a way, though, because he didn't look all strange and different like I imagined he might have. He looked like he had a smirk on his face, which made me smile.

We had to stay out there for a while to sort out all the details with his body, so we booked into a motel. And we held a funeral at the War Veterans Club where he always went, and they played a song by George Glenn Jones, an American country singer me dad loved, and everyone stood up and saluted him. It was amazing.

We had him cremated out there. It was hard doing that, but we decided it was the best way. That way, we were able to put some of his ashes under this tree in America, in Texas, as it was the place he had always dreamed of living. He had made his dream happen near the end of his life, so we decided to continue that for him. I would like to think we did him proud and gave him the kind of send-off he would have wanted.

Then we took the rest of the ashes home with us. It was Pat's and my way of dealing with things, to make a joke of everything. And we were laughing about what would happen if we got pulled over at the airport and asked to explain this box of ashes hidden in our hand luggage!

Back in the UK, we had a funeral at Padgate Church of England, across from The Stocks pub. Then I had all these crucifixes made up for all his kids, with the rest of the ashes divided between them.

It was all so sad, but I was just glad I had got back in touch with him to have known him for the last two years of his life, and then to have been part of everything when he died.

As for the rest of the family, well, I was especially glad that Pat and I had been able to get close again. At times, when I was a kid, she had been more of a mum to me than Mum had. She was two years older than Mum, and although she had her own issues, she looked out for me and protected me when she could. In fact, I sometimes wished she had been my mum – she was my everything when I was a little girl. So it was great that I had had her back around, ever since I'd been back in touch with Dad.

I was also pleased that my children, especially Molly and Lilly, had had a chance to get close to Dad. Although Max will never remember him, the fact that Dad met him and held him is something I will always be glad about. A few months after he died, I came home to find our Molly crying. When I asked her what she was crying for, she said, 'I miss Granddad Arnie.'

'Oh darlin'!' I hugged her and felt myself well up. 'I miss him too, and that is normal. But he had a great life, and he is still happy and looking out for you. So just think about good memories you have of him and smile!'

And she hugged me back and gave me a little smile up through the tears and it really broke my heart. It was so sad, but in a strange way it was nice. It meant that he really had made an impact on her life in the short time she had known him. I was just sad that both the kids – and myself – didn't have longer with him.

Summer of Drugs

No matter how much I told myself to be glad about these small blessings, there was no getting away from the fact that Dad's death hit me incredibly hard. The whole summer after Dad died is a complete blur for me. The kids were away some of the time in Ireland and Gemma looked after the other two a lot of the time, and I just disappeared, wallowing in my own misery – encouraged to stay there by Mark.

Frustratingly, and despite all of my best intentions, bit by bit I had slipped back into taking coke again after Max was born. It felt like the same cycle as for Heidi. Once the motivation of protecting the baby inside me had gone, it didn't take much for me to accept a line from Mark. And then of course it spiralled.

The happy, calm period for Mark and me had been short lived, and we had started swinging wildly between blazing rows and make-up sex, then moments of being loved-up before another row happened. So with that, my grief over Dad, and my sense of loneliness, it started to seem like coke was the only thing that cheered me up. There were times when it was like coke was my only friend.

I've always said that I did coke in binges – I couldn't do it every day, or I'd be dead. But I would have a session that could go on for a couple of days, then it would take a few days to come down and recover and sleep it off, then there might be a week or two gap before the next binge. That summer, though, it became more intense and everything just rolled into one big haze.

I remember one session, the longest I have ever been on, and it lasted seven days. By the end, when I had slept but had just kept topping myself up with more lines, I was a hallucinating, mental wreck.

And of course Mark was doing the coke too, and would sit there literally for days on end on the Xbox. I would look over and see him growing thinner and thinner, and staring gormlessly at the screen. It was becoming a living nightmare.

He never got affected by it as much as me, he was a bit more in control – in control of his own habit but also of mine. When I asked for his help to get out of a session, it didn't feel like he was helping me. Whenever I tried to say that I was going to, needed to, have a break for a while, I would start finding packets left in obvious places, like they had been left there to tempt me, in me shoes, or by the bed. When I said, 'Why are they there?', he'd make out it was a mistake, then just tell me to have the one line and I'd be fine. But I couldn't, and he knew that. I could say no to one line, but once I had one line I would be chasing the buzz.

It got to the point that I was scared to stop taking the coke, because I couldn't face the comedown. A comedown is the period when the effects of the drug are wearing off, and your body effectively kicks back at you for what you have done. It is like you crash, and feel physically run down, but the worst thing for me was the depression and paranoia. I guess it makes sense that if you take the high a low is going to follow. But I couldn't handle them, and they got worse over time. I would be curled up under my duvet, crying and struggling to keep the crazy thoughts going through my mind from taking hold.

So to stop myself having to deal with that, I would carry on taking more and more coke. Eventually I would have sleepers – sleeping pills – to run me down, Valium to get me to sleep and then, when I woke up, my white friend would be there and I would be back where I started.

Other times I stopped only after I had an epileptic fit. I think altogether, including that first one at me mum's house, I had seven fits. My nose would be bleeding, my lips would turn purple, and my eyes would go back into my head. I would lose all memory of what had happened, and wake up not knowing where I was, what day it was, or anything.

Sometimes I would hope to have a fit just to force Mark to stop me taking more drugs. I thought if he saw me fitting badly enough, he would say, 'Right, enough is enough. I love you and you can't keep damaging yourself like this.'

But he didn't. Instead he would be good when I had a fit – I would come round and he would have me in his arms and be looking after me – but he never told me to stop. Instead I'd get up and have another line, and he would do it with me. I sometimes wonder if he looked after me when I had a fit, not because he cared, but only because of how bad it would have looked on him if I had died when he was there. How awful is that, to think your husband would be capable of that kind of thinking?

Sometimes I wanted to push it, to hit rock bottom so that I could be taken away somewhere even if Mark didn't want me to go. If I OD'd, I would have to go to hospital, and they would have to put me in rehab, and then I could hide and get clean and get better. Other times I actually wanted it to kill me, because I just couldn't see any other way out. Recently I saw a psychic who knew nothing about my epilepsy, and she said to me that actually I died twice having fits. I stopped breathing, and it was my dad who brought me back. I don't know if that's true, but it is a nice idea, that my dad is watching over me.

Even sitting writing this and remembering it all makes me feel like I have a panic attack coming on. What I put my body through back then makes me feel so sick and horrified and so massively ashamed now.

But what made the drugs worse was the fact that I hadn't changed my medication after I had given birth to Max. I was still on Chlorpromazine, the drug that I had been prescribed for my bipolar during pregnancy and which was now completely wrong for me and my body. The effects were completely different on me now. It was slowing me down too much and making my mind all hazy, but I never thought about it because I never used to put my health first, which is stupid. I didn't realise what was happening at the time, but someone – in particular Mark, who was in charge of giving me my medication – should maybe have realised that what I was on, was not right.

I think it was around this time that my speech started to slur, although it was very gradual, so it was only people I didn't see for a long time who would notice. Mark and the kids and I didn't realise it was happening, as we were used to it.

I knew I was living a double life. My life with the kids, who I loved to bits, and my life with Mark and drugs, which I kept completely separate from them. They never knew about that side of me, and I was determined they wouldn't be affected. So if I was on a bender, they were either away or they were just told that 'Mummy isn't well and is sleeping' or 'Mummy is busy working' – and they never questioned it. Sad as it is, I think Mark, Gemma and I did do a very good job on that front, protecting the kids. Because I honestly don't believe they ever thought anything different to what they were told, or felt upset by it, or questioned it. Living this lie became second nature.

*

The other thing that I had a growing niggling feeling about around this time was our accountant, Dave.

It had been back before Christmas, at the end of 2007, that I had first started to wonder if my money was being looked after in the best way it could be. The press and the public had always given the impression that they believed Mark was with me for my money, and that he was quietly rinsing me of it, but it was not something I had ever taken any notice of, and I had continued to let him look after the majority of the finances.

At one point, to help, he had taken on the services of an accountant called David McHugh. We had met David through a not-for-profit organisation that I had put some money towards, called Pink Ladies. It was a Warrington-based cab company aimed at making women feel safe when they were driven to places. It seemed like a good idea and I was happy to back it.

Through that, we had met David, and Mark and he became very pally. Soon he was offering to look after my finances for free. David was the father-in-law of the footballer Robbie Fowler, and for some reason, in my head, that link meant he must be legit and that I could trust him. He said he didn't mind doing the accounts for free because the publicity would generate him other work. I thought, 'Well, if it is good for both of us, then let's do it!' I didn't give it any more thought than that because it never occurred to me that my hard-earned money wouldn't be safe in his hands. I was heavily medicated along with everything else and just went along with it all without question.

That began to change as I started to get uncomfortable with just how close David and Mark became. It felt like I was getting shut out of conversations about money. They redirected my mail to David's office, and Mark reassured me that David would get all my bills and things, and be able to deal with them straightaway.

At first, it seemed like a nice idea, and a weight off my shoulders, but after a while I began to realise I didn't have a clue what was happening. I was cut out of the loop.

There had been various stories in the press about me owing huge amounts of tax. I had asked Mark and David about them, and they both said it was fine and things were being exaggerated, and that I easily had enough money to pay off my bills. So I didn't push it, I just accepted what they told me, and put it down to the usual media spin – looking for a story on me when there wasn't one.

At the same time, David had told us about an investment he was keen for me to make. He told me not to tell the Pink Ladies, but he was working on a project he thought would interest me.

Mark told him to lay it out for us, so he took us out to the Orkney Islands, telling us this was the latest place to invest. It sounds completely daft now, but at the time he flew us out in a helicopter, champagne on board, no expenses spared, all of that. And he gave us this spiel, which sounded great, about a new hotel and complex that was being planned, and all the money we would earn if we invested. Eventually Mark agreed that we would put £150k towards it.

The whole thing felt weird to me, but I was really trying to stick to my rule of letting Mark look after the money so that he felt like we were on a level. And, to be honest, I didn't have a lot of choice in it, as he had got stronger on that front, and no longer asked me about spending money but would just do it. He was confident with our accounts, and I felt I had to trust him.

All I asked was that paying out for this wouldn't affect my ability to pay the tax bill which kept getting mentioned in the paper. They laughed at me and told me, 'Definitely not!'

*

And then suddenly, around this summer, when I was at my lowest, the tax bill that had been rumoured in the papers came along – for real. I told Dave to just pay it, and when he didn't, I started asking for answers.

He told me it would be paid any day, but it never was. There was always a reason, like we were waiting on payments, or money was being moved around and was tied up, but he was going to untie it, or whatever. As each week went past and it remained unpaid, things got more ridiculous. Sometimes I would kick off, sometimes ignore it, and sometimes cry about it. But mostly I still didn't really believe there was a problem – I easily had the money to pay it off, so it was just a matter of making it happen.

I repeatedly asked him for proof of where my money for the Orkney Island project had gone, and it was never forthcoming. I didn't push it too far yet, as I was giving him a chance to come up with answers. But it really didn't seem as if there were any that I would want to hear. And, to be honest, my head wasn't in a place to fight. My mind was getting so fuzzy it was easy for David to talk me round on things, because I would lose the thread of the conversation half way through. I just wanted to be told it would be paid and I didn't need to worry. That wasn't going to happen, as I soon found out the hard way.

On 21 August 2008, I was declared bankrupt at the London Bankruptcy Court, with my future earnings and repayments to be dealt with through a trustee. I wasn't at the hearing, and I never really understood the ins and outs of it, but my initial tax bill had been £417k, and it had been paid except for £82k. For whatever reason David could not produce that money, yet he told me it had been paid. For less than the price of one of Mark's precious cars I had been made bankrupt.

I was confused, ashamed and angry. I knew I earned enough money to have easily been able to pay my tax bill. Ultimately, of course, it is my responsibility, but I knew I had done nothing wrong other than hire and trust the wrong accountant.

The court allowed me a reasonable amount each month to live off, to pay my mortgage, school fees, bills, buy food, and so on, then the rest went to pay off my debts. A trustee was assigned to me to deal with my case, and I felt like she thought I had hidden the money away myself under a mattress or something! And despite my requests, she didn't investigate David.

The funny thing was, in terms of day-to-day life, it didn't affect me too much. I have never been a big spender, and generally have just spent what was necessary. Even my idea of a meal out was the local Chinese or pub. I wasn't the kind who lived the extravagant showbiz lifestyle. It was actually Mark who had to tighten things up, because he had been splashing the cash on cars and motorbikes and new business ventures. It was really him who had to change the way he lived.

But I had other fears hanging over me from it. I was terrified of losing my house, and it was up for constant debate in the courts. My trustee wanted me to swap to a three-bedroom terraced house. I know that is not the worst thing in the world, but with four kids who are all used to more space, I fought against it. There was also a threat that me mum's house, which I had bought for her and which was still in my name, was going to be taken off her, which was horrible. Even if we weren't on good terms, there was no way I wanted her to be turned out of her own home because of me. For the next couple of years, it was a constant worry for me.

Unexpected Family

I was becoming more and more scared about leaving the house and going into the outside world. It was partly a side effect of the drugs, but also I was becoming paranoid about what the public thought – it felt like I was getting a full-scale assault from the media. Everyone hated me. I'd obsessively Google myself and read what the websites were saying about me. And the more I read nasty comments on my weight, my appearance, my parenting skills, my relationship, whatever, the more I sank into a feeling of worthlessness.

Mark would tell me, 'Everyone out there is evil fuckers, I'll keep you safe in here.' I was literally not leaving the house unless I absolutely had to for work.

Instead my link to the outside world was Facebook, I was on there all the time. Sounds great, doesn't it? But I really had no other friends. The only people I talked to were there. I used to play Poker on Facebook all the time, and I would chat to the person I was playing with. On one occasion I'd been playing with this woman for a week, just talking and playing Poker. And then a message came through from her in a totally different tone: 'Kerry, I really need to talk to you, it's quite serious.'

I was suddenly on edge. What had happened to our chilled game of poker? 'What is it?' I asked.

'My niece used to go out with Mark,' she said.

133

'Right…' I said, feeling a sense that this was not going to be something straightforward, or what I wanted to hear.

'She's got a kid, and the kid is Mark's.'

Wow! I felt my head spin, and I was struggling to breathe. I knew he had Keeley and I had accepted her, but a child I didn't know about was another thing. Did Mark know? Was it a boy or a girl? How old were they? How would this affect us? I had hundreds of questions whizzing round my brain.

She told me her niece's name and I sent her a message on Facebook. 'Hi, I'm Kerry, Mark Croft's wife. I think we might need to talk.'

She replied very quickly, but was dead discreet and private. 'I don't want to discuss this on Facebook, and anyway, it's got nothing to do with you.'

'This has got a lot to do with me,' I replied. And we eventually ended up talking. She said she had a son who was a bit older than Heidi. She had brought him up with her ex-partner, thinking he was his, and they had had another kid together before they split. Then he wanted a DNA test and it came back that her son wasn't his. She realised the only other person it could be was Mark.

There were two things about that which broke my heart. First, that it was a boy. I was devastated 'cause I'd always wanted a boy, and I thought Max was our only one. So although we both had children before with other people, a boy was the special new thing we had together. So to find out he's got another boy left me distraught.

And the fact her son was only a few months older than Heidi made me wonder if he had been with this girl while he had been with me. If the baby had been conceived while Mark and I were together.

'If this is Mark's son, can we please get a DNA test?' I asked, and she agreed.

So I confronted Mark. 'First I know about it,' was his reply, although he admitted he had been with the girl.

He agreed to do the test, and it came back 99.9 per cent certain that he was the dad. But he wasn't interested. I said, 'Mark, you have to go and see him.'

But he was like: 'No, he's not my bloody kid.'

'Mark, the test proved it.'

'Well, I've got my family, I don't want any others.'

I was really against that. I never had my dad and anyone can see how messed up that made me. And you can see how distraught I am over Molly and Lilly not having their dad around. I kept saying, 'Mark, this is so wrong.' But at the end of the day it was his choice, and there was no convincing him.

Strange though it sounds as well, I have made a conscious choice to never sit down and work out the exact dates. So I don't know if there is a crossover. I know the boy is only a few months older than Heidi, so it is quite possible, although Mark has always told me he had split from this girl before anything happened between him and me. At the time I just thought I couldn't face knowing, so I ignored it and focused on the kid and what to do about him instead. Even to this day I have never worked it out, 'cause I imagine I will only find out something I would rather not know.

Meantime, I was getting to be friends with this woman. I was being the bigger person and apologising for Mark. She sent me a picture of her son, and he was beautiful, and I sent her one of Heidi and Max. This was their half-brother, for goodness sake!

We were filming our MTV show at the time, and some of this got recorded for it. And I remember watching when it got aired, and Mark saying to the camera, 'I don't want owt to do with this kid. I'm not interested.'

I was so, so upset. How the hell could he say that on national television? One day this kid is going to grow up, and maybe for some biological, or health, or psychological reason is going to look for his dad and end up watching the show, and seeing what he said about him. How could Mark be so cold? This is his child! I was gobsmacked and so sad for the child. Yes, maybe a lot of that was because it did bring my own memories back, but that just meant I understood better how this boy could be affected. I told Mark all of that.

'Well, if I got involved, she is going to come after you for child support 'cause we are married, and you don't want that, do you?'

I was so angry. 'Mark, that is not the point. This is your son. Max and Heidi's brother. You have to make him part of your life.'

But he wouldn't. I have never met his son, as I don't think it is my place to do so. The woman and I still talk, though, and keep in touch on Facebook from time to time. I've told her if she needs anything to let me know. I think she is strong for bringing him up alone, as is any woman in that situation.

Heidi and Max don't know about him yet. I don't think it's appropriate right now because they are so young. Heidi is one of those little girls who remember everything you tell her, and she'll want to bring it up again and again and discuss it, and it's not my place to discuss it with her. Really, it is Mark's place to deal with it at some point, although who knows if that will happen?

Maybe when they are older they will read this book and learn about him, and if they want to go and research their brother and meet him, I'll be there for them and will help them. I'll be honest, it will be really hard for me too when they do that, but he is their brother at the end of the day. I've got half-brothers and a half-sister, and I know how important they are to me.

It was Mark's reaction that horrified me so much. I was disgusted, embarrassed, humiliated, and ashamed that I had married someone who could react like that. It was one of those real cold moments where reality kicks in and I looked at Mark from an outsider's viewpoint and wondered what the hell I was doing. But I didn't want my kids to be without their dad as well. And I couldn't see what else to do. So like every other doubt that had ever arisen about Mark, I crushed it down over time, pushed it to the back of my head, and tried to get on with my life.

Where is My Money?

Everything was getting out of control. I needed to try and have some time away from cocaine to clear my head. I had to stop accepting that this was my life and letting it tug at me, always finding its way back into my life. I couldn't do this anymore.

So I stopped taking it, and as always once my head began to clear, I started thinking. Without my life being given over to coke, I couldn't just pretend that everything was great and happy, and I started wondering about my money again. I knew something was wrong. The incident with Mark's son created a spiral in my mind and I knew I didn't trust him yet. I needed to understand what he had been doing and quickly.

I started with the investment into the Orkney Islands, which still hadn't come back. I said to Mark, 'Something is not right here. Once and for all, I want David to show me some papers and proof of where my Orkney Islands money has gone.'

'Babe, stop being paranoid!'

'I mean it, Mark. I want to see what he has spent it on. I have asked this time and again – you hired him, make him do it!'

But the pair of them couldn't supply anything, and it felt like they just came out with excuse after excuse. Eventually I was handed some documents, but even I, who was no expert in the financial world, was pretty sure they looked fake, and flimsy, as though a child had drawn them up.

'Mark, these aren't real.'

'Oh come on, Kez, you're fucking mad, you. You must be on a come-down or something 'cause you're not talking sense.'

'I am, Mark, and you know it. I've not taken coke in weeks, my head is clear!'

But he would argue and argue and it got so draining. And although I was no longer distracted by cocaine, my head was still so fuzzy from my bipolar medication that I felt I couldn't keep up the fight. I didn't have the energy to follow through my thoughts, because the meds were so draining. It was a cycle that I couldn't escape, but at least I had an edge from not taking cocaine and so I was not going to be a pushover anymore.

The next day we were driving along and having yet another conversation about Dave and whether he was legit, and Mark started shouting at me, 'You are fucking nuts! He is an accountant, he knows what he is doing, whereas you are just stupid! How can you question him? He does it for a living!'

I sat there thinking about how I didn't trust Mark, and how I wasn't even sure he was a nice person, and I could see how my world had been gradually collapsing around me since I had been with him. All that was left of me was a shell and yet for some reason I suddenly felt a surge of strength and, coupled with the newfound clarity, I knew I needed out. I had had enough. So I turned to him and said, 'It's over. I can't take this anymore, I want you out.'

He went mad. Slamming the wheel he screamed at me, 'You leave me, I will destroy you. I'm going to tell everyone you are a little fucking smackhead.'

He was literally spitting and frothing at the mouth he was so angry. And although I'm quite hard, me, and have taken a lot in my life, there was something scary about the way he completely lost control. I was shaking and could tell he meant every word he was saying.

He was in my face as he spat out, 'Who'd want you after you've had four kids? Look at the state of you, you're nothing but a junkie.'

But I stuck to what I was saying. Something in me told me that this time, it was time for me to go. 'Mark, I mean it.'

And I did. Until he said, 'When I have told everyone all that about you, do you think you'll keep your kids? Not a chance. I will make sure you never see them again.'

And that was it. He knew my weak point, and he had gone straight for it. In a moment, the walls of doubt and confusion quickly rebuilt themselves and I had crumbled and given in. I went quiet and instantly backed down. 'Right, you've got me. I'm yours. I don't want to split up, you win.'

It was easier – and really the only option I could see – to surrender. So I went home, took a line of coke and forgot about it. Getting lost in a world of cocaine was my only escape, and before I knew it I had fallen into a cycle again. Take drugs, decide I needed to get clean, start thinking about things, argue with Mark, give up, and go back on the coke. How was I ever going to fight and beat a guy like Mark? Was this really who I had become?

This Morning

Then *that* interview on *This Morning* happened.

It's so weird, no matter how many times I put forward my side of what happened that day, there are still people who doubt it. But you are reading this book, why would I lie about this now when I'm telling you all about the drugs I have taken? Why would I tell you I wasn't drunk, if I was?

And come on, it was 10 o'clock in the morning. Why would I be drinking and going on a live television show? That would be ridiculous. I don't drink alone or to just get drunk. It's just not my thing.

What had happened was that I had come to London for a few days for work. As for drugs, I probably had been on a bender a few days before, but not while I'd been down in London. I have always been very good at stopping drugs when I know I am going to be working. Anyone who has ever worked with me, filming or on shoots, will tell you that they have never seen me touch drugs. Besides, Iceland went through a phase of drugs-testing me when I was shooting with them, because of all the stories, and I always came back clean, because I would be professional and give myself enough time off it before I went to work.

On 21 October, I went to the Riverside Studios in Hammersmith, to film for *Celebrity Juice* – the comedy chat show with Keith Lemon. Anyone who watches that knows how much he can rip into his guests, so I was dead nervous, and didn't talk much for fear of lining myself up for a ribbing! I was just like: 'Hiya' and 'Yeah' and kept everything to a minimum, but if you watch it back you will see my speech was fine – and I was sober as a judge.

Celebrity Juice finished filming quite late, but we went straight back to the hotel afterwards and got there about 11.30 p.m. I took my medication then, which is four hours later than I'm supposed to take it, but I knew it made me slur my words and get really drowsy, so obviously I didn't want to take it while filming *Celebrity Juice*.

After I took it, we went straight to bed, then I was up first thing the next day at about 5 a.m. The next morning after those medications you're still so... well, it takes you a while to kind of come around, and your speech is slurred.

Looking back, I suppose I shouldn't have gone on the show, or someone should have stopped me, but I never noticed the way I spoke, and Mark was used to it, so I don't suppose it occurred to him.

It wasn't long into the show and I felt it all start to go wrong. I'd been on *This Morning* several times before, and had always enjoyed it, and I thought it was a good show. And I had known Phillip Schofield for quite a few years before that day, as we had been at the same agency and had the same manager.

But early in the interview, he started saying to me, 'You don't seem right to me sitting here now. Your speech is a bit slurred. How are you feeling?'

I replied, 'Is it? That's probably 'cause I'm on medication at night time, which I took at 11.30 last night, didn't I, Mark?'

I was feeling cornered and unsure – I couldn't even tell it was slurred, and was so used to Mark answering questions for me and helping me out, that I kept looking over to him for reassurance.

But it was Fern Britton who really got to me, when she started asking me about a recent article in a magazine. It had talked about the various drinks I had had during a photo shoot in Spain. She said, 'The interview did say things like that you had a great deal to drink… It said you went to get ready with a bottle of champagne and once that had gone you were feeling better, and they wanted you to jump in the pool and you were tempted when they said, "Have a shot first and a champagne afterwards."'

'I don't understand what you are trying to say.'

'I suppose, and I'm going to be frank with you here, a lot of people say when you have an addictive personality and you get rid of one addiction, it's replaced with another. Is it alcohol?'

'No, not at all!'

I was furious. I had been in Spain two weeks before for a photo shoot and had got drunk, and for that she was implying I had a problem with alcohol. I was there in Spain, at 28 years old, without my kids and with a girl mate, letting my hair down after I had just worked my arse off. Of course I am going to have a few drinks, down a few shots! For goodness sake, where is the harm in that? I felt like she thought I should have been arrested for it or something. And I was getting so frustrated. I didn't see why I should have to explain myself for having had a few drinks on holiday. I was so angry, because I really hadn't been drinking that day of the show, and drink was and is not a problem for me.

I would place a bet that a lot of the people who were judging me for that interview go home every night and drink two glasses of wine, or even a bottle – and that is also a form of alcoholic dependency. And it is something I don't do. Yet I immediately thought, even in the middle of the interview, 'Shit, this is going to be all over the papers tomorrow.'

And as for the people who thought I was on coke during the appearance... coke doesn't make you slur your words, it makes you talk quickly and all hyper, you can't stop talking dead fast. It does not make you talk slow and slurred. I'm sorry, but I've taken enough of it to know exactly the effects!

At the time, I didn't really even realise that I was slurring. I was so angry and pissed off with the whole thing. My attitude was like: 'It's their fault, the people on *This Morning*, there is sod all wrong with my speech.'

I have watched it back since, and it really upset me. I see now why people thought what they did – I sounded like I had had a stroke. But it was purely down to medication. I was on 150mg of Effexor, 7.5mg of Zopiclone and 350mg Chlorpromazine at the time – go Google them and you will see that slurred speech appears as one of the first side effects on practically every description of the drug!

Not that I should have been on Chlorpromazine by then. That had been prescribed while I was pregnant with Max, and was supposed to just be for while I was pregnant, as my usual drugs had to stop because they can be harmful to the baby. But I didn't think about it and had just continued to take it – and, of course, when you are not pregnant it affects you completely differently. But I never used to put my health first or I would have remembered to change it. That is something I know is stupid and is something I have worked to change since.

Now that I have watched the interview and accepted what I sounded like, I understand why Fern and Phil were concerned. But what makes the whole thing so upsetting for me still is that when I mentioned my bipolar, I don't feel like they took it seriously. I had never really spoken about it, apart from briefly in my last book, so for the first time on live TV I was acknowledging my battle with the illness. But neither Fern nor Phil said to me, 'What is bipolar?' 'What medication are you taking and why?' 'How does it feel to live with that?' Not anything that would have allowed people to know more.

It's weird. If I had gone on the show limping, or with a limb missing, people would have understood and sympathised with me. But because they couldn't actually see any physical signs that I wasn't well, they didn't believe it, they didn't understand it.

Generally, mental illnesses are really poorly understood by most of the population. A psychiatrist has said to me in the past, 'Let people know you've had a drug problem, let them know you've had the occasional drink, just don't let them know you have mental issues because they will not understand it.' And sadly I think that is so true.

While I like to think I am helping to raise awareness of it, it feels like most people don't listen. Stephen Fry did a whole TV documentary about bipolar, called *The Secret Life of the Manic Depressive*, which was great – and all everyone said at the time was how brave he was to discuss it, how he was raising awareness, and so on. Obviously I agree, but what upsets me is that when I draw attention to it, I am mocked more than anything. People tend to focus so much on the negatives about me rather than the positives, especially in the press. It's always an attitude of 'Oh, it's messed-up Kerry' as though that explains it all away. Even today I'm described by the press as 'troubled reality-TV star' as though I am not allowed to move on from my past. And that was frustrating, especially around this time when I really wanted to make people understand that actually I was suffering a mental illness.

*

The week after my *This Morning* appearance, Max Clifford gave an interview to *heat* magazine, and I felt so desperately let down by him. He didn't defend me at all. Instead, he tried to distance himself, and said he was worried about my drinking. Like I said, that wasn't a problem I had, and I thought Max knew that.

I felt so angry and betrayed by him. This was the man who had given me away at my wedding in Italy, and now he was implying to the public I had an alcohol problem, when I needed him to defend me the most.

Looking back, I think he was like the viewers of *This Morning*. Because he couldn't see physical signs of my bipolar, he struggled to really understand it. It was something out of his control, and Max doesn't like to be out of control.

And the fact that he hadn't been down at *This Morning* – well, I think he felt guilty about that and so tried to pull back from it. I think he, or one of his team, should have been there with me that morning. I felt like it was their job to see me through things like that, and had they been doing that, the interview wouldn't have happened; they would have seen the state of me and stopped me going on air. On my MTV show, you can see me screaming at him down the phone at how let down I felt.

I think the whole *This Morning* saga was just the last straw for Max and me. Mark had already convinced me that Max was setting me up, and he was making me suspicious of him. He planted a lot of seeds of doubt about him in my mind. Looking back, it was more the case that Mark knew Max had his cards marked and knew full well the kind of person he was, so he didn't want him to have so much influence over me. And because of the way Max let me down, it felt that everything Mark had told me must have been true. As always, Mark was able to get his way. Ugh, it was just so complicated.

Well, when I had that phone bust-up with Max, that was that. That was the end of us working together. And it was the end of our close relationship altogether, which made me miserable. He was one person I always thought I would be able to depend on. Yet another father figure out of my life.

And thanks to the TV appearance, I also lost one of my favourite jobs – my column with *OK!* magazine. As well as all the shoots I did with them, I had a weekly column, which I loved doing. Each week a reporter would ring me up and I would talk through what I had been up to, and they would ask me about any particular story or for my opinion on different events in the news. Then they would write it up, either my agent or myself would read over it, and it would go in the next week's magazine.

But a week after my *This Morning* appearance, I got a fax terminating my contract. It was a real kick in the teeth, but I suppose they were just following public feeling, which at that time seemed very much against me. I was gutted to lose that, though.

I took on a new PR to replace Max. I went for a guy called Sean O'Brien, who was an ex-journalist. He seemed to understand me and have some good ideas for how I could get my career back on track. Plus we clicked when we met, so he seemed like the best choice.

Everything was just becoming too much for me. Shortly afterwards, I went on one of the most distressing benders ever. After taking line after line, I was sat in my room on my own, going over and over everything that had happened in the last few months. My husband cheating on me, being held hostage, going back to The Priory, Brian trying to take the kids, my money going missing, Mark finding out he had a son he didn't want to know, and then, of course, *This Morning*. And all of it appearing as stories in the newspapers, allowing people to judge me for it, but with only one side of it being put out there.

I sat there that day and thought how it was just too much, and I couldn't see a way out of it. And I needed Mark to help me. I needed to be able to lean on Mark, and for him to make things right for me, to tell me he loved me, to show me he did, and to save me.

And I was sitting taking lines to try and make myself feel better, while I went over and over my misery. Where had life gone so horribly wrong?

Then I had an epileptic fit because I had taken too much. And when I came round I went into the bathroom and got a razor and cut my foot with a razor blade. I didn't really do it properly, and it was one of those safety razors that stop you doing too much damage, but it was the only thing I could think to do. I've never been a self-harmer, and obviously I wasn't trying to kill myself by just slicing at my foot, but I suppose it was a cry for help. I wanted Mark to come in and be shocked, and say to me that what we were doing was so wrong, and that we needed to stop, and that we'd work it through together. It was my cry for help to him to take me to hospital. I wanted to have hit rock bottom so I could turn things round, and then the only way would be up.

But he walked into the room and noticed what I was up to, and hardly reacted. He just went, 'What are you doing?' Nothing changed.

I said to myself, 'He really doesn't love you. Look how little he cares, that you can cut yourself, and he as good as ignores it.' And I got more depressed and upset and was crying all the time. Looking back, that makes me so angry with myself. I know I am a stronger and better person than that. But I was like some broken, beaten animal, cowering in the corner, with no sense of how to get out. I was almost at rock bottom. *Almost.*

After I had been up for days on end and hadn't bathed or showered, and was filthy and smelly and tear-stained, Mark finally picked me up and put me in the bath and washed me. For a split second I thought, 'Oh my God, he really does care about me, he really does love me to do that,' and I calmed down.

But after he washed me, he went off to set up another line for me. That was not love, to wash me and then feed me coke. That was complete and utter control.

Forgiving and Forgetting

Right at the end of the year, something good came out of all the badness. It had been two years since I had spoken to Mum, and at the time I had decided that that really was it. After she had made that decision to sell me out, I didn't want anything to do with her ever again. She had tried to be in touch several times, but I had never been willing to give her the time of day.

It still makes me mad if I really think about it, but at Christmas 2008 I decided to put it behind me. I don't know exactly what it was made me do it, though I think it was probably losing Dad that year. You realise you have only so much time, and having regrets isn't good. Even with everything she had done, I'd never have forgiven myself if something had happened to her and we hadn't been reconciled. Plus I thought it was right for my kids to know their grandmother.

Mark, the girls and I were going round to our Pat's house on Boxing Day, and I suddenly just decided to go for it. So I went, 'Hold on, while we're here, let's go and knock on her.'

We drove round to hers, and weird though it felt to be doing the familiar walk up to her front door, I didn't let myself think about it. I felt like I was on a mission – and that was it! When she answered I didn't say, 'Hi' or anything, I just went, 'Here's your grandkids.'

Mum couldn't speak. I don't think she knew whether to laugh or cry, but she got Mark and the kids and me through to the front room. She was in there with a couple of friends, but they quickly made themselves scarce. I was really offhand and stroppy with her, and I could hardly look at her, because I still had so much resentment there, so it was Mark who did the talking.

He said to Heidi, 'Tell Nana about you and Max.' I could see me mum just completely melt. She was really happy Mark had called her 'Nana' and not 'Sue' to the kids.

Heidi was nearly two, and Max was eight months, but until now she had seen them only in magazine shoots and on television, so for her it was an especially important moment.

Then after a bit of doting over the kids, she disappeared upstairs and came back with a present for me, a pair of pyjamas. She said, 'I bought these for you just in case you came round. I have hoped you would every single day since we fell out.'

And I have to say that melted me a bit. The visit was a starting point in mending our relationship. She had missed a crucial time in Heidi and Max's lives – and mine – but she was so keen to make up for it after that. And from there, we just took it really slowly. We were glad to be back in each other's lives, despite everything. And although looking back to before our fallout, I'm sure she sold a lot of stories and tips on me, more than I realised at the time, I think after we made up, that was the end of it. I think two years of not seeing me or her grandkids did it for her – it wasn't a risk she was going to take again. And our relationship just slowly developed.

Max and Heidi wouldn't accept her at first – to them she was a complete stranger, and they didn't know what to make of her. They idolise her now, and she idolises them. It took a while, but they love her to bits and she became a brilliant grandmother. She is a much better grandmother than a mum, I guess because she doesn't need to have much responsibility. She can just spoil them and play with them and have fun, and she is brilliant with them, she really is. She loves them as much as she loves me – if not more! She and our Molly are especially close. Molly calls her Nana 'Nou', and me mum adores her. She always says to me, 'I didn't know it was possible to love someone and feel as protective of them as I did of you when you were born. Then Molly came along, and well, I feel exactly the same about her. I'd kill anyone who touched her – or any of the other kids. They are my life.'

And it was true. I also think it was good for her, seeing them growing up, and watching my relationship with them. I know she has realised she didn't exactly do her job as mum with me in the best way. She tried her best, but there was a lot she could have done differently, and I know she has realised that now.

As for Mark, she and he seemed to get on well again. They had a laugh together – that similar humour they had meant they amused each other. She told him she didn't retract the stuff she said about him in the *News of the World*, despite his denials in the newspapers of being a drug dealer, she knew he was her dealer and still didn't think he was good for me, but he shrugged it off, and they moved on from there. Mum had no other choice I think, as it was the only way she was going to be back in our lives, and it was clear she was willing to do whatever it took for that to happen. I do think it had broken her heart, those two years away from us.

So despite everything else awful that had happened in 2008, it ended on a good note.

Who Can I Trust?

As I went into 2009, the big thing for me was still whether I could trust Mark or not. I still hadn't got to the bottom of the money issue, but he was already setting up other money-making ventures in a bid to bring in some cash. At one stage there was a car valeting company; another time he started a company renting out fruit machines to pubs. Neither really got off the ground.

But on the trust front, there were more and more issues with other girls seeming to come up.

I was getting girls getting in touch with me, saying they had slept with Mark, and they wanted their money. When I would confront Mark, he would deny all knowledge.

'Mark, why has this girl Becky [or whoever] texted me to say I owe her money?'

'No idea. I don't know any Becks.'

'She says you slept with her, and said you would pay her if she didn't go to the papers.'

'Well she is a liar, then.'

'But she has my number somehow?'

'I've no idea, Kez, must be from a friend of yours. She will be after money, ignore her.'

'She says she has texts from you as proof.'

'She'll have made them up. She is just a fame-seeker, babe.'

'She has photos of you together.'

'They'll be old.'

'But you don't know her?'

'Photoshopped. It's not true, just fucking drop it and stop falling for their tricks!'

Sometimes I wouldn't believe him, and get upset and cry for hours, or fight with him, and look through his phone. But mostly – maybe because it was easier or maybe because he had completely brainwashed me by then – I believed him. I really believed that he was being faithful to me and that these girls were all desperate, hungry for money and fame. You see it on my MTV shows. I get the papers and just dismiss the stories, and you can see that I really don't give them the time of day. That wasn't put on for the cameras, it really is how much Mark had convinced me.

I can honestly say I have never met anyone like Mark, who can look you in the eye and just come out with the most bare-faced blatant lies and have not the slightest wobble about telling you them.

But I don't know how he convinced me with some of the girls. Like one, in early March of that year – looking back it was so blatantly true, yet I refused to see it. She was called Samantha Riaz, a girl from London, who said she had slept with him the year before. She had texts and even a phone call as proof, and everything she said seemed to match up. And yet *still* I refused to believe it! I look at the Kerry from back then and think I really was brainwashed. Manipulated into thinking and believing only what Mark told me.

Then, in March 2009 a friend of mine, Debbie McGovern, got in touch. She said: 'Kerry, I think you should know something. I've bought £25,000 worth of your Orkney Island shares off Mark, as it seemed like a good idea. He said you needed to free some money up.

'He told me you needed the cash for school fees and things, and there was no other money, but that he hadn't told you. But I feel a bit weird if I hide it from you, so I'm giving you the heads-up.'

I was shaking with anger, and started looking into it, but there was no explanation of where the money had gone – or a lot of other money as well. I went to the cash point and tried to get some money out, but couldn't. It was like I had been cleaned out. I asked Mark to give me a copy of a bank statement so I could have a look, and he went mental and asked for a divorce. It was insane. I had gone from wanting him to have some control of the finances so that he didn't feel pushed out, to being completely out of it myself, and not knowing where any money had gone. And here was Mark asking for a divorce because I questioned him.

I know Mark, and I know that by getting in first about a divorce he wanted to shake me up, and scare me into submission, but this time I was past that point. I went absolutely mad. All the doubts I had been trying to suppress, surfaced, and I began wondering if all along he had been stealing money from me. Why would he mind showing me my own bank statement unless there was something in it that he didn't want me to see? Up until then I had thought there was something strange to it, but I had veered more towards thinking it was just that him and David were dabbling in some kind of ropey venture. Experimenting with my money, maybe, but not actually stealing it.

We had a huge row, and he left the house, telling me it was over, and I was hysterical. I didn't know where to turn. Our Pat was great at this time, and stayed with me, and the nanny Gemma did what she could to help, but neither of them really knew what to do. I was beside myself. And my mind was so hazy from all the medication, I was struggling to follow through my thoughts and work anything out.

So I called in a new financial advisor to investigate: Frank Cochran, from a company called Celebrity Financial Planning.

As soon as word got out that Mark was out of the house, the paps descended on my home in force, and people were getting in touch to offer advice. And you know what? Not one of them was backing Mark. Everyone used it as an opportunity to have a go at Mark and accuse him of all sorts. People were e-mailing, texting, calling, claiming he had my money in all different accounts, that he was stealing off me and cheating. I felt like I was going out of my mind. I couldn't stop crying, I stopped taking my bipolar medication in an attempt to get my mind clear and see what was going on, and I called in a divorce lawyer. I changed my Facebook status to single, so people knew this time it was more than just the usual row. Except for Mark, that is. He just seemed to think this was one of our usual kick-offs, and assumed I was going to give him a call and get him to come back home. It was normally me who made the first move when we had a falling-out, but not this time.

I was terrified of being on my own, that was true. Despite everything, Mark was the one who calmed me down when I had panic attacks and gave me a cuddle when I was feeling down and vulnerable, and I really wasn't sure I was strong enough to go it alone. But my fury at the idea he might have been stealing off me kept me going. I just focused on trying to get to the bottom of it, while pushing ahead with plans to divorce Mark. I even got my new accountant Frank to announce my decision to divorce on 13 March. He stood on the drive and made a statement telling the world.

As well as the upset I was going through at the idea of what he had done, I was feeling completely stupid. People had tried to warn me about Mark, people had criticised him and I had refused to listen, and now I felt like everything they had said was coming true. I felt like the whole world was looking at me and laughing: 'We told you so.' I desperately wanted to be proved wrong, to be told it was all a big mistake and that Mark had been doing the right thing.

A few days later, he came home. I didn't expect him, he just pulled up on the driveway and walked in. He rarely made the first move after a row, so it showed he had started getting scared of what was happening. Not that you would have known it, he was all like: 'Y'alright Kez?' as though it was just a normal day of our lives together! 'Listen. I swear I've only ever had your best interests at heart and I can't believe you think I would do anything like that with your money. If you can find proof that I have stolen off you, fine, I accept it, and we can divorce. But there isn't any, 'cause I haven't.'

So I kept pushing ahead to try and find the evidence, while at the same time praying I wasn't going to do just that. I wanted to believe my husband wouldn't do this to me, and that actually it was just people who were jealous of us, or who had a problem with him, trying to stir things up.

There was also that little bit of me still defending Mark, no matter what. Because so many people were coming out against him, it fired up that bit of me that gets defensive of him. I felt like they were all turning on him, and it made me want to protect him in a weird way. In the same way that people knocking him when we first got together only pushed us closer. As my resolve weakened, all the stories against him made me want to go back to him.

Especially when, as it turned out, no one was able to supply any proof of all the accusations they were making. It felt like it was more a bullying campaign than helpful people trying to make me see the truth.

Even Frank Cochran came up with nothing – there was no evidence Mark had stolen from me.

So I agreed to give things another go, and I made an announcement confirming that to the public – Mark and I were back together. With him back in the house, I went back on my medication too.

Stupid, stupid girl, you are obviously thinking, and so am I, writing this now. But I also know at that time I was such a mental wreck that I probably wouldn't have survived on my own. I was so completely and utterly dependent on Mark, I could hardly dress myself in the morning without him there. He was like my carer – although not always a very good one!

I took a few days out and went to a spa with a friend. While I was there I had to do an interview with the *News of the World* on the phone, to tell them my relationship was back on track. I was so defensive, because everything they asked had a kind of double meaning, as though the reporter was trying to trip me up every step of the way. At that point I just hated all the press, and what I thought they were doing to me and to my marriage.

But even after I had defended him, getting Mark to pick me up from there turned into a huge argument. He had to do it because he was the only one who could drive the cars we owned by this time. Bit by bit, as Mark had sold and bought new cars, he had bought only manual cars – and I have a licence only for automatic cars, so I couldn't drive any of them. Which meant I couldn't go anywhere without him driving me there and therefore being with me. I thought it was a nice gesture and was him looking out for me, always being there. But it meant I was completely stranded without him, and so more and more reliant on him.

Mark also took my mobile phone away from me, so he had control of all my calls. I didn't mind that – I actually thought it was nice he was dealing with all my business for me. To be honest, by this stage I was paranoid about talking to anyone, and thought everyone except for Mark was bad, so actually it was like he was doing me a favour. He even spoke to my PR agent Sean for me, so he knew all my business and PR plans before I did – and often without even letting me know what was said. It was yet another control thing, but at the time I was quite happy for him to do it, as it was a sign he cared, wasn't it?

And we still had great sex. Every row would be followed by make-up sex and we'd be happy for a few days, but I knew it wasn't enough.

So that was the dynamic in our household. I did have some support, though: Gemma had moved on from just being a nanny to being one of my best friends. Not only did she work for me, but we started socialising together. We would tell each other our problems, and she was a great girl and I loved her to bits. One night, quite a shocking thing happened, which would have repercussions down the line.

The boys went for a night out – Mark, his brother Stuart, who was round ours a lot, Gemma's boyfriend and a few other lads. The kids were away, but Gemma, myself and a few other girls stayed in, and hung out in the cinema room. We were just chatting and drinking.

When the lads came back, everyone went off to bed one by one, except Gemma and Stuart, who sat up talking. Well, in the end they ended up kissing and got it on. Both of them dumped their partners, Gemma got her boyfriend to move out of our house, and Stuart moved straight in!

And I did like Stuart. He was a good lad, and as far as I know he never sold out on me. He was Mark's half-brother, and they were

quite different. Stuart's humour was even harsher than Mark's
– he could say something that he thought was funny, but which
was really quite nasty and crushing. But generally we never fell
out and got on well.

I was really excited about it. There seemed something kind of
complete about it. She and I were so close that to have her dating
Mark's brother made us this nice little foursome.

Just as Mark and I were getting ourselves back on track, a story
appeared in the paper about me. This time they were saying I had
a hole in my nose. Well, other than my nostrils, that just wasn't
true. They got a weird-looking picture and ran with it. Then there
were details next to it from a source claiming I would get through
7 grams of cocaine in one binge. 7 grams? No way could I have
done that on my own, which is what the story implied. To get
through that, it would have been a group of us.

I didn't care too much about what this story said, but what I
did care about was where it had come from. There was only one
person I could think had done the story, and that was our Pat. She
had gone quiet on me since Mark had come back after our recent
row and there were a few accurate details that let me know it was
only someone close who could have done it.

I never knew for sure, but it felt like confirmation when a few
days later *heat* magazine came out and it carried an interview with
her. She was telling the world her opinion on Mark's and my
relationship, and the way I was raising the kids. I really couldn't
believe it. Pat was my everything when I was a little girl. Then
she did that to me. My real mum had betrayed me – and now the
woman who at times had been like a mum, had done the same.

I had given Pat a job as my cleaner. And maybe that's where
it went wrong – they always say you shouldn't hire your family,

don't they? Soon after she started working with me, Pat and her girlfriend Vicky split up and Pat was drinking a lot to get through it. She would sometimes get quite abusive after drink, and I know there was one night she had quite a falling-out with Mark over it. She was dabbling in cocaine too and I guess she just wasn't handling life very well. I wanted to support her through that – a break-up is horrendous for anyone. But I also needed her to keep working.

But she kept calling in sick and not turning up for work. I said to her, 'Pat, if you don't come in, I can't pay ya! I know you are my sister, but you can't keep having days off. I need you to come in and clean.'

I think that is what the interview stemmed from. Maybe she thought she was entitled to behave like that, and she wanted revenge on me for not just paying her regardless or something. I don't know, because then this story came out in the *News of the World*. I found out about it at just gone midnight, and I rang her up straightaway.

'Pat,' I said. 'How could you do this to me?'

'I don't know what you're on about,' she said.

I was devastated. 'I know it was you, Pat. Why did you do it?'

But I got no answer, and she has never once tried to apologise to me for it.

Even today I still don't know how I feel about her. I have so many good memories of her, and I know sometimes she was the best person in the world, but to have her betray me like that....

She saw me when I was at my worst. When I was with Mark in the bedroom, off my head, then crying and sleeping for hours on end. It was such a horrible, awful, dark time. And for her to turn on me when she knew what I had gone through was total betrayal. I always wonder if me dad knows what is going on and what he would think of her for doing that to me.

Out of his five children, four of them have sold stories on me. The one who hasn't, Vic, owes me £20,000. I lent it him a few years back when he was about to be evicted from his house and I haven't seen a penny of it since. It feels like they have all taken advantage of me in some way, and put the chance to gain some money over family ties. I've got no contact with anyone from his family now, which is so sad, but I don't know what else to do. You can't just keep forgiving people who stab you in the back.

Losing My Dad
All Over Again

One night in April 2009 I got a phone call from my PR agent, Sean. 'Hi, Kerry' he said. 'I don't know how to tell you this, but the *News of the World* have found out that your dad has died.'

'What you on about, Sean?' I said. 'He died last year, what does it matter to them now?'

'No,' he said. 'Your real dad, Ronnie Armstrong.'

Well, I've never revealed my real dad's name to anyone so I knew straightaway he was telling the truth. I was devastated. I cried more over this man I never met than anyone ever. I wasn't crying for the actual person, as I didn't know him, but more for what he represented – for the dad I had never known and now wouldn't have a chance to know, and for an end to all the secret dreams I had that one day I could be a proper part of his life.

Sean said that the family knew about me because the reporter had knocked on the door of one of the daughters and told them. Previously no one in the family had had a clue, but they had done an interview about it.

Well, I was shaking like a leaf. I was terrified. And I kept thinking about this poor woman Joyce, whose husband was not long dead. She had just found out that her husband, the man she loved and had so many beautiful memories with, had had an affair with somebody. It can't help but tarnish her memories. And on top of that she discovers she's got a step-daughter – and worst of all, the biggest kick in the teeth of all, is it's Kerry Katona!

The only basis she has for knowing anything about me is all the shit she has read about me in the papers. Can you imagine what she was thinking? I wouldn't have blamed her if she'd run a mile. In fact, I think I expected her to just that.

For me, rejection is a massive thing. I've had so much of it in my life and I have a real fear of it. But Sean said that they wanted to meet me.

I did a DNA test to prove I was Ronnie's daughter, which came back confirming it, and then a meeting was set up in a pub. I went along with Mark, and I was so, so scared. I honestly think that going there was one of the most frightening things I have done in my life. I didn't want to allow myself to have any expectations, and I really hoped that what they had read about me wouldn't put them off, because I wasn't that person.

I walked through the door and they were all there: me dad's wife Joyce, my older sister Lynsey, and my younger brothers Ian and Paul.

I knew it was them as soon as I saw them because they looked so like me, especially our Lynsey, and I just burst into tears. But I was smiling at the same time, and they were doing the same.

I didn't even know where to start, but we started commenting on each other's appearances, and working out what features we shared. I guess it was the easiest starting point.

Joyce was quiet, though, just standing looking at me. Then she told me, 'You look more like Ronnie than the rest of the kids do!'

They all kept saying, 'Looking at you is like looking at Dad' and they were so lovely, I couldn't stop getting upset. Not just from sadness, in a good way too.

I told Joyce, 'All my life I have wanted to find you all, and come knocking on your door, but that fear of damaging your lives and you rejecting me has stopped me.'

She looked at me and shook her head, and said, 'We would have welcomed you with open arms.'

And that killed me. My fear of being turned away had stopped me having known them for years. I always worried Dad would have answered the door and said he was happy with his family and didn't want to know me, but the way they were talking, it was as though I could have had a relationship with my dad. And that is a hole that is never going to be filled.

I don't want to sound like I'm making excuses for myself, but I do think that all my life I have been trying to fill that hole, maybe find a replacement for Dad. I think it explains the men I have chosen, the drugs to hide behind, the need for someone to look after me, because I looked after me mum and myself from when I was tiny. I was three the first time I saw her slit her wrists. Ever since then, I have felt worthless: if my own mum doesn't think life is worth living for me, then why would anyone else think I was worthy? At times I think, 'You selfish cow, how can you do that to me? Am I not good enough?' But I know she was going through her own problems. She suffered from bouts of manic depression all through her life, and as I know well myself, there is often not much you can do when your mind is starting to go down certain routes.

That's why I have had the names Molly and Lilly tattooed on my wrists. To remind me never to do anything stupid to myself that will damage their lives.

But now, suddenly, so late in life, I had this whole other family. And they are so, so nice and loving, and Scouse!

I also have two older brothers, Wayne and Jason, from Dad's

first marriage before Joyce. I have had some contact with them but not yet met. Hopefully that will happen one day too.

After that first meeting with Joyce and her kids, I started seeing them more regularly and building up a relationship, and I love them to bits now. They invited me over to the house, and showed me dad's ashes, and told me things about him and his life.

I do still get envious and feel like a bit of an outsider: every time I go round, they will be telling all these stories about their happy life together with my dad. Obviously I don't begrudge them it, and I love hearing my brothers and sister talking about their memories, and just being there for each other, but I am always wishing I was part of them. While they were doing family things and having this great upbringing, I was living in a refuge or foster home, or watching me mum being stabbed, or I was being beaten up myself.

I think that is why I've got a big family myself. I never wanted to have one kid – I'd have another 10,000 kids if I could afford it! I really would, because I never want them to be on their own. I think the childhood I went through would have been a hell of a lot easier if I'd had a sibling to go through it with me. So I always want my children to have each other for support and friendship, and for them to have loads of good memories growing up together and with me. I was always determined to put my mark on this world, which I've done through them: they're my babies, they're my mark on this world. A big complete family is all I've ever wanted.

A New Way of Thinking

For so much of this time, it felt like no one was really looking out for me. But, thank God, behind the scenes, there were people who had my best interests at heart. Without my knowing it, my agent Sean had got in touch with two psychotherapists called Nik and Eva Speakman. They are a married couple and have developed a lot of their own methods for treating people.

They were introduced to Sean through a mutual friend. He asked them if they would be interested in working with me, as in his words, 'Kerry is in a really, really bad way. I am worried we are actually at the point of life and death with her if someone doesn't step in and sort her out, and I think you might be the pair to do it.'

It turns out that they had previously watched my MTV show, and said to each other how sorry they felt for me, and how they wished they could work with me on my bipolar. So they jumped at the chance when Sean asked them. The only problem, they had been warned, would be getting past Mark and through to me as he was very protective, or controlling, depending on how you looked at it, and was resistant to outside interference.

I knew nothing of these discussions, and was off in Majorca on holiday with Mark. After everything we had been through, it was a break for the two of us, and I came back feeling very loved-up. A day or so later, I went to a meeting that was set up for Mark and me, and Sean and the Speakmans, and we had a chat. They both have long blonde hair and friendly faces and are in their forties. But I'll be honest, I don't even remember that first meeting. A lot of this period of my life was a complete haze and I have days and weeks of that period of my life where I can't remember a thing.

According to what Nik and Eva told me afterwards, they were shocked by what they saw that day. Apparently they kept trying to ask me direct questions, and either Mark would chip in and reply before I had a chance, or I would look at him to get him to reply for me. I had lost all ability to speak for myself. And they said my speech was slurred and I was really spaced out – as though my body was there but my mind was there for only brief spells.

The thing that distressed Nik and Eva the most – and I know this will have been true because I did often think it – was the one thing I did say with clarity: that I wasn't going to live past 30, that I was confident I would die before I reached that age. Given I was just over a year away from that birthday made it doubly shocking.

And you know what? Mark sat there and agreed. He wasn't shocked either, but said, 'Yeah, I don't think she'll make it past 30 either. She's a mess, look at her.'

But despite the wreck they saw before them, Nik and Eva wanted to carry on working with me. I must have liked them because they came around the house a day or two later. Mark wouldn't let them come round when he wasn't there, but they came a few times, and just chatted and became friendly with both of us. Sometimes I was open to it, other times I was curled under a duvet on the sofa, unable to cope with the world, and barely able to function, let alone go through therapy. And they did comment on the state of the house at the time, and that the people around me seemed to be letting everything get into a mess, which can't have helped me. Me on the sofa with my duvet, while grubby mugs and plates of old toast built up around me.

I have a vague idea that I would spend days curled in bed or move down to the sofa, but that was about it. Mark did everything else, like giving me my medication, and telling Gemma what to do, what food to buy, getting the kids from school and all those kinds of things, because I no longer believed I was capable of it. He told me I wasn't, and I totally believed that myself as well.

According to Nik and Eva, there was a time during one of their visits when Mark came in and got me to sign a load of blank cheques. I don't remember it, but again, it is quite possible. I wouldn't have questioned it, because he had my best interests at heart, didn't he?

The first time I have a really clear memory of time with Nik and Eva is when I had to go to court in Manchester at some point in July. For some reason Mark couldn't come with me, but they did, and it was the first time it had just been the three of us. I really appreciated them coming to support me, and as I had no car at the time I needed a lift to what was yet another bankruptcy-related hearing. I was having to go to these as a follow-up to having been made bankrupt. I was scared and confused, mainly because I didn't have a clue about my money or where it was, or what I was supposed to do about any of this. I needed Mark to come to these hearings and explain things to them, but of course he was having none of it.

After the hearing, Nik and Eva came back to my house. I didn't realise it at the time, but they have since explained to me the technique they were using on me. I thought they were just talking, but they were working on what they call 'schemas' in my mind. Schemas are beliefs we have within us that can relate to a part of our past, even when we were very young children, and can often mean we do things that aren't actually logical when thought about clearly. So, they were trying to open my mind to think differently about certain issues in my life, which were perhaps negative, and rebuilding my confidence by trying to get rid of the bad schemas.

Nik once explained it to me. One example: with me, whether I like it or not, slitting my wrists when things are bad was always an option in my brain. Because by association, and having seen my mum do that as a child when things got too hard for her, my mind will have learned the link. Times are tough equals slitting wrists as an option for dealing with it. By contrast, someone who had never even heard of someone slitting their wrists is extremely unlikely ever to consider it. So schemas are about readjusting your mind, which makes sense to me.

At the time they were very focused on making me regain my confidence and independence, and trying to make me less reliant on Mark.

'Why do you think Mark didn't come to court today?' they would ask. And then they would spend time complimenting my career and telling me how incredible it was that I had achieved all these things by my age. And little by little things did start to soak in – I felt like the penny was beginning to drop.

One thing they also pointed out was that I didn't have my own car, and that for practical reasons wouldn't it make sense? And I started thinking about the fact Mark had bought only manuals despite knowing I couldn't drive them. It was like little seeds of realisation about his control started to grow.

To help me, Eva took me to the airport and hired a car in her name with me as a named driver – I couldn't even hire it myself, as I didn't have access to my credit cards or money anymore. So she did it for me, which was extremely kind and trusting of her.

They also had a look into David McHugh for me, and pointed out that he wasn't a qualified chartered accountant, and that he had been done in the past on several counts of dishonesty. But somehow none of it was said in a way that was passing judgement, it was just like they gave me the heads up to make my own mind up. And, to be honest, as far as the money was concerned it only added to what I already had started to work out myself deep down, but had been ignoring.

When Love Turns to Hate

One Sunday morning, 2 August 2009, I went off to record for the Iceland adverts. I was clean as a whistle – I was always dead professional with the shoots for them. The only thing that got in my way was my bipolar medication, which meant my speech was really slurred in the morning. Combine that with the fact I naturally talk really fast, and have a strong northern accent, and my words would just be totally garbled, so I would have to calm down and wait for the meds to clear. But the Iceland producers were really good about it – they knew that was the case and would fit filming times around it, never filming too early in the day.

So this day I was on set, getting ready to film a new set of adverts with singer-turned-presenter, Coleen Nolan, who I love to bits.

My stylist Lorraine was with me as well, as I sat in hair and make-up, getting ready, and the three of us were chatting away. I was feeling all happy and loved-up at the time, and had just sent Mark a text saying that I loved him, when my phone rang and it was me mum.

She went straight into a massive rant: 'Have you seen what that scumbag has done?'

'Mum, what you on about? It's Sunday morning.'

'Look in the paper. I'm gonna kill him.' And she hung up.

I used to dread Sundays, because it was the day the papers were most likely to have some kind of scoop or exposé – sometimes true, sometimes not, but 99 per cent of the time, pretty damaging. The times when they could have written 'Kerry on a break from coke' or 'Kerry and Mark happy and in love' – well, it wouldn't have sold, would it? A lot of the time I'd stay awake till gone 12 o'clock on a Saturday and check what went up online on the Sunday newspapers, but as I was working the next day for this filming, I had gone to bed. Plus I hadn't been expecting anything to come out.

I called Mark, 'You seen the papers? Is there a story in there about you? Mum just phoned and went mad. What is it, Mark?'

But he said, 'I don't know what you're on about. I haven't seen the papers yet.'

I didn't know what to do. But I thought that I should stay professional, so I stayed where I was, and Coleen and Lorraine went off on the hunt for the papers for me, as they normally have some lying around on set. I just sat there trying to stay calm, but really shaking, and with my mind racing like mad through all the possibilities.

After about ten minutes they both came back into my dressing room and said, 'Kerry, we've seen the paper, and we've had a vote on set. We don't think you should see it until you have finished work for the day.'

I was like: 'You're joking!' But they weren't. 'Ah no, that means whatever is in there must be bad.'

I love Lorraine and Coleen to bits and I knew they would have my best interests at heart, so I listened to them and got on with the day. A long, 14-hour day where me mind kept going through all the possibilities, but where I would drag it back to focus on the job at hand.

As soon as we were wrapped up, I left and drove straight to a petrol station to get a copy of the story. And as I pulled on to the forecourt I could see straight away which paper it was. On the front of the *Sunday Mirror* was a grainy picture of Mark all over some girl, with the line: 'The pictures that will break Kerry's heart. Sleazebag husband gropes strippers.'

I remember being so mad I punched a wall in the garage. It wasn't because I was upset, in an 'Oh my god, he's touching another girl, I'm so jealous' way. But more the humiliation! I couldn't believe he had done it, after everything I had been through with him, after everything I had done for him. To let me endure seeing pictures like that on the front of a national newspaper, knowing the whole country was looking and probably laughing.

How Mark thought I wasn't going to see it, I ain't got a clue. And I don't believe he didn't know about it. My agent Sean would have called him the night before for a statement, as papers always have to put the stories to you, to check if you want to comment. Even if he had tried to get through to me, though, Sean wouldn't have been able to speak to me. The 'kind' gesture of Mark's which meant he looked after my mobile all the time meant that he would have answered Sean's call and could have given any excuse he liked as to why Sean couldn't speak to me.

I was so angry. In fact, I hadn't been that angry with Mark ever. It was like I had reached the point of, 'Enough is enough!' After everything I had given him, done for him, and all the love I had shown him, how could he do that? I just couldn't take yet another letdown from him. And as I drove home, my rage from the garage just kept building and building.

So as soon as I walked through the door, I didn't stop to talk or give him a chance to explain – I knew he would only have some ridiculous excuse – so I'll admit, I really went for him, I just couldn't stop myself this time. I hammered him, punched him, the lot. It was like every bit of hurt, confusion and humiliation from the last two years, since that first Clare Bonello story, was now coming out. Not that he held back, either. He grabbed me and threw me across the room, and I hit a table, and ended up with a massive bruise on my leg that hurt for days after.

I was screaming and crying 'Why are you doing this? What am I doing wrong? Do I not make you happy? That is it, get out!' And I think he knew it was game over, so he left. And I got in touch with a divorce lawyer.

There is only so far you can push someone before they snap, and he had pushed and pushed and pushed, way beyond the point where most normal people would break. My massive regret about the whole incident was that Heidi was in the room. She was only two at the time, so too young to remember or even realise what was going on, but still, it really bothers me today that she was there. Luckily it was a one-off – violence between Mark and me wasn't something the kids ever saw any other times. That was the only time I went for him, and Mark never really laid a finger on me apart from that. But it wasn't right, and it makes me feel horribly ashamed.

Twists and Turns

For ten whole days I had no contact with Mark. Then – and this is the first of several twists, so try and follow it through as best as you can! – this guy gets in touch. I had met him a few times before, as he supplied Mark with drugs, and he said he also did some work for the *Sunday Sport*.

He called to say that one of the strippers had come in to the newspaper offices to try out for a photo shoot, and that he had interviewed her as part of it. And he said he had to ask her lots of questions about her past and that she was open with him because she thought the publicity of all the Mark stuff meant she was going to get the job. But it was what she was claiming that was interesting: she admitted to him that the whole stripper incident was a set-up, that she and this other girl had set out specifically to snare Mark.

So I'm listening to all this, interested, and starting to believe it, as it fitted with what Mark has always tried to claim about other girls. But I was very hesitant: I really didn't want to be taken in again. And even if he had been set up, it didn't mean he was entirely innocent anyway. So I asked this guy what proof he had.

'Tell you what,' he said. 'I've written out the whole conversation, everything I've asked, and everything she has replied is here on a bit of paper. How about I come and give it to you, and you can make your own mind up?'

Well, with those ten days to cool down a bit, I decided I needed to get to the bottom of this, and I was calm enough by then to hear this guy out. I wanted to see exactly what Mark had been up to, so I agreed. This guy came to my house, and we're chatting, and I asked to see the paper. The kids were home, but were out in the back garden playing, so as to give us space to chat, and Gemma was keeping an eye on them.

'I've got some coke here, do you want some of that first?' he said.

I shook my head, but he said, 'I'm not giving you it until you have had some coke. You are well uptight, and you need to be relaxed before I hand this over, as it might be pretty shocking for you.'

'You have some if you want,' I said. 'But I'm not going to, I don't want one.'

I was having a dry spell at the time, keeping my mind clear so I could work all this out.

So this lad went to the bathroom and had a line in there, and came back, and said, 'I've left one for you in there. If you want this paper, go do it.'

When I repeat that all now, it sounds ridiculous. Why the hell would this kid be so keen for me to have coke? But at the time I was just focused on wanting to see the paper, and if doing a line would get me it, then fine. So I went 'sod it' and went in the bathroom, one line, sniff, done and dusted, and then went back out and got the evidence I wanted, and he left.

So I read this sheet, and everything is in Mark's favour – the girl openly admits they set him up, they got paid for this and that by the newspaper, blah blah.

And as I read it, I felt bad. I didn't think in any way at all that Mark was innocent, but it seemed as though he wasn't as out of order as I had originally thought. It did seem like he had been set up, and let's face it, that only happened to him because of my fame. No newspaper would want to pay two girls to make him look bad, if he hadn't been married to me. So in that respect, I felt like it was actually a bit my fault.

And I thought about it for the rest of the day, and decided I'd give him the benefit of the doubt. Because despite everything, I was missing him, and not sure I could cope on my own. So I called him and we talked, and everything he said fitted perfectly with what this piece of paper said. So the next thing I know, Mark was back home and we were getting on with our lives. For a couple of days, anyhow. Soon I needed his support more than ever, as a different story was about to come out.

On 15 August, Sean phoned Mark, who passed the call over to me. 'Kerry, the *News of the World* have got a video which, they say, is you doing cocaine. I've no idea if it's you, I don't want to know, but you can't really tell either way, so we can deny it.'

He sent me the video to look at, and it's me doing that one line in the bathroom, which the guy who claimed to be from the *Sunday Sport* had got me to do.

My heart sank and I started shaking. I knew how bad it looked and how much criticism I was going to get for this. After all the denying I had done in the past about my drug habit, there was no getting out of it now. Partly because I was in denial myself. Although I was taking coke, I didn't see it as a problem at this time – and publicly admitting stories were true, would turn it into a problem. And also, well, it would hardly have been good for my career, would it? But when it was there so blatantly on film, I knew I couldn't pretend.

So I went, 'Yeah, it is me. I can't deny that. Anyone who watches my reality show can see that's my bathroom. But I know who has done it, which little shit has sold this video.'

And I hung up and said to Mark, 'This is so bad. I'm screwed. But it's that lad you know, he totally set me up. He must have put the camera in, got me into the bathroom to do a line, then took it again just before he left. I was sat there listening to him, falling for everything he was saying, hook, line and sinker, when he was using the info he had on you that I wanted, to get to me.'

Mark agreed and went mental. Then he phoned the lad up in front of me, and was really sticking up for me, going, 'What the hell have you done this to her for? You really are scum!'

And I thought it was great. Rather than have a go at me for being stupid and getting caught out, he was really sticking up for me.

As for the story, there was absolutely nothing I could do about it. I had been caught and that was it. So I just decided I would have to hold my hands up and roll with whatever came off the back of the story.

By coincidence I had already booked tickets to go with the kids to Tenerife for a break the next day, so as the papers were hitting the shelf, we were getting out of the country. Mark joined us a day later. Angry though a bit of me still was with him about the strippers, I was still happy to have him there. He seemed like the one person I could rely on, my security.

And the bad news just kept coming. While I was out on holiday, Iceland got in touch to say they were terminating my contract. They said the drug thing was the final straw for them and they couldn't be seen to have someone who did cocaine as one of the faces of their brand.

They released a statement saying, 'In recognition of the relationship we have developed, we will continue to try and help Kerry to ensure she gets the most appropriate support, should she require our assistance.' So actually, they were quite nice about the whole thing, and I did understand they were in a hard position. But I was so gutted to lose that job. I actually really enjoyed it, and all the people I used to film with – the celebs and the crew – were lovely. Not to mention the fact that I was paid a lot of money for it, so it was a massive financial loss, as well as a shame on a career and personal level.

I was just so lost and confused about the whole thing. How had I managed to get myself into such a mess?

More Consequences

I came back from Tenerife a few days later, terrified to be back in the UK and facing the media and the public. And being away hadn't really made things better – there were all sorts of consequences of that video still to come.

First up, eight days after the newspaper article appeared, I was arrested. I was taken to a police station and cautioned for possession of cocaine. I didn't think there was any point in denying it, as the video made it quite clear. But it was just plain embarrassing.

The next day, on the Tuesday, I got a call from someone at Pownall Hall School, where the girls were supposed to be starting in September. They had been at Alderley Edge School For Girls on Wilmslow Road, but I had thought it was too expensive and felt a bit stuck-up, and I wanted to move them elsewhere. I had looked around and opted for Pownall Hall. It was just down the road in Wilmslow, so they could even walk to school, and they had passed all their exams with flying colours and had been accepted.

But on that Tuesday, the headmaster called me in for a conversation. I didn't like the way this seemed to be going, and sure enough, when I arrived he said, 'Look, I don't know how to put this, but there have been a few things in the press lately. And now parents have been complaining they don't want your children to come to this school. Unless they are taken off the class list for next year, other parents are going to pull their children out. So I have quite a problem on my hands.'

I went mad and really kicked off in the office. 'Why are you doing this? Because I've been in the paper with drugs? Have you done a police check on all the other parents? I guarantee there will be some right stuff in some of their records. I guarantee there is a list as long as my arm, it just happens not to be in the press. How dare you punish my kids for what I've done!'

It takes a lot to push me to my limit, but this man really did. Bring my kids into it, and I see red. I will never stand back and see my kids suffer – and I think any good parent would say the same. When I have reached that point of seeing my children affected, I lose it. Mark used to know when I had reached that point, and even he would sit back and not say a word, and I think this headmaster took the same approach.

'Do not condemn my kids because of my stupidity!' I ranted at him. 'Oh, and by the way, I have not been charged, so you don't have a leg to stand on. You don't just have a problem on your hands with other parents, now you will have the biggest lawsuit, 'cause what you are doing is plain discrimination!'

Then I stormed out. Oh, it makes me so angry even thinking about it today. I can feel the fire welling up in me. I was livid. The girls had left the other school, had a farewell party for all their friends, and I had bought them all their new uniforms. They were really excited to be starting off on a new adventure. I was so angry – and sad as well. I really thought a headmaster would have more strength to do what was right, rather than just to bow to peer pressure caused by people believing things they had read and rumours they had heard – and then punishing my children for it.

As it turned out, the headmaster might have done me a favour because I managed to get my girls into a different school called Cheadle Hulme, which was a great school. Molly ended up getting a scholarship and being moved up a year, and I was so proud of her. If I needed any proof that my lifestyle wasn't affecting them, that was it!

But back to my horrendous week... On the Thursday, I had the trustee on the phone asking for certain documents that were wanted in connection with the bankruptcy. This was a full year since the court hearing and I really couldn't believe that arguments around it were still going on. I kept trying to say they needed to talk to my accountant David because he had sorted everything out, but it seemed like he wasn't helping them or supplying what they needed.

I had just about reached a limit on my money and not knowing where it was. And all my fears that I was being completely screwed over by David came bubbling to the top. Was it his fault that I was bankrupt? Was he the reason I was going through all this? Had he stolen my money? And why the hell had it taken a year to get it sorted? I was ashamed, upset and angry, and I wanted answers. This wasn't how my life was supposed to be.

So I stormed round to David's offices in the Hawthorne Business Park, working myself up on the way. When I got there, I kicked his door open, I was so furious. And I yelled, 'Where's my money? What are you doing to me?'

He refused to answer or help me out, but just said, 'Please leave.'

'Why has all this happened? Enough is enough!'

'Please leave.' He repeated.

So I pushed his desk in frustration, and a cup of coffee that was sat on it went over him. I never actually touched him – the guy is like 6' 7" and about 50 years old!

Terry, this other guy in there, then grabbed me and dragged me out kicking and screaming.

I was so angry that although I was supposed to have a doctor's appointment after that to get a strange mole on my leg checked out, I skipped it and went to meet Gemma and Mark in the pub for some food. I was sitting there ranting about what had happened, saying, 'I have a good mind to go to the police and have that man who grabbed me in the office arrested for the way he treated me. That was so out of order!

'And while they are at it, they can arrest Dave. I don't care what you say, Mark, there is something not right with that man!'

But Mark told me to calm down, so I tried to, and decided not to do anything rash with the police just yet.

After we had eaten, Gemma went home, and I thought I had better go to the doctor after all, so Mark was taking me there when Gemma rang.

'Erm, Kerry, I don't know how to say, this, but you better come home.'

'Why?' I asked. Thinking there was no way this day could get any worse.

'Erm, there are like 15 reporters outside, and photographers, and camera crews.'

'What! What is going on?!'

'Well, erm, there are also two police cars. They've come to arrest ya!'

'What!! Please tell me you are lying?' I actually just started laughing. What else could I do? Only two days before, I had been in the police station thanks to the drugs. Surely they didn't need to see me again.

I was still laughing when we pulled up outside the house. I was arrested on Monday, my kids got kicked out of school Tuesday, then Thursday it looked like I was about to be arrested again.

I walked up to my front door and said to the officer that he'd better come in. He did and started the whole spiel. 'I'm really sorry, but you have the right to remain silent, Anything you say....' And all that.

I was laughing again, but this time with nerves, and then as he carried on talking I felt myself getting angry.

I cut him off as he spoke: 'This guy, this David McHugh, is a crook, he ripped me off. You need to arrest him. And his friend Terry assaulted me, I never touched him! You are arresting the wrong person.'

I said I had to make a call and started to walk to another room. You would think I was going to run away the way they reacted, all jumping to stop me.

But then they calmed down and let me, and I called my agent Sean. Ah, poor Sean, the things he had to deal with as my PR!

'Sean, I am being arrested. Again.' I could almost hear the energy disappear out of him down the phone. He must have wondered what the hell he could actually do to help my image when things like that kept happening. He must have had the hardest PR job in the country at that time!

Then I went back to the other room and told the police officers I was ready to go with them. I begged them not to put cuffs on me – I think that would have been the final straw – and I walked with them back out to their car. The camera flashes were going like mad as they ducked me into the car, and once I was in there, I just burst into tears.

The whole thing was so unfair. There are many times in my

life when I have done something wrong, but this incident with my accountant Dave was not one of them. The police officer even told me that Dave claimed I had assaulted him, and that it was something to do with drugs. It had nothing to do with drugs at all; that was just an easy way out for him, as it was such an obvious weak spot at that time. All I had wanted was answers about my money and I didn't get them.

When we got to the police station, they took my jewellery, my laces, my belt, my necklace, everything. They put me in a cell with a plastic mattress like you get in a gym, with just a toilet and a camera to keep an eye on me. I was treated like a criminal.

And I was left there alone for 14 hours. I spent the first few hours crying, thinking how the hell had this happened to me. In five years I had gone from winning *I'm A Celebrity... Get Me Out of Here* and basically being a bit of a nation's sweetheart, to, well, to this.

But after I had cried myself out, I started looking around, and I think I just went into shock. I put my feet up on the bed and started talking to myself and laughing. It was such a crazy situation, I think I was getting hysterical.

In the evening the sergeant knocked on the cell door and came in.

'Are you alright, Miss Katona?'

'Yes, but can I make a phone call, please. Not for a lawyer, but to ring my kids. They were expecting me to pick them up from school today, but their nanny had to do it, so I want to make sure they are alright.'

'Not a problem,' he said, and gave me his mobile.

Gemma answered and passed the phone to Molly.

'Hiya, Molly!'

'Where are you, Mum?'

'I'm just doing a bit of early Christmas shopping baby girl.' Do not ask me how that was the first thing that popped into my head. It was August, for goodness sake! But I just went with it.

'Ooh, have you seen anything nice for me?'

'Oh Molly, the amount of stuff I have seen for you!' While I was talking, the tears were flowing down my face, and she didn't have a clue.

'I've got so much shopping to do, and then a bit of work this evening, so I am going to stay in a hotel, but I will be back real soon in the morning. Love you.'

Then I had the same conversation with Lilly, and to this day, they don't have a clue that I was doing anything different. And that is how I wanted to keep it – a child doesn't have to know everything happening in an adult's life. What was the point in making them worry about something they had no control over?

The police decided to let me go at about 3 a.m., and Mark picked me up. I just remember walking out of the cell looking like shit, and Mark was just stood there laughing. For a second I was mad, and then I started laughing too.

I was like: 'Can you bloody believe this?' and he just gave me a massive hug and we both just collapsed in fits. It was the only thing we could do.

We checked into a hotel in Manchester for the rest of the night, then went to The Trafford Centre in the morning. I was determined to keep up my pretence to the kids and turn up with bags full of early Christmas presents! But I remember walking through the shopping centre, still in the same clothes as the day before, and going past a news stand and the front cover of every newspaper was my arrest with a picture of it, me in my jeans and black shirt, with Caterpillar boots and my glasses. I can still picture it now: 'Kerry Arrested... Again!'

I was mortified, and trying to hide my face so no one would see me as I walked through the centre.

The charges were dropped, of course. There was nothing else the police could do – 'cause they weren't true!

One More Twist...

But then, of course, because this is Kerry Katona's crazy life, yet another twist happened in the story. The lad I thought had planted the camera, got in touch with me through another friend. His message said, 'Kerry, I need to see you and meet with you. I did not do that video, and I can prove it to you. Meet me and let me explain.'

I didn't believe him. But then I went for a drink with Gemma that evening in an attempt to relax, and she asked me, 'Who do you think really put that video in the bathroom?'

'It's got to be that guy, I suppose.' I shrugged, feeling too brain dead from everything that had happened in the last month to put any more thought into it.

'Please don't say I said this, but do you remember that camera that Mark bought off eBay a bit ago, that little camera that was like a pen?' And she just looked at me.

'I didn't even think of that, Gemma.' I said, feeling strange.

'I'm just saying,' she said. And we changed the subject.

But that conversation had made me feel uneasy. I didn't even want to consider the possibility that Mark had anything to do with it – I don't think I could have handled knowing that. But still, the nagging feeling in me was enough to make me wonder whether I should give this guy time to hear what he had to say. There had been so many twists and lies and strange discoveries, that I just felt like I had no idea of telling what was the genuine truth any more. So in the end I thought, 'What the hell' and decided to meet the lad and hear what he had to say.

Looking back, I realise it was very brave of Gemma to say that to me, and another one of those moments when I realised how loyal she was.

So I agreed to meet the lad at a hotel. Well, this is when the biggest twist of all came into play – not one I had been expecting at all.

He came in, and this time there was no messing around with coke or chitchat. Straightaway he handed me a piece of paper. It said exactly the same as the piece of paper that he had given me before – the apparent transcript of his conversation with the stripper – but this time there was a difference. It looked like it was in Mark's handwriting.

I stared at it, but I didn't get it. 'Why does this look like Mark's handwriting? I don't understand.'

He claimed that basically Mark had written down all the questions and answers. He had faked the interview to try and win me back round. He had known that I would have to believe he was set up, to forgive him.

Then he got this lad to copy them out in his own writing – all the bit of 'I asked her this' and 'She said, "we got paid that"' and 'Mark was really reluctant to do anything', and so on.

If what he was saying was true, Mark had invented the whole thing. He had been with a stripper, but then got this lad in on his lies to try and convince me he was innocent and therefore win me back.

It also changed things in terms of who was responsible for the video, and put a massive question mark over that. This lad could still have done it off his own bat. Or Mark and he might have gone in on it together. Or Mark could have been totally responsible for it.

I was in shock. But terrible though it sounds, I knew, deep down, that Mark was probably capable of it. I could imagine he might think this story about the strippers, where it looked like he was the victim, would get him back in my good books. Then the coke video would cement it – me at my lowest, needing him to lean on, because everyone else had rejected me.

But I'm his wife, the mother of his kids. I couldn't believe someone could do something like that to another human being, let alone his own family. I had no idea which of them to believe.

Of course, I went home and confronted him. But typical Mark, even if he had done it, I'd never have got a confession out of him. One thing I had learned about Mark over the years was he could lie and lie, to the point where he convinced even himself of what he was saying. So he argued, and twisted everything I'd said, and played with my head, and made me think I was going crazy. He started to convince me that all of these things were in my mind, and that it was my bipolar making me imagine things and create scenarios that didn't exist.

Then, when it had gone on for hours and I felt drained and like I couldn't go in circles on a point any more, he'd be like: 'Just have a line.' I would, then I'd forget what we were even arguing about, and somehow I'd feel myself starting to slip back to our old life, and I realised I was beginning to file this incident at the back of my mind with all the other mysteries about Mark that were left unanswered.

But that whole month was the final wake-up call. Too many completely horrendous things were happening. And questions were being raised all the time, which I just couldn't afford to ignore.

Looking back at my old self, I can't believe it took that long – it is like when you are screaming at characters in a film to wise up: 'Leave the bad guy, stop believing his crap and be strong, run away!'

So finally, finally, I realised something had to be done, and this time, I really did start to find the strength.

Coming Out of the Mist

One day, Nik and Eva introduced me to what they called the Circle of Trust. You have to imagine yourself in the middle of a circle with five rings coming out from you, and put people you know into those rings. The people you trust most are in Ring One, the people you would never trust at all are in Ring Five. I put Mark in Ring Four, and I remember Nik gently saying to me, 'So you hardly trust Mark at all, and yet this man is in your bed every night, and looking after the most important things in your life. How does that work?'

They would plant little seeds of thought in my mind. 'Why do you think Mark has bought only manual cars?' 'Do you think everyone around you is here for the right reasons?' Never direct accusations, or telling me how to think, but just little questions that opened up my mind.

All the time it was like there were signs that I was going the right way, by trying to break out of my reliance on Mark, and work things out for myself.

It was my 29th birthday, 6 September 2009. Something about the fact that the next year I was going to be turning 30 really made me stop and think. Although I was nearly at the end of my twenties, I still felt in my head like I was 16. And while sometimes I had taken on huge responsibilities, and done things well beyond my years, sometimes I acted like I was 16 too. But I remember on my 29th birthday I was reassessing my life, like you tend to do at birthdays, and I thought to myself, 'You're an adult, Kerry, start acting like one.' And that was a turning point in my mind.

From then onwards, much as I had plenty of slip-ups and things that didn't always go right, I kept pulling myself back to that. I wanted to focus on my babies, and on making myself a better person. And that meant being without the drugs. More importantly, although I wasn't quite ready to face it at the time, it meant being without Mark Croft.

Nik and Eva were also encouraging me to come off my medication. They never directly said it, but it was clear that is what they believed themselves, and they did say it would be good to cut back. They pointed out that what I was taking included antidepressants, as well as antipsychotic and hypnotic drugs. That is a hell of a lot to handle, not to mention when it's mixed with a cocktail of cocaine and drink.

Now I need to handle this section carefully, because I am aware the medical experts would not agree with me, and I also know I probably did not do things the way some doctors would advise.

I had started to think over some of the ideas Nik and Eva had put in my mind. They never told me something as fact, but sometimes they cleverly asked questions that got me thinking, like: 'Do you actually believe in bipolar?' Which was something that got to me.

Nik told me that he didn't take any medication, other than the odd Anadin if he was in real pain, or an antihistamine if his allergies got too bad, because he liked to be in touch with what his mind and his body was feeling. Which in itself was a different way of thinking. I had always worked on the basis that medicine was there to make you better, so if you needed it, take it. And I had never questioned what doctors or psychiatrists prescribed me.

He got me to look at medication as a money-making scheme – while it is necessary sometimes, pharmaceutical companies do gain out of people needing it – and that was a bit of a realisation for me. I had never really had people talk to me like that before. Nik was the first person who has spoken to me as though it wasn't just a given that I had bipolar, and that I should take medication and be on it for the rest of my life.

I thought about it a lot. And the more I went over it, the more it made sense, until I decided that was it, I wanted to give a med-free way of life a go, and see what happened.

So one day, I just decided to stop taking my meds. I can't remember the exact date, but it was soon after my birthday.

I didn't cut down, I didn't speak to doctors about it, I just made the decision in my own head. One day, I took my usual dose; the next, I took none. Now I don't recommend people do it like that, even if they want to stop. Looking back, I know that was dangerous, and it did have side effects. But it was the only way I knew how to do it. It is also the way I am – once I have decided something, I go for it.

Mark was not impressed. He even called up the doctors at The Priory on loudspeaker one day and told them, 'Kerry has come off her medication and is refusing to go back on it. I'm worried. What am I supposed to do?'

The doctor said, 'She needs to go back on it. It is the only way to control her disorder.'

'No, nope, not a chance,' I said, and I stuck to my ground. As far as I could see, this was my only way out of a life that I knew was doing me no favours.

And sure enough, little by little, it was like a cloud of fog cleared away from my mind. Everything that had always been a bit of a blur before, started to clear and refocus, like I was coming out of a coma and into consciousness. It happened gradually, but it was like I was regaining awareness, like I was able to think again, and feel emotions. They weren't always the best emotions, but at least they were mine, they were real.

The problem with the medication is this: bipolar means that sometimes you are ecstatic and giddy, and other times you are down and sad, and the medication theoretically works by keeping you somewhere in the middle. Which sounds good in theory, but most of the time it just means you are left feeling numb and docile.

You don't feel anything, it's just really weird. At least, that was the case for me.

It's hard to describe the numbness, but imagine it like this: If your closest relative dies, you want to cry, you feel a pain deep inside like you need to let it out and sob and grieve. But somehow you can't, because there is something blocking it, and the feeling stays deep down, and on the surface you stay very calm. That is the closest way I can think of to describe how it felt to be on that medication.

Coming off it was scary, don't get me wrong, especially as it meant I was having to face up to a lot of things I had been able to ignore before. I was suddenly going, 'Woah, hold on there a minute!' about certain things happening around me, which before had just washed over me. But even knowing, 'This isn't right', about certain things, felt nice in a way, exactly because I could feel it. Which in itself was a new thing.

Coming off my medication, though, I could almost see the panic in Mark's eyes. He could see me changing on a daily basis, and he didn't like it. It was as though he was losing grip of me.

I started wanting answers. I would go through statements and letters, and now I was aware, I could see half of them were not real.

It was like a child had drawn them up, rather than a government official, or accountant, or whoever it was supposed to be.

But rather than answer my questions, Mark would turn it round on me.

'Where the hell is my money, Mark? This doesn't make sense.'

'Look at you, you need to get back on your meds, you. You're being right snappy. You're becoming nasty and arguing all the time.'

'Where has everything gone? You hired David. Well, what has he done with everything?'

'You are paranoid and imagining things. I'm going to take you back to The Priory and get you sorted out.' Anything to deflect away from the questions I was actually asking him.

But the real me was coming back through. I am not a stupid person under it all, and once I was starting to look into these things, I stuck with it. Rather than realise something was happening but then go back under in another wave of medication and/or cocaine like I had done before, I now followed it through.

The Kerry on medication who would just say, 'Yeah, whatever' and for ease just go along with whatever Mark told me, now started saying, 'Hang on a minute, Mark. Do not tell me this is a real statement from David McHugh, because it isn't!'

Time and again, David was central to the rows. Even though he no longer worked for us – after getting me arrested, that was the end of it – there were still all the problems from when he had done. The money just wasn't there. And time and again Mark couldn't answer anything.

Of course there was still coke, though. I might have cut out my meds, but I can't say I did the same for the drugs. I would still get caught up in benders over the autumn. Sometimes I was just too tired to argue. Sometimes I just needed a release or to enjoy myself for a bit. But after a bit, I started to cut back even on that. I knew there was something going on, and I knew I needed a clear head and my wits about me if I was going to get to the bottom of it.

Several times in my relationship with Mark, I said to him, 'Let's go to rehab, you and me. We'll go together, kick this addiction, and we'll come back a much better couple.'

But he always just said the same thing, 'I don't need rehab for drugs – and nor do you.' He put me off the idea any time I mentioned it, and just handed me a line until I forgot about it.

I think he knew if I went to rehab I'd come out so much stronger, and he didn't want that. So throughout the autumn of 2009, coke continued to be present, even though I was still continuing to cut it down and resist when I could. At times I wondered if I was even addicted to it, or if I was actually addicted to Mark and the coke just came as part of the package. Even to this day, people have suggested to me that they thought that, and who knows, they might be right.

I also started to see what people had been telling me for so long, that I was so dependent on Mark. The reality was, he was in total control of everything – and if I was going to get my life back on track, I needed to get my own control back.

Around this time I was approached by *Celebrity Big Brother*, which was made by a TV company called Endemol, and at the time was being shown on Channel 4. They offered me a huge amount of money to go on the show, which would have been great for sorting out my debts and getting me back on track. I also really liked the show and thought it would be fun to go on it.

So I said, Yeah I would do it, no worries. But I had to get through psychiatric tests first. So this doctor, or psychiatrist as I suppose he was, came round my house to see me. I already knew

My babies are my world. We always have so much fun together.

Me and the lovely Sharon from GI Jane Boot Camp.
Love ya babe.

Me at boot camp, which I go to at least twice a year. Boot camp helped change my life. I would even say it saved me.

Getting to grips with what the ice really meant!

On my way . . .

Dancing on Ice was a big step up in me realising I could turn my life around, with the likes of Dan helping me beyond words.

Happy with life and look where I was headed . . . hello *Big Brother*!

So happy I got as far as I did. I had so much fun in the *Big Brother* house.

Me and Paddy Doherty. I don't know if I would have survived in the *Big Brother* house without him!

Danielle and me have become such good friends. She really is like my twin sister!

Molly as fearless and cool as ever!

Helping the Dreams Come True gang – very inspirational people.

At Birmingham Pride – my first proper gig in 10 years.

Happy times with the amazing *This Morning* team. It's crazy how things have come full circle, but I am so happy to be where I am today.

him because he had interviewed me for *I'm A Celebrity... Get Me Out Of Here*, so I figured there would be no problem. He had a computer with lots of questions, which you had to answer either yes or no.

They were weird questions, though. 'Do you think you are being watched?' 'Do you think people are talking about you?' I sat trying to think which answer they were looking for and then I decided I should just be honest. Because the answer was 'yes' to questions like that. Did you see how many paparazzi were outside my door at that time, or how many gossip magazines were discussing my life each week?!

I think I passed those questions, but then a producer called up and asked if they could have access to my medical records. I thought, Yeah, I have nothing to hide. I have been quite open about my past medical history, especially after everything that happened on *This Morning*, so I said, 'Yeah, go on, have a look'.

Well, I was down as bipolar, of course, and they rang my doctor to discuss if going in the house would have any impact.

At this point I was still completely off my medication. Instead all I had was a psychiatric nurse who used to come and talk to me once a week, like therapy. But the doctor said to the producer, 'Well, we don't advise her to go in the house without any medication, it would not be a good idea for her.' So the producer called me back and said, 'Take your medication and you can come in'.

I was furious. I hadn't put in all that effort to come off something that was clouding my mind so much, just to have to go back on it to get on *Celebrity Big Brother*. So I said, 'I'm sorry, but I'm not going back on that stuff. You saw on *This Morning* the effect it had on me!'

But they stuck to what the doctor said, and I refused to back down too, so I never got to go on that series. It made me mad, that they took the evidence of what the doctor said over what was in front of their eyes. I guess that is what society does – believes doctors are all-knowing on everything medical, and never question them. But when I have seen some of the other people who have been on that show – like prostitutes, and people who have been in jail – it really makes me question it. I wonder how they got through because I was definitely more sane than them!

Bootcamp

Strangely, the thing that was really going to turn my life around came from a completely unexpected source. Right at the start of 2010 I got a call from a reporter at *Closer* magazine, who wanted me to do a diet and fitness feature. Not exactly my thing at the time! They wanted to send me to GI Jane Bootcamp for two weeks to lose weight and they offered to pay me to do it. I'd heard about bootcamps before and they didn't exactly appeal. All I knew was you spent most of the time having to exercise, instructed by ex-army trainers. I wasn't particularly interested in the idea, but I needed the money, I had bills to pay. Not that I was going to see much of it – it was just going to go straight to the trustee anyway. But it was proof I was working, I was trying to earn money. No one wanted to work with me because of the whole cocaine issue. So I felt like I had no choice.

I wasn't happy with my body. I thought I looked like a whale, as I had put on all the weight I had lost from the liposuction. I weighed 10 stone 3lb and I felt like my perfect weight was definitely a good stone less than that.

I didn't want to leave the kids for two weeks, and part of me was afraid to be away from Mark for that long as well. We were never apart for that long in our whole relationship, except perhaps once when Mark took his motorbike and went across Spain with a friend. But I would never go away without him unless it was for work, or of course when I had visited me dad. I hardly left home without him being there. And I was so dependent on him, it was actually a frightening prospect to be on me own for that long. He didn't want me going, either. But he realised too that I needed the money.

So I agreed to it and met up with a magazine photographer to do some 'before' photos so that there was something to compare my 'after' figure with. You know the kind I mean – those ones that go with every weight article, where the celebrity has to look as fat and unhappy as they can!

'Yep, stand there, push your belly out.'

'I *am* pushing it out.'

'Well, push it out more!'

And I was in these unflattering clothes with no bra, and kind of slumped with a depressed look on my face.

And then I was ready to go! They sent a car for me. It was 10 January, and there was really bad snow blocking up a lot of the roads, but we managed to make it down. The camp is in Sittingbourne in Kent, and is in a big country manor house set in its own grounds.

But when I got there, no one else had! The snow meant no one else had made it, so it was only me and a trainer called Stevie P. He was older and looked a bit like Russ Abbott and was lovely. It made me wonder what the hell I was doing there!

Then a lady called Sharon Smith arrived. She had founded the bootcamp in April the year before, and was to do the cooking for us that night because the chef had been stranded in the snow too. She told us she was going to make us chicken soup, but it turned out she had lost the chicken on track to the bootcamp, so we had chicken soup without the chicken! But that gave us a laugh and we bonded straight away. In the end she fed me a crisp butty, 'cause that is all we had – not exactly bootcamp food, but I was happy with it!

They worked out we'd have to reschedule for a different week, but we stayed for three days, waiting for the weather to clear because now I was snowed in there and couldn't leave. We couldn't really do much exercise, but I ate the set meals that I was supposed to, which added up to around 1200 calories a day of fresh food. I couldn't believe how little they were. I was like: 'Is that it? Is that all I'm getting? I'm still hungry!' I was so used to eating more that I thought I was being starved!

And after three days I was able to go home. And I just sat and ate everything I possibly could. Burgers, take-aways, kebabs…. I knew I would be going back, so I reckoned this was my way of stocking up on fuel!

I spent a lot of time over at me mum's too, as she was not in a good way. She was going through a court hearing to find out if she would be evicted from her home. I had bought it for her back in 2001, but it had always been in my name. Then with my bankruptcy troubles, it looked as though she would have to be evicted to pay back some of the money. I felt awful about it, but there wasn't much I could do, other than hope her solicitor could work some magic.

The day I was leaving to go back, I went over to see her. There was another hearing later that day. Mark had promised to go round to keep her company, but instead he just gave me a load of coke to give to her, and left her to it.

When I got over there she sat there doing it, while I was just crying. I told her I didn't want this life but I couldn't get out of the rut. I didn't know how I was going to change anything. And then even though I didn't even want a line of coke, I had one. Not that one even affected me by then, so I kept going, and by the time a car came up to take me to bootcamp, we had done the whole bag. I was high as a kite, off my head. I didn't even enjoy it by then, it was just habit. And actually, no one could even tell I was on one, because I was able to control my behaviour to a point.

I started at bootcamp properly on a Monday, and I'll be honest, I absolutely hated it. We were a group of eight women with two trainers – Stevie P and another guy called Kev Green.

The daily routine was to get up at 5 a.m., and be out on a march by 6, then an hour later we were back for a breakfast of porridge or muesli. Then it was back out and exercising. It was something different each day – say, circuit training or an assault course. Then we would get a snack break at 10 for 15 minutes, and they would give us a rice cake with a bit of Philadelphia and salmon, or it could be a piece of pineapple. But whatever it was, we were savouring every little bit, nibbling it tiny mouthful by tiny mouthful, because we were starving and didn't want it to end!

Then we would go back out again on another kind of exercise and come back from 12 to 1 for lunch. Because the weather was so cold at that time and we kept getting rained on, we always wanted something warm, and sometimes we got it – soup or a stuffed pepper, say. But other times it was salad and we would be gutted! All the portions were measured out, and tiny – at least in my mind, as I was used to much bigger portions! Then it was back out again for something like boxing or weights. Then a snack at 3 p.m., perhaps a yoghurt, and by then we were so hungry we were taking as long as possible over it, and even licking the lid and the inside of the pot to get every last bit! A final fitness session of the day, perhaps a fitness test, before we were allowed to finish. Then it was back for dinner of say a jacket potato or pasta, and then there was just about time for a bath before everyone just collapsed into bed!

Now I'm a very weak person for exercise, so I always need pushing, and at the beginning I was always at the back of the line for the walks. But I struggled even with that. There were women much older and fatter than me, much more capable of doing the exercise. I couldn't even walk up hill I was gasping so much. I thought, 'I can't do this, I'm going to die, you're going to kill me.' I felt like Goldie Hawn in *Private Benjamin*, and it didn't help that I was in so much pain thanks to previous injuries. I had fractured my coccyx when I was in Atomic Kitten, and of course had broken my pelvis when I was pregnant with Heidi. Although I have put on weight from having kids, I am actually only little, I'm naturally petite, so I wanted to get back to my true size. But it was painful and I just kept thinking, 'I really can't do this.'

On the first day, we did this exercise where we were given these walking sticks and told they were our guns. And we had to put this army camouflage paint on our faces and put up our hoods. I thought they were really winding me up here, and wondered what I had got myself into.

Then we went out into the grounds, and we were in the snow and crawling on our hands and knees and my fingers were freezing and I felt plain miserable. Then out of nowhere, Stevie P jumped up on this roof, and Kev Green jumped out from behind this tree, and they were pretending to shoot at us, shouting, 'Get down men!' And everyone was taking it dead serious and diving to the ground. I was lying on the ground, just looking up at the sky, and thinking, 'Is this actually for real?' I really thought Jeremy Beadle was going to jump out of his grave and go, 'You've been framed!'

I had no idea how I was going to put up with two weeks of this.

But over the coming days, I started to slowly change my mind. And I think the bit that did it for me most, was the morning walks we did first thing.

For a start, there were no paparazzi. At that time I was used to having between 15 and 30 camped outside my house every single day at Wilmslow. It was just constant: as soon as you opened the door, or got in the car, they'd be clicking away. But there, I was a nobody, I could be who I wanted. It was just me, walking in the middle of Kent with all these amazing views and country lanes. And walking through them at that time of the morning, it was just nice to reflect.

As for the other women, they were one of the nicest bunch of women I have ever come across. We were all ages and sizes and shapes, but slowly we started to bond over the exercise. It took me a while to come out of my shell, but we would be on the morning hike and start opening up to each other because of the natural high we were getting from the exercise.

And I can say, hand on heart, it was probably the first natural high I had had since I was 14 and me mum had gave me my first drugs. Up until then, if I am really honest, people who didn't take drugs were for me the ones who weren't really normal. But this exercise gave me a high that I had never had without putting something up my nose.

As I walked each day with these women, we started to talk. And I realised how isolated I had become from other women. I started to see that in the four years I was with Mark, I had had no social life. I didn't really leave the house except to do work, I just stayed in all the time. I never went out with a girl mate for a bottle of wine and a gossip, and it wasn't like Mark ever took me out for dinner or anything. My only friends were Mark's friends, and they were all bang on the coke and pills.

But despite the realisation, and me telling my mum before I left how unhappy I was, I still couldn't stop defending Mark. I would tell everyone early in that first week, how Mark was my soul mate. How he wasn't the way people thought he was. When it came to the public and people I didn't know well, I would defend him. I think I was in complete denial, but I also didn't want people judging me for being with him. And the more I said it to other people, it was like I was trying to convince myself, because deep down I think I knew he wasn't what I was making him out to be.

But I listened to the other women at the bootcamp, talking about their stories. One woman was a carer for her mother, and had a daughter as well, and felt like she had no life of her own. One had triplets and was completely run off her feet, and another had her own business to run and children to look after, and just needed bootcamp to get some time for herself.

And slowly, day by day, inside my own mind, I was starting to think very differently. I learned to be stronger, watching the other women.

Take my roommate. I hadn't realised when I arrived that I would be sharing, so I walked in and told this woman she was in my room – and she told me that no, I was in hers! It turned out we were sharing. At first I kept myself to myself, but she started to talk, and told me she was in her fifties and from Barnsley. She told me how she was an alcoholic, and that she was getting off the drink while she was there, and she had the DTs (Delerium tremens, which means a tremor caused by withdrawal from alcohol). I learned her marriage wasn't good – her husband had been violent and controlling, so she had started drinking in secret. But she had got herself into such a mess that she had left him and run away to come to bootcamp. I felt really sorry for her, for the life she had led, but admired her too, for her strength in finally taking things into her own hands.

And the more I talked with everyone, the more I enjoyed it.

By the Wednesday, I was in so much pain. Six hours of intensive training each day adds up, and my body was aching.

'Black Wednesday' it gets called because everyone suffers badly by then. You hear everyone screaming in pain from the aching in their muscles which makes every movement hurts. Even going to the toilet and bending your legs to sit down is agony. Getting into bed, all you can hear is yelps from the other rooms – it sounds like all your neighbours are having an orgy! And everyone thinks they are worse off than everybody else!

We had to do a fitness test and I was crying and crying, and saying I couldn't do it anymore and I wanted to go home.

But that is where the trainers were so good. Stevie P was really understanding and able to get through to me emotionally and support me. I developed a really good bond with Kev, who was just so encouraging, understanding and supportive. I was open with them about my drug problem because I could be, and it didn't feel like I was judged for it, more that they pushed me in the right direction. I still had that way of thinking in me, deep down, that people who didn't do drugs were weird and I was the normal one. Kev got me to see the healthier other side, what it was like not to do drugs, and that I was the one in the wrong.

Most people go to bootcamp for one week, so at the end of the first week everyone was leaving except for me. They left on the Friday, and I was really sorry to see them go. I had felt myself get close to several of them, especially my roommate. I have kept in touch with her since, and she never went back to her husband but set up a new, happier life for herself. I'm so proud of her. It was amazing the strength bootcamp brought out in her.

After everyone left I had 24 hours off before the next lot of people arrived, but there was no point sending me home – and, to be honest, I didn't want to go home. I was loving it by then!

Closer magazine came to take pictures at the halfway point, of me exercising and with the trainers. The reporter and photographer said they were dead impressed with how I was getting on, and I lent them some of my clothes and got them to have a go at the assault course.

Mark also came down with Max to see me and spend the night. It was when I saw him there that I knew how much my feelings had changed. I didn't want to be near him, or for him to touch me, and he could see that things had changed too. I was all organised and together, and off my medication. I was standing there, doing my ironing, and he was like: 'What's going on with you? This isn't the Kerry I know!'

I said, 'I've changed, Mark. You are going to have to accept it.'

'Well, don't lose too much weight.'

And then I realised he didn't want me to get slim. That was yet another way of controlling me. If I was fat, frumpy, miserable and unhappy, he would be in control of me. The amount of times he called me 'chunky' or 'whale' and yet when I did something about it, he didn't like it. It was a case of, Put me down, he gets stronger.

That night, I couldn't even sleep with him. Everything in me cringed at the idea, and I admit I used Max as a bit of a barrier! I was like: 'Max, get here!' and spent the night with him in my bed, hugging him. I could see the conflict building between Mark and me, and I had no idea what was going to happen. All I knew was I was happy when he left.

Then the second week started. Well, the change in me was incredible, even if I say so myself! I was at the front for all the exercises, I was like the teacher's pet in the group, nearly turning round and pulling faces at the people behind I felt so superior! I felt liberated and was like: 'Oh my God, this is amazing!'

It was in the second half of the second week that I found myself admitting, 'I actually don't want to go home. I'm scared of what will happen, because I want to stay clean, but I know as soon as

I am back in that house he is going to have me back on that shit, and I don't want to be. But I don't think I'm strong enough.'

Coke was like a comfort blanket for me in a way, and I knew as soon as I was back in a tougher environment with Mark, I would need it to protect me again.

As for Kev, well, I did really fancy the guy. I knew he was married, and he would talk about his wife Sarah and say he was happy, but without much enthusiasm, so I didn't really believe that he was.

One night, when we were all sat about, we started having the craic and tormenting the trainers. And I said to Kev, 'What do you do when you fancy a bird? Do you go up and talk to her?'

And he said, 'No, I'm dead shy me, I just kind of stare.'

I went, 'Yeah, I've noticed that', and started laughing. And he just went dead red. He is quick-witted, but I could see him liking what I had done really, thinking, 'Wow, you've got one up on me there!'

There was a real chemistry between Kev and me – I admired him and took notice of everything he said. It was a sexual chemistry as well as a mental one, but I tried to ignore that, and he was very professional too. I was obviously married, and so was he, and they had kids together. So nothing at all happened. In truth it was just a flirt and there's no harm in that surely!

When I was weighed at the end of the two weeks, I had lost 14lb and was down to nine stone. And my body shape had completely changed, I just looked so much better. And it wasn't on some stupid diet, either, it was sheer hard and healthy work! Really, it was my attitude that had changed. In the beginning I was like: 'This is going to kill me, I can't run up that hill,' but I learned I could push myself to the limit. It's not going to kill me – it's going to bloody hurt and there will be blood, sweat and tears involved – but I'll be a better person for having done it.

I even did a six-mile run. Look at me, that's a long run! And that sense of achievement was overwhelming.

I had my own private presentation at the end with Kev, Stevie P, Sharon and the other staff. And it got really emotional and everyone was in tears. They told me that they had loved seeing me go from someone with such low confidence and self-esteem into the strong person who was leaving them. They told me, 'You are a special person and you have done so well, and we are all begging you to keep it up.'

I got so upset. It was really lovely. The guys there, well, it is not just shouting instructions, it is like they are really there for you on all levels.

Before I left, Kev gave me a real good final talking to about drugs and said to me, 'If you get back on that shit, you know you are letting me down, you are letting yourself down.' I have to say, it inspired me.

When we said goodbye, he gave me a kiss goodbye on the lips, just literally like a peck, but I could feel the chemistry, it was electric. And we both kind of pulled back and looked at each other, and it was like we both realised it was dodgy and we were on dangerous territory. But I'd never kissed another man on the lips since I got married and felt what I felt for Kev. It was really weird.

And the whole way in the car afterwards I thought about it, and how much I had enjoyed it, and I started making more and more of it. But I realised I couldn't.

So when he sent me a text after we left bootcamp, saying that it all felt very strange for him, and that I should stay strong and was a very special lady, and that he felt really empty inside leaving me.

I was really touched, but fell into banter mode instead. I replied, 'What was my time, gay boy?' 'cause he hadn't given me my time for our last activity. Not that it calmed the texts. In fact, after that we were texting all the time.

But I had to put those thoughts aside, because when I left bootcamp I had something else to focus on first: I had to do a photo shoot with *Closer* magazine in their London studios, to show my new body after the two weeks. They had the one I had done before I went all ready to print alongside this one, to let readers make a comparison. I also had to record an advert: 'Read my story in *Closer*', that kind of thing.

I wasn't allowed to go home first, though, in case I snuck off and ate loads of kebabs or something and ruined my new look!

They put me in this black swimming costume with heels – and I'll say it myself, I looked really good.

Mark drove down to the studios and turned up to the shoot with the kids, and I was so pleased to see my babies. But the first thing Mark said was, 'You've lost too much weight, you have, you'll have to get another boob job.'

Straightaway I just felt this ball of fire in my belly and I thought, 'Ooh! I really, really don't want to be with you.'

Fighting Back

Back home I tried my best to keep up the lifestyle I had been taught. It was obviously harder on my own without the trainers to motivate me, but they had taught me habits to try and get into and routines to follow.

So about 5 o'clock every morning I was up and on my herbal tea, and out jogging, and then eating healthy meals like fish, chicken, or rice and vegetables for dinner.

I hate the word 'diet', as a diet is like a chore to me. But I saw it that I just watched what I ate, and made sure it was healthy.

I also had to get out of the habit of eating the kids' leftovers – as a mum, that has to be one of the worst habits to get into, and one of the hardest to get out of too. Cook their food, and what they don't eat, you eat! But I stopped doing that, so I was losing more weight, and getting even healthier.

Mark didn't like it. He couldn't control the new Kerry in the same way, and I was getting into a lifestyle that was completely alien to him.

He would sit there and go, 'Look at you. You're getting moody, you need to get back on your medication, you do. You've changed and I don't like it.' I probably was snappy, 'cause I was off my medication, but that was just something I knew I had to ride through.

Well, sorry, Mark, but I had changed for the better. Where was my support? As my husband, he should have been encouraging me, telling me I was doing great, and helping me out if he could – or even joining in!

Gemma, though, was lovely and really supportive of the new me. I remember she actually cried one day, soon after I was back. She said to me, 'Kez, this is the best I have ever seen you. It's amazing. I have never seen you like this and I am really proud of you.'

It was brilliant to hear. Gemma, who had been with me through all my ups and downs, and really has seen me at my lowest, could see that this wasn't just a fleeting moment of 'Oh, I'm sorting myself out.' It was the start of a real permanent change for the future. Bootcamp had been like the last chance saloon for me.

Stevie P and Sharon would both send me motivational messages, and Kev in particular was giving me a lot of support, both emotionally and on the exercise front. He was texting and calling me, and telling me, 'Don't let Mark get you down. Get up in the morning, go training.' He would send me lists of exercises and instructions: 'Three sets of this, four of that.' That kind of thing, and I did it. I became quite dependent on him, and it was like he was my sponsor.

There was nothing going on with Kev – we weren't planning to run away, or have a relationship or anything – but by having feelings for him, I felt like I was mentally cheating. I'd never had feelings for anyone other than my husband the whole time we were married, so in my head this was putting up a big question mark. It was a massive deal. I had had so many unbelievably good-looking and nice men try it on with me when I was married, but I always rejected them and stayed with Mark. I already knew Mark and I were over, it was just a case of making it happen, and this was like a final push. I knew if I was thinking about someone else, it wasn't working and I needed to get out.

Kev showed me what life could be like, and along with exercise and bootcamp, and everything Nik and Eva had done for me, he gave me the strength. He showed me a different kind of life, where you get a thrill out of exercise and achievement, whereas Mark would have gone, 'You want a thrill? Better have a line, then.' Now I had the two options in front of me, and although it would have been very easy to have gone back down the coke route, I thought, 'I actually prefer the version of life Kev has shown me.'

But the absolute final straw for my marriage came when Mark tried an old trick of a casual mention of a line to try and subtly draw me back onto the cocaine. This time, though, I was far too alert and strong to fall for it.

My diet had obviously changed a lot, so I was constipated. Five days after I came home, I asked him to go down the shop and get me some laxatives because I hadn't been to the toilet and my tummy was swollen.

You know what he said? 'You know what'll make you go to the toilet, don't you? Do you want a line?'

It was that phrase that turned my blood cold. I'd just put my body through two weeks of hell – and a third week working on it myself back home – and was getting myself on the proper straight and narrow, and I felt on top of the world. And he wanted to bring me back down?

I exploded and we had a massive row. I had reached the point when everything he did made me cringe, and if he ever touched me, it just made my skin crawl. To be strong enough to say no to coke, I had to be away from coke. So after that I was doing anything to be out of the house and I was getting my life together.

He kept saying, 'This ain't the Kerry I know, this isn't you.' And

I'd get angry and say, 'This is a good me, Mark, I'm exercising and eating healthily. I feel great. Support me, change with me.'

But Mark was never going to change.

I had started filming a documentary called *Kerry and Me*, to be aired on Channel 4 later in the year. It had been set up by my agent, so I didn't know much about it, other than that it was a one-off programme, taking a look at my life in the limelight.

I haven't watched it back, but from what I have heard I don't think the show did me any favours. The crew was up with me at 5 in the morning, watching me jogging, and I'm in the kitchen with the kids, all super-cheery and hyper, which is the way I am, but people thought I was still on drugs. By then, though, I had been clean for three weeks.

As I was filming it and talking to camera, I was still working everything through in my mind, and realising that those moments where I didn't want to be with Mark had by now become a constant. There was nothing about him that was keeping him there for me. So while he was sat in the kitchen, I found myself in the living room with the crew, telling this to the camera before he even knew. I hadn't meant to do that, but I was asked about him, and was feeling so repulsed by him at the time that I couldn't lie. There was a bit of me thinking that if I said it on camera, it was going to be shown to the public, so I would have to go through with it. Somehow, doing that meant it was going to become reality.

The final crunch came at Lilly's seventh birthday. We were having a party at home, and I couldn't bear to be around him. I just thought, 'I need to get this man out of my life. He is not good for me, and I need to end it before Heidi and Max are old enough to be affected by their dad leaving.' So that evening, after everyone had left and the kids were in bed, I found myself turning round to Mark and saying, 'I don't want to be with you, I don't love you anymore.'

I don't think he believed me at first, then he asked if there was someone else. And when he said that, I couldn't look at him. Because although I had done nothing wrong with Kev, I felt I had mentally cheated. So I told him about the kiss. He didn't take it well, which given all the times he misbehaved during our marriage is a bloody joke.

But anyway, we were screaming at each other, and then I basically kicked him out. I knew that was it, but I don't know if Mark got it. Not that I can blame him – we had broken up so many times, it must have been hard for him to know that this time I really meant it!

But *I* knew I meant it. That first night he was out of the house I looked around and realised I was alone. But I also realised that I was okay with it. The future was going to be hard, but I knew in me that things were definitely moving in the right direction, and I could be proud of myself for finally taking that step.

Mark Fights Back

Mark was furious that I had broken up with him. He couldn't believe I had actually done it. But I pushed ahead and filed for divorce.

The kids didn't question for a while where Mark was, as they were used to his coming and going. I was really worried about telling them, and spent hours working out what to say, to make it as easy for them as possible. But when Molly and Lilly eventually asked, I just said, 'Look, Mummy's not with Mark anymore.' They really just seemed to shrug it off. I remember Molly saying, 'Look, Mum, as long as you are happy, we are happy.'

My eyes filled up as I looked at them both and realised that they made things so simple for all of us – if I was okay about it then they would be better than okay about it. Simple as that. To be honest that's how they've always been since… if I'm fine they're fine, and vice versa.

One thing I realised then was that despite me thinking he had been a good dad – and he had been in that he had been around and had gone to events like parents' evening – he had obviously never created a real emotional bond with them. It was literally a shrug of the shoulders and a hug and the subject was closed.

He was keeping himself busy with a new girlfriend too. As soon as I had kicked him out, he went straight out on a date with a barmaid called Sharon Thorpe!

They became a couple very quickly, but in the next breath he would come round and try to make things up. But I was always dead factual with him. I would just use those times to say things like: 'Mark, you're going to have to get me a car' because he took the only car off me when he left. So from having ten cars, none of which I could drive, I was down to none.

At the time I was keeping myself busy by focusing on the positives. I knew that that was the best way to make sure I didn't let myself slide back and give into Mark's demands. So I decided I needed to go back down to GI Jane, because of how much it had helped me. I would concentrate on helping to promote it. I was so grateful for what they had done for me, and if I could encourage other women to go there and receive the same treatment, I would be happy.

I decided to go down there for some meetings with the owner, Sharon, and as I left, I said to Gemma, 'Don't let Mark in the house.'

But he came round, and she did let him in, and he raided the house, and took loads of stuff, including the computer. I was furious when I got back. I was especially angry that the computer was gone. I guarantee, because he was a computer whizz, that he knew there was probably all kinds of evidence on there against him in terms of girls, financial problems, everything. So of course he wanted it back, and Gemma let him take it.

I realise it must have been a tough position for Gemma to be in, but as my employee, and not Mark's, I thought that what she had done was completely out of line. I told her so, and we had an argument.

It was only then that I learned Mark was actually living with her and Stuart, as they had moved out to their own place just a few weeks before.

Looking back, I still like to believe Gemma was on my side at this time, and deep down was loyal to me. Not only because we were closer friends, but because she worked for me. But with both Mark and Stuart in the same house as her, I feel like they were able to get to her, and they got the better of her. That is how I see it anyway, because I think she really did have a good heart.

A day or two later, I had to go back to GI Jane again, to do all this press promotion that we had set up. I hadn't spoken to Gemma since our row, but I sent her a text saying, 'You have to be in work tomorrow.' She replied saying she wasn't coming in. So I said, 'Gemma, you know this has been in my diary for three weeks. If you are not coming in to work tomorrow, you are fired'. And she wrote something about suing me. Then she didn't turn up, so I went ahead with my threat and sacked her and that was the end of our friendship too.

We had been real friends. It was so sad. She really was part of the family. But actually, that is a dangerous thing for a nanny. At the end of the day, she was still my employee and I was her boss. So when that line is crossed, it is kind of hard. It was the same as Pat being my cleaner: once the divide becomes blurred, it is harder to define your relationship with each other. And if your lives become too entangled, it is very hard to take a step back. I think that is what happened with us. Not that I realised it at the time. I was just enjoying her friendship and appreciated her loyalty and company. Especially as there were so few people I was getting that from!

I will be honest, I really can't have been the best boss at times. She knew everything I was going through, and the extent of the drugs I was doing. So I could see that she did have it tough at times, and she did well. She really did have my best interests at heart and I trusted her with everything. I am pretty sure she never sold a story on me. Given the rarity of that in the circle around me, I really have to thank the girl.

She really had been a constant positive in my life, and it felt like somehow Mark and Stuart had got between us. But maybe it was always going to happen – the relationship of employer and employee had broken down, and you can't have someone working for you without that.

So, of course, I was left in a mess with no nanny. I had Mum, and friends helping out with the kids, for the next couple of weeks. Then a friend told me she had heard that my original favourite nanny Cheryl, who had been sacked by Mark, was back in England and available for work, which made me very happy. My friend rang her when I was away, and when I got back to the house, Cheryl was there! I knew even before I saw her, because as I walked through the door I just saw everything was in complete order.

And as she walked out the kitchen I gave her a huge hug, and was like: 'Cheryl, I have missed you so much!'

It was amazing: she was exactly the same, the kids were over the moon, and what can I say, life was perfect again! Cheryl was – and is – amazing with the kids. She was, and is, a rock in my life and despite the hurdles we've had to overcome she is a big part of the kids' lives and mine. They love her, and she is so protective over them and me, she really feels like part of the family.

At the same time as Cheryl's return, there were other changes. Poor Sean had done a great job with my PR, but in my mind he was so closely linked to Mark and my life with him, that I felt like I needed to move on and get someone else to look after me.

I had tried to contact a woman called Claire Powell a few months before this. She did management and PR and I had known her back in my Atomic Kitten days, when she PR'd things like the *Smash Hits* tours. But she had told me she wasn't interested in looking after me when I was with Mark.

After he had been gone for about a month, though, my phone rang and it was Claire. She got straight to the point: 'Is what I am reading in the papers true?'

'Mark is gone and I am as clean as a whistle,' I replied.

'Can we drugs test you?'

'Not a problem.'

So I met up with her and her husband Neville Hendricks, who was also her business partner, making their company CAN (Claire And Neville). We had a bit of a chat, then they handed me a contract they had drawn up for me to work with them.

I looked at it and saw that it included regular drugs-testing and also me signing that I would stay away from Mark.

'That's pretty extreme, isn't it?!' I asked.

But Claire was adamant. 'We will not take you on if you are with him. It is for your good and ours.'

The contract effectively meant me handing over control of my private life. But like everyone else, I suppose, they had seen the damage Mark had done to my image over the four years I was with him and they weren't prepared to work with that. So I signed it, and that was it, we were working together.

Working with Claire and Neville was like gaining new foster parents. When you meet foster parents for the first time, you've got to sit in their house and listen to what they say, and learn to abide by their rules. It's scary and hard to adjust, but exciting at the same time. Because of the way they took on that almost parenting role, it meant I was able to lean on them and at first everything worked out great. They had great energy for me and could see that I was together and willing to be just as driven as they were.

*

One of the first things they set up for me was a TV series called *Kerry Katona Coming Clean*. Once again I had a camera crew in my house, filming me day to day. The idea was it would show me in my new life, post Mark, getting myself back on track. This time it was to run on ITV2 rather than MTV, which meant it would reach a much larger audience.

I was happy to have a crew back in my home, as most of the time I enjoy making reality shows. I knew it could also be my way of putting across why I split with Mark, and it would be yet another way of encouraging myself to stick to it. I wasn't going to let my weakness be documented to the public!

A couple of days after they had started filming, we were all sat in the lounge when there was a knock at the door. I went to answer it.

It was Mark stood there. The conversation went something like this: 'Alright, Kez. Have you stopped being daft yet?'

'What are you on about, Mark?'

'You know I love you. I want to move back in and give things another go, you, me and the kids.'

'Mark, I can't. It's over.'

'Oh come on, you need me.'

'Mark, I don't. I've decided I don't need you in my life.'

And with that he flipped. 'Who the hell do you think you are? You won't last a week without me. Don't try and pretend you are someone you aren't. I'll make sure the public know the real Kerry Katona, and you will be left with nothing!'

'Get away from my house before I call the police! You are nothing but scum, Mark!'

'Don't you dare talk to me like that. You will regret this Kerry!'

And with that I slammed the door in his face. I was shaking and couldn't believe that had happened. But at the same time I was proud of myself for staying strong.

I went back into the lounge and the film crew were literally hiding behind the sofas. They were terrified!

It wasn't the last time it happened, either. He would come round every few days, some days to convince me to get back with him, other days to, well, I think just to give me pure abuse. And each time the poor crew hid while Mark and I stood screaming at each other!

I was so glad I had signed that contract with CAN, which stopped me from taking any more drugs. Although I knew drugs and Mark were both things I needed to give up, I think mentally, despite everything, I could have slipped without that to keep me in line. So I am forever indebted to Claire and Neville for putting me in that position.

It sounds awful, doesn't it, that I might have ever gone back? But Mark still had a kind of hold over me. It was scary to think of life without him. Before I had met him, I was a very independent, strong-willed person who dealt with everything on my own, but when I was with him, he had stripped all that away, so that I was completely and utterly dependent on him. Whether it be financially, emotionally, medically, through drugs, confidence... you name it, when it came to me, he controlled it. So it was very hard for me to say to myself, 'Hang on, Kerry, you've been through a hell of a lot in your life, you are strong enough to do this' – and then to actually believe it. But now that was finally happening. I was becoming the real me again.

And I admit, I did have weak moments. One night I was lying there and the kids were all in bed, and I felt so lonely. I felt all my resolve dripping out of me, and I rang Mark up, crying, and going, 'I love you, I miss you, but it's in my contract I can't see you!'

He was like: 'Fuck the contract! Let me back in the house and let's start over.'

But this time, whether it was the contract, the inner strength I had found at bootcamp, or just that I could now begin to see a proper future for me, I didn't listen and I stuck to my resolution.

Mark never asked to see Molly and Lilly again after he left, and they didn't ask to see him. But as for Heidi and Max, we were sharing them between us at this time. At first, it was amicable. We didn't have an official arrangement, but although they were with me the majority of the time, they would visit him a lot as well, and I was happy about it.

Or at least I was happy for the first few weeks, until Mother's Day. Mark had agreed to bring Heidi to me mum's house that morning, where I had gone, as obviously it was an important day for all us girls to spend together.

But he didn't come round with her, and when I rang, he started going mad. 'No way! She's staying with me today. Why do you think you can have her back when it suits you?'

He was mad, and I don't know why – perhaps he just wanted to spite me by keeping her away – but the nightmares of Brian's mum keeping them that time in Ireland came flooding back and I felt panicked. I had to get the police involved before I could get her back. But even once Heidi was back with me I was determined that Mark should still have contact with the kids, even if I trusted him even less. So I made myself treat that Sunday as a one-off, and carried on as we had done.

It was hard for me, definitely, to know the kids were spending time with Mark and Sharon together. I would keep close contact while they were there, and one day I called and asked Heidi what they were doing. 'Baking cakes with Sharon and Daddy in the kitchen,' she told me.

'That's lovely, darlin',' I said, and I was glad she was happy. But it left me with a strange feeling. To know Mark was doing things like this with the kids and Sharon, or that the four of them were going swimming together, was really hard. All I ever wanted was that kind of family, but he had never wanted to do that kind of thing when he was with me. It felt like it must have been my fault. Or perhaps he had been really in love with me and wanted us to work, but somehow my money and fame stopped us being a nice normal family. The thoughts went round and round my mind and kept me up at night.

But then I realised there was the cheating and the lying, the mental games. I couldn't be held accountable for all of that. The realisation added another layer of reinforcement to my vow never ever to go back there and allow myself to be controlled like that by anyone ever again. I had signed the contract with CAN, but I made an even stronger one with myself, which I can never break.

As for the drugs, I really thought to myself, 'This is my last chance. Everyone already expects me to be back on drugs, so I'm going to be drugs-tested. If I slip up, I'm screwed, my career is over. It's going to be publicly known I'm on coke, and my last chance of working with CAN or anyone else will be gone.'

My cocaine habit was so linked with Mark. I know I could never have continued being married to Mark and stayed clean; that was never going to happen. I honestly believe, as sad and awful as this sounds, if back in my years with him, I had gone and put a bet on at the bookies about who would have died first from drugs or alcohol – Amy Winehouse, Whitney Houston or myself – I'd have put me. It's not even something I have realised in retrospect. It's something I knew at the time, but I just couldn't see how to stop it happening. It was like I could see myself spinning towards death.

But instead, I haven't touched coke since that final session with me mum, just as I was to head off to bootcamp. I'd never have believed then that that would be the last time I would ever touch the drug, but it was! Cocaine, which had been so much a part of my life for the last few years, was now properly a part of my past. I am really proud of that!

Night-time Escape

I filed for divorce from Mark on the basis of his behaviour, but he wanted to contest it. I thought about it, but realised it would have meant dragging it out, getting witnesses and going to court, and I had no money for that – plus I just wanted to be free from him. So I said, 'Look, I just want to be divorced. If that is what you want, fine, we can divorce on difference of opinion or whatever.' So that's what we did.

I was filming for a show called *Celebrity Wedding Planner*, where I was helping this woman plan her marriage. We were standing in a wedding shop in Liverpool surrounded by dresses, discussing what she should wear, when I got a text from my solicitor, 'You are now officially divorced from Mark.'

I was over the moon to be free, but my God, the irony! There couldn't have been a more ridiculous place to receive the news. And of course I got a pang of sadness, that another marriage hadn't worked out for me, and that my kids were now going to be without their dad in the house. But mostly, I couldn't have been happier or felt freer!

I knew I needed to do something to get myself far away from Mark – not just mentally, but physically, because the fact he was still turning up at my door at all hours was just horrendous. I thought about moving into a hotel in secret, just to escape him, but I knew that wasn't really a long-term solution. I needed to move house, away from the area. I didn't care where I moved to – I'd have moved to Timbuktu if there were flats available there.

Then one day Claire sat me down and said, 'Why don't you move down south? Neville and I think it would be a good idea to get you completely away from your old life.'

'Wow, that would be a massive change for both me and the kids,' I said.

'Well, a lot of the work you are going to be doing will be in London, so it will be easier for you, and it means you can see the kids more often with less travelling. And they will get a good life down here. It would also be good if you were closer to us, and as far away as possible from bad influences and old memories.'

I didn't have to think about it for long. It made sense to me because by then things with Mark had started getting really nasty. I honestly felt scared to stay. Also I had no real friends up north. I had pushed them all away when I was with Mark – or he had cut them off from my life. I had been spending time only with his friends, and I didn't trust any of them, I am sure most of them were siding with Mark. Also, me mum was still doing coke, so I didn't really want to be around her while I was getting myself strong again.

It also looked like the house was going to be taken off me because of the bankruptcy at some point anyway, so I was going to have to move. Why not make it down south? It could be like an adventure and a whole new start! I thought the kids were young enough not to be affected by the move, and they are all such outgoing little characters that they can always settle in well and make new friends wherever they go.

So I agreed to move down south and started organising for it. It was actually brilliant to have something to throw myself into, and at the same time I was still exercising – I looked so skinny and good!

I kept driving down and staying at Claire's and we were making plans for where I was going to live, and what we were going to do with my career. I was getting excited about the process of starting afresh, in spite of it being so scary.

I started getting back in touch with my friends up north, the people I had isolated myself from, and I sent them messages to say I was separated from Mark and it would be good to see them. I had a leaving do and lots of them came, and I remember panicking, wondering if I was doing the right thing. Just as I was starting to get back on my feet up north, I was about to uproot and start all over again.

I had told Mark what I was doing and he was not happy about it, but by then, as far as I was concerned, he didn't even have a say. So I pushed ahead with the plan, and started packing. And I was so scared doing it by myself, and quite heartbroken to be leaving the house – because no matter how bad some of my memories of the place are, there were also plenty of good ones, especially of my babies growing up and spending their early years there. And I did love the house itself.

We had decided to leave in the middle of the night so that Mark didn't try and stop me at the last minute or anything crazy, and also so that the paps didn't get pictures. I wanted this move to happen before anyone had realised. I lay there in the middle of the night, still dressed, just before we left, with Max in bed with me with his bottle. And I was looking round at the boxes sitting piled up, waiting to go, and the rooms looked so empty and soulless, and I couldn't stop crying. I was giving my house over to a trustee as part of the bankruptcy agreement, and I knew I had lost everything.

I had one last cry that night in the old house, but I didn't let the kids see me. Then I took a deep breath and wiped my eyes and put on a bright chirpy voice. 'Right, kids, we're going on an adventure! Come on, in your pyjamas, let's go!'

I piled up the pillows and a duvet in the back of the car and Molly and Lilly climbed in sleepily, while Cheryl took Heidi and Max in her car, and we were off. And I've never been back.

Once I was on the motorway and heading south, the further I got, the freer I felt. It was like a weight was being lifted off my shoulder with each mile. Every trace of my old life with Mark started to fall away as the distance between us grew. And as the signs for London started appearing, I could finally accept it. I was free of him! I was my own person again, responsible for what I did with myself. Although that was scary, it also felt amazing!

So while the girls dozed on the back seat, tucked up under the duvet, with Lilly leaning into Molly, I smiled to myself, thinking of the future. For the first time in a long time, I was feeling really, truly positive about it.

Life Down South

We went and stayed at Claire's house for two nights, while we finished house hunting, eventually settling on a place in Godstone, in Surrey. It was hard because I wasn't finding a place just for the kids and me; it needed to have accommodation for Cheryl too. But one was perfect. It was a seven-bedroom barn conversion with a duck pond, which the girls loved – a proper English place!

The day we got there, the kids all leapt out of the car and into the house, arguing excitedly about who was having which room. All the boxes from the last house were already piled up, waiting for our arrival. I looked at them and thought, 'Wow, the stress of this move is not over, it is just beginning!'

The most stressful things in life have to be moving house, divorce, getting off drugs, bankruptcy, getting your kids into a new school. Most people don't experience all those things in a lifetime – well, I was going through all of them at once! Looking back, I don't know how I did it, but I was feeling strong, and independent, and set on getting my life in order. Every day was exciting again and my time was full of things that needed doing. Warrington was a long way away...

Determined though I was, I'm not going to lie: living down south was hard. Getting the kids settled, and worrying if I had done the right thing, moving them away from what they knew, was one of the hardest things. But they seemed to be adapting fine, and were happy and none of it seemed to faze them at all, certainly not in the way it affected me at times.

Things were good but very different in so many ways. It was really difficult adapting to Claire, and her way of living and doing things. I hadn't seen her in ten years and I had to change to fit around her way of life, and it was hard. I remember saying to her in one moment of frustration, 'I want to go home! I don't fit in down south. I'm not like your other clients who have done well down here, like Peter Andre or Katie Price.'

But she told me, 'Of course you are different, and that is why people like you! It is the real Kerry Katona the public like, and we are going to make sure they see her again. Stick with it, and you will love it!'

The fresh start was exciting as well. One of the first things we decided to do was a big interview with *Fabulous* magazine, which came free inside the *News of the World*. I was to do a warts-and-all type interview about my drug use. The main reason was that although people already knew I had been caught doing drugs, they didn't know the details or the extent of it. Also, Mark had already done a vile interview with the *News of the World*, where he had said I was dead to him, and then listed off lie after lie about our life together. As though he was the person who had suffered throughout it!

So this time we decided it should come from me. I would talk about my life, including the drugs, in the one interview, then I could move on with a fresh start.

It was hard, though, and I was brutally honest for the first time. I told the magazine about doing drugs in the upstairs bedroom while the kids were downstairs, and how I had known it wasn't right but didn't know how to stop. It felt like it feels now, writing this book – very painful, because it was like it was happening to someone else instead of me and I now had to see it all for what it really was.

In the end, I was actually relieved when the magazine was on the shelves and the public could read it. It meant Mark couldn't hold anything over me by threatening to leak everything. I felt vulnerable too, as I was revealing things I had kept hidden for so long. When it came out, I think, people already knew in a way what was happening, so I didn't get too much of a hard time over it. I wouldn't have blamed anyone for having a go at me. All I knew was that they couldn't have more of a go at me than I was having at myself... constantly.

It was good to have got the interview out of the way, but the big problem was money. I didn't have a pot to piss in – if it wasn't for CAN Associates, God knows what I would have done. They got me a house, helped me pay my bills, kept my kids in school... all the basics I needed to keep going, to survive. But it was difficult to adapt to the way they did things. All my money went to them directly, and then out of that they paid all my bills.

According to my bankruptcy agreement, I had an allowance per month to live on, but CAN took some of that for bills and I was given what was left. I was effectively given pocket money. It's a weird way of life for an adult!

I was also struggling with the loneliness. It hit me the first night in the new house, when I was in my big double bed on my own, with no idea how I was going to cope, and I cried myself to sleep. The next morning I was positive and full of ideas, but it was the same every night, and I think I cried myself to sleep every single night for the first six months in Godstone.

I had Claire helping me, but you're never going to get someone's attention as a manager 24 hours a day, and I knew she had other clients like Peter Andre and other people to look after, so I struggled for a while.

I never once considered going back on drugs, or going back north, but it was a huge change and I knew that no one believed I would stick to it. The newspapers, people on forums, even my old friends and Mum, were like: 'She won't do it, she won't stick it, she'll go back up North.' And although I had a wobble, and there were times I seriously thought about it, I decided I wouldn't be going anywhere.

Bit by bit, I started building things up again and started to love my new life.

Best of all, my relationship with my kids got better and better. It was the best it had ever been because I was able to be completely focused on them, and we got closer. We would play silly games, or go out for food or go bowling. Other times I would do their homework with them – or, at least, I would make sure they were doing it!

Molly had learned to play the piano and was developing a beautiful singing voice. She would say to me, 'Mum, watch!' and get me to sit and listen while she played little songs she had learned or made up herself. Then after I'd told her, 'That was beautiful darlin', you are doing so well,' she would give me a grin, and wind me up: 'I definitely got my singing talent off Dad, though, didn't I, not you!' Cheeky bugger!

Other times I would sit them down and I felt like I was able to make up for the time I had lost with them, when I had been locked in my bedroom, or sat on the sofa, unable to function. It was phenomenal and one of the highlights of life down south. I had more energy and time to give them and our bond became stronger than ever. We had so much fun, planning things to do and places to go, always giggling and loving spending all this new time together. A cloud had truly lifted.

The relationship with Mum had also got much better than it used to be. She came down and spent time with us. I think she could see the changes in me, and it started to put ideas in her own mind. So she decided to give up drugs too. She said to me, 'Right, if our Kez can do it, so can I!' And despite the doubts I'd always had about her ability to come clean, I really hoped that she would be able to do it and make me proud.

She still had her moments when she was bloody hard work, though. She'd get funny if she thought I hadn't given her enough of my time. It was like she forgot I had a job and four children, and they were – and are – my priority.

And she still thought, even when I was clearly bankrupt and had no money, that I could pay everything for her. Like the first time she came down south to visit me and the kids and stay for a few days, she said to me, 'What time are you sending the car for, Kez?'

'I can't afford £500 for that, Mum! Get the train like everyone else.'

'I'm not getting the train down on me own. Send a car!'

I couldn't afford a car just so she gets a nicer journey down, but she didn't seem to grasp that. I guess it is hard after she was used to years of me having that kind of cash, which I suppose she – and I – thought would be there forever. She still suffers from some of the effects of depression, and doesn't like to be on public transport alone.

I do still pay other stuff for her, though. In the end, unfortunately, my bankruptcy meant that, like me, she lost her house, which was awful. Now she is on housing benefit, but that doesn't cover the cost of her place so I pay the rest. And I pay things like her Sky and her electric for her. If I go up to stay, I'll give her £100 for food shopping, that kind of thing. The distance of me being down south, though, did mean that our relationship was improving and becoming more adult. I think she was proud of me and it had given her her own new lease of life.

In April 2010, I had to go to court with Mark for custody of the kids. I had hoped we would be able to keep things amicable, but he wasn't happy I had moved, and instead suddenly applied for full custody. So off to court we went. I told the court I was happy with shared custody, as I wanted the kids to have access to both parents, but he kept fighting for full, so of course I was going to fight that to the death.

Needless to say, I ended up with full custody; with an agreement Mark could have them for a weekend every two weeks.

Facing the Past

Claire was doing a brilliant job, getting my head back on track, and me back on the showbiz circuit in a good way.

She was taking me to premieres and events, and she didn't try and change my character. She did get me to rein in certain things that she thought I should change and which she was very picky about.

'Stop sticking out your tongue at the paparazzi every time they take your photo. It was fun and cheeky when you were younger, but it's repetitive and unoriginal now! Act like the classier mum you are.'

I know it's a strange thing I do, but despite the millions of photos I have had taken of me over the years, I still get embarrassed, and I think pulling a face is a kind of defence mechanism.

I remember the very first premiere I went to with Atomic Kitten. It was for the film *The Beach* with Leonardo DiCaprio, and we were walking down the carpet. Geri Halliwell was in front of us in this beautiful dress, and she stops in front of the paps, and does all these poses, working her way through the textbook ones of leg out, of turning her back and then looking back over her shoulder, and so on. I was waiting for my turn, and was like: 'Really? Who does that? I so can't!' So I just went and pulled lots of stupid poses and funny faces to hide my embarrassment. And I guess that has continued ever since. Even today I feel a bit of a wally, and my legs will shake on the red carpet. There are still days I feel completely out of my depth and think, 'How am I doing this job?'

At one awards do, we met the executive producer of *This Morning*. He said, 'We want the first interview with Kerry about her new life.' I was like: 'Yeah, let's do it, I'm alright now!'

But Claire said, 'No, she has got to learn to walk again before she can run, she's not quite ready yet.'

She did a brilliant job in that way, knowing when was the right time to do things.

Another great thing that Claire got back for me was my *OK!* column. I had always loved doing it, and was devastated when I had been dropped from it. I had really missed it, for a few reasons. One, let's face it, it is a steady source of income. But also because it is nice to get my opinions out there, and it is the one place where I have control over what is said, so I am able to set the record straight on a lot of things going on in my life, without it being manipulated or turned into a story that just isn't true.

I like the people I deal with over there. I have always got on well with Richard Desmond, who owns the magazine. He is very sharp, and we have a laugh together. Then the girls I speak to for the column – mainly Chrissie Reeves – have always been very good to me. We have become close enough that I went to her wedding this year, which was wonderful. *OK!* magazine are extended family to me in lots of ways.

I also started filming for a reality TV series called *Kerry Katona: The Next Chapter*. It was being recording by CAN TV and was to go on ITV2, and it was supposed to show just that – the next chapter of my life. My life down south in my new home with the kids, and basically me rebuilding myself. I was more than happy to have cameras following me around again, as I always enjoy it, and had missed it!

I loved the crew. They were a constant in my life, and were round all the time, so were like my bestest friends. We had so much fun and it kept me occupied. I find it difficult not to be doing something. If I have a day off, I'm not sure what to do with myself, and I am dangerous in my own company – I'll come up with all sorts of crazy thoughts! It's difficult because not everyone has a job like me, where you work odd days and hours, so the show was good for me.

One very difficult decision I made during that series was to allow the children to watch my TV show *Coming Clean*. It was a spur-of-the-moment decision, but one that I was sure was right.

The show was being aired, and I had discs of it at home. The camera crew were there, and one day Molly said to me, 'Mum, can we watch it?'

'No darlin',' I said. 'There is stuff on there about Mummy that I don't want you to watch until you are older.'

'Are we on it?'

'Yes, of course you are, it's about my life, and you are the most important part of that.'

'Well, then, we should be able to watch it!'

And to be honest, I thought she had a point. Plus I realised Molly, who was 9 by then, and Lilly, who was 7, were old enough that their friends in the playground could talk about the show, and it wasn't fair if they knew nothing about it. I know I had always said I never wanted them to know about that side of my life, but I now realised it was impossible. They would have to know about it one day, and I would rather it came from me. Besides, now that way of life was in my past, rather than the present, it was like a different thing. It wasn't something they were having to live through, it was something about their mum's past, which they could learn about, and hopefully learn from.

So I sat the girls down and we all watched it together. I had a real knot in my stomach, wondering what they would make of it. And it was all about the cocaine, and me talking about trying to cut myself. I sat behind them as they watched, with tears streaming down my face. I was ashamed and afraid of what they would think.

When it ended, they both turned around and gave me big hugs, looking totally confused.

Molly went, 'Erm, Mum, when did this all happen? We never saw any of this!' Lilly was equally confused. 'Mum, have you been leading a double life?!'

And in a strange way that made me feel so good. The fact that my children really never did know what was going on… well, it was exactly the way I had wanted it to be. They genuinely didn't have a clue, so I knew I had kept their innocence, as I had wanted.

I explained to them what I had gone through, and said to them, 'If you ever want to ask me any questions about it, or if you ever hear anything from your friends or on the television and you want to know more about it, or if what you hear is true, you ask me. You can talk to me about anything, and I want you to know I am always here for you, and you are the most important people in my life.'

And they said, 'Mum, we love you' and gave me another hug – it couldn't have gone any better. They dealt with it so well and I was so proud of them.

Shortly afterwards, Molly came home from school.

'Mum, we were studying your subject in school today.'

'What was that darlin'?'

'Drugs!' she said, and started giggling.

She has a right cheeky humour, does Molly! But I had to laugh, and I was glad she felt she could talk to me like that.

New Friends

As a PR company, CAN tend to operate quite differently to anyone I had worked with before. They are much more involved in all aspects of your life, not just the business side, and have a lot more control over everything you do, from career choices, to who you date, even who your friends are.

They were always very keen for their clients to hang out together. I think the idea is everyone increases interest in each other that way. For example, Amy Childs appeared on my reality show *The Next Chapter*, when she came out of *TOWIE*, and Nicola McLean came on it as well.

By linking everyone up, it also means you have a bit of a support network. And my two closest friends that I made down south definitely happened that way.

The first is Peter Andre. The first time I met Pete was obviously when we were both in the jungle, for *I'm A Celebrity...* and he automatically became like a brother to me. Even though he is older than me by eight years, he was kind of like a younger brother 'cause he's so childlike. I became friends with Katie Price at the same time, and when they got married, she asked me to be her bridesmaid.

People have always misunderstood my relationship with Kate. She's a nice girl, but we have never been close. It was just that we got on reasonably well and would see each other at events and photo shoots. But we never had a deep close friendship – or a falling-out, for that matter. A few strong words were exchanged in magazine articles over her opinion of my relationship with Mark, but that was it. Nothing really happened, it all got very blown out of proportion. I know if we ran into each other none of that would matter and we'd have a proper chinwag and catch-up. She texted me after Christmas this year to see how I was doing, and if I bumped into her, it would be good to go for a drink. But that is about the extent of it.

I've always had a soft spot for Pete, though, and we got closer when I moved down south. I knew that if I was ever down, Pete would be the best one to get on the phone and he became a genuine friend. And CAN's way of working really works for Peter. Incredibly, he has been with Claire for 16 years.

The other person I got really close to was Danielle Brown, who was on CAN's books at the time. She is a good northern lass and maybe the fact we are two northerners living in London helped us get on, but we just clicked.

Danielle is the sister of Mel B from the Spice Girls, and is a very strong-willed, honest and funny girl, as well as one of the most loyal people I have met. I know she has my back and I have hers. I love her to bits, I really do. And her mum says I have brought the confidence back out in her, which is nice to hear. I am so close to her mum Andrea as well as Danielle, who has become like a sister to me, and it breaks my heart to see what they are going through with Mel.

She has fallen out with them because of issues with her husband Stephen Belafonte, who seems to be pulling her away from them. Watching Mel and her fella is like déjà vu for me, because I feel like I am watching Mark and myself. It's like, everyone else has a view on him, but she doesn't agree, and the more people tell her they don't like him, the more it pushes her into his arms. Not that I'm insinuating he is the same kind of person as Mark, of course. I feel sorry for Mel, because it can be so isolating. And I say as much to Danielle and Andrea – as much as I feel their pain, I can relate to Melanie too, because of how bad it is to be on the other side, even if you don't realise it at the time.

As for the other clients in CAN... well, they were all fine, but I wouldn't call any of the others close friends.

Take Amy Childs. She's a lovely girl, a sweet girl, and when we have gone to events we've had a giggle, but we don't hugely click. We have a laugh together, but we are just too different. She is such a girly girl, and I am not. I am not someone who can spend four hours putting on my makeup in the morning. Quite frankly, I can't be arsed! I would rather dress for comfort than fashion.

One time, Pete, Amy and I were sent to Dubai for a working holiday. I think Pete was filming for his show, I was doing an *OK!* magazine shoot, and Amy was doing pictures for her calendar. Amy and I were sharing a room. The first day, we got up to head out for a spot of sunbathing, and I was there in my bikini and bandana, without a stitch of make-up, and Amy emerged, with big eyebrows, false lashes, layers of bronzer.

I looked up and went, 'Are you having a giraffe?'

And she's all like, 'What, babe? What, honey?'

'It's like 100 degrees outside! Get in the bathroom and take all that shit off!' And she laughed at me, and I laughed at her, and she just kept it all on. It is just how different we are. She is fun, but wasn't someone I would especially hang out with were it not for the job.

*

Over the summer I filmed a fitness DVD called *Real Fitness*. It was a mix of exercises and was aimed at busy women, especially mums, who needed to fit in exercise around their daily life. Between filming that, building up my new life and filming for my TV show, I was really busy, which was lucky, as Molly and Lilly had gone off on holiday to LA with their dad, Brian, and I was missing them like mad. But I was glad too that they were getting to spend time with him.

Then, when he came back to drop them off, he came in. He never did that, but this time we sat out on the patio and had a brew, and we had a laugh and a joke.

He had called me a 'pig-faced mole' earlier that year on Twitter when he hadn't liked something I had said about him. So I went, 'Do you still think I'm a pig-faced mole?' to break the ice. And he laughed and told me how one of his fans had made a mask of my face like that.

Molly kept looking at us, and then whispered to me, 'Mum, this is really weird.'

And I went, 'I know!' None of the kids, even her, can really remember us together as a couple, which I think is really sad. I'd like it if they had some memories of their parents together. So I was really excited about it, for the kids to see us together and getting on.

I had great hopes after that day that it would happen again. But it was a one-off. A few months later a magazine used an old quote of mine, Brian got annoyed again, and went back to being bitter, and when he passed by at Christmas he didn't come in.

A major milestone happened for me near the end of that year. Claire eventually agreed it was time for me to do an interview on *This Morning* – my return to that sofa as it were, for the first time since that disastrous day.

Phillip was to be the interviewer again, but this time with Holly Willoughby instead of Fern, which I was happy about, as Holly is lovely. But it was still one of the hardest things I have ever had to do and I was terrified. What if I made lots of mistakes and said daft things? What if the public still didn't like me, and didn't believe I had changed?

I got there really early, to be sure no mistakes happened, and I chatted to Phil and Holly before the interview. She told me, 'You look amazing!' and Phil told me, 'I'm really proud of you for the changes you seem to have made in yourself', so that set me more at ease before the cameras were rolling. Phil added, 'Just be yourself and be honest. We are not trying to trip you up, just to get a real feel for where you are at in life now', which sounded fair enough to me.

It was weird to be sat back on that same sofa where things had gone so wrong, but before I knew it they were filming, and it all seemed to go really well. I held my hands up, and admitted my mistakes, and didn't try and throw blame around, but just talked through what had happened in the previous few years. I had been clean for nearly a year, but to go on there, and talk through everything... well, it took a lot of nerve, but I got through it. And viewers gave a great response, which I was so happy about.

I wore a new white dress and had my hair all styled, and looking at the footage of me then, and the first time round, even I can see the difference is incredible. It is like two different girls. I can't thank *This Morning* enough for that opportunity to make things right again. It was a great experience.

Dancing on Ice

Filming for the first TV series of *The Next Chapter* finished up in the autumn, and although plans for a second series were already underway, I was still scared about what I was going to do next, and still feeling lonely. But then Claire called me and said, 'You are on the next series of *Dancing on Ice*!'

I couldn't believe it, I was so happy. For me, it wasn't about entering a skating competition or becoming a professional, or winning it. It was more that this was my first big TV show since *This Morning* went wrong. It was an ITV1 show, which was a big deal, and I had been hoping for exactly that. Producers believing in me and trusting me to go onscreen again… well, that was the best thing about it and it really gave me some of my confidence and self-belief back.

Not that I had the first clue about how I was going to do the actual ice skating bit. I had been on the ice only a couple of times when I had taken the kids, and spent most of the sessions with them going around the edge, clinging to the sides!

The first thing I did was meet Christopher Dean and Jayne Torvill. Can you believe it? I'm only bloody getting taught to skate by Torvill and Dean, the top of the top! How awesome is that?

They revealed who I was being partnered with, and I was over the moon when it turned out to be an amazing professional skater called Daniel Whiston, who was just an absolute star. He had won the show twice with his previous partners, Hayley Tamaddon and Gaynor Faye. No pressure, then! But he was a northerner and had a great sense of humour, so I knew we would click.

We started training in the October, with the idea that we would be TV-ready by January, when the show would air. We trained for two hours every single day at an ice rink in Slough.

I was really nervous on the first session and wobbled my way on to the ice. I think Dan spent most of those two hours just holding me up! But the one thing I had on my side was that I had just done my fitness DVD, so I was in great shape. Probably lucky for Dan too, as he was going to be lifting me so often!

He was really good at boosting my confidence, and so was the coach Karen Barber. And I really got into it. After a few sessions, I realised I was really enjoying it. It was like I got on the ice and left all my troubles behind, and could be someone else for the two hours we were training. I had to focus, so there wasn't room for any other thoughts.

I trained so hard for that show. Even though I was slim and toned at the start, all the work was taking it to a new level. The exercise was just making any extra weight fall off, which in turn made me more confident and happy.

Christopher and Jayne choreographed the routines that you were to do, and chose the music, while someone else designed your outfits. It was all decided for you. Jayne sat me down when she was telling us what we were to skate to in Week One, and she put on the music. It was Adele's 'Make You Feel My Love', and I just burst into tears I was so emotional. I love that song, it is so moving, and it makes me think of my kids. And we tried to make the routine as sensual as possible to fit with the romance of the song, so I had to do a lot of staring into Dan's eyes, stroking his face, and wrapping my legs around him!

Finally, after Christmas, it was the big day. I was absolutely terrified as it approached.

I got dressed into a sparkly blue dress – it didn't seem to cover much at all, and I felt really exposed, despite the tights. Dan was in a matching blue top and trousers, and he kept giving me reassuring hugs.

My kids were in the audience with a banner saying, 'Mum, you are our ice queen'. I think they were as nervous and as excited as I was. I really didn't want to let them down. It was the first time they had ever seen me do anything like that: when I was in the jungle, they were both too young to know what was happening. So I was proud that I was making them proud!

They loved my costumes too. All the sparkle and colours – it was like playing at dressing up.

It was the scariest thing, skating onto the ice for the first time in front of an audience and the judges: Jason Gardiner, Robin Cousins and Emma Bunton. As we stepped off the side, Dan hugged me, 'You can do it, you are a great little skater, now let's show them that!'

My knees were literally knocking, but we got through it with a few wobbles, and no falls, so I was really proud! I couldn't catch my breath afterwards, and as host Phillip Schofield tried to interview us afterwards, I was lost for words – I think for the first time in my life! I eventually managed to joke, 'Give me the jungle any day!'

Jason described what we had done as 'tender and controlled', so it felt like we had got off to a good start. Then it was back to the ice rink the next day.

The routine continued like that for the next few weeks, and in between I would do the odd television appearance, my favourite of which was *Loose Women*. Back when I was 22, I had been on the panel with them, discussing daily issues, but after I left, I hadn't been back as a guest until *Dancing on Ice*. So that felt like it was yet another important TV show and another set of producers who were willing to give me that chance to be on air again, and I loved it!

One of the other *Loose Women* panel, Denise Welch, was also doing *Dancing on Ice*, so we had a real gossip about it. She's great, is Denise, a real laugh.

But back in the rink, it was like I couldn't keep up with the other contestants. I would improve each week, just not at the same speed as them. A few weeks in and the judges started saying, 'You are relying too much on Dan. It is like a dependency, not a partnership.'

I was just amazed I had got that far, to be honest, and I was genuinely really enjoying it. Maybe that was the problem, though: I was having fun, while others were being serious! Backstage before the competition, Dan and I would be having a laugh with rapper Vanilla Ice and his partner Katie Stainsby while the others would be stretching and warming up in silence. Oops.

By Week Seven, I knew I was going to be gone. So much so that I had booked a holiday for the kids and me the week after in Majorca! I didn't let them come to the show either, as I knew they would get too upset, so they were up staying with me mum.

And true enough, we didn't have the best routine. I nearly fell in one of the lifts – I like to pretend it was Dan's fault for nearly dropping me. And afterwards cheeky Jason said to me, 'Your skating ability is clearly on the endangered species list, as it is practically extinct.' I always think his comments are funny, except when they are aimed me!

I was upset to be out, but I knew it was my time. I thought I had done really well, and saw it that I was so blessed to have that opportunity. It was my own personal battle to prove to everyone

I was alive, healthy, had got my personality back, and that I am a survivor. I'll admit it as well: of course I want the public to like me. In some ways they are like my family and my support, and it matters to me what they think. I had lost so much trust and respect from them in the previous couple of years, and *Dancing on Ice* felt like I was starting to gain them back.

My kids were more distraught than me that I was gone from the competition! I rang them as soon as I was off the ice. Lilly answered and could hardly speak for crying.

'Mummy, why are you out?'

'It's only a TV show, baby!' I soothed her. 'It is absolutely fine. I did my best, but it was my turn to be out.'

'I'm so proud of you!' she managed to get out between the sobs.

'And I'm so proud of you too!' I said.

That made me so happy. Because I really want my kids to be able to say, 'Kerry Katona? Yeah, she's my mum. She's made mistakes and I'm proud of her' – rather than forever feeling they have to duck their heads down when my name is mentioned.

The whole *Dancing on Ice* experience was amazing. I'd do it all over again, if I didn't have to skate!

My Saviour

O ff screen, however, while *Dancing on Ice* was happening, there was something else very important happening in my life.

I was driving home from the ice rink one day, when I got a text that would change my life forever. It was a strange one-word text, which came from a number I didn't know, and it just said 'tap'. For some reason, I knew straightaway it was Kev, the trainer from bootcamp.

He was getting in touch with me because he had split from his wife.

Well, that was it. He came over, we started talking, the chemistry was there as strongly as ever – and now with no partners in the way, we started seeing each other. And although I have always denied in every interview and article since that anything happened between us, that wasn't true, because I fell in love, and fell in love hard.

I wanted to keep it secret for a few reasons. Partly, I felt like people might judge the fact that we were both separated rather than divorced. But more importantly, I always think the longer you can keep a relationship private, the better. It gives you more time to get to know that person as an individual without the pressure that comes with media coverage.

I always get: 'Kerry wants more babies!' 'Kerry is head over heels already!' 'Kerry demands her man proposes'. All that kind of thing is written about me. Or even worse, the talk is about my weight – the romance has made me either too fat or too skinny. It is relentless. So I always think if a new relationship has any chance of succeeding, you need that time to get to know each other before the whole world knows about you – and has an opinion.

November and December 2010 passed in a blur of happy times with Kev, and we were together all the time. We would go for walks and talk, but we never went out much so that we could keep things private. And when we were at home together, nothing else mattered.

One of the best things about Kev was how safe he made me feel. When he gave me a hug, he would just hold me, which made me feel so protected. He hadn't fallen in love with the Kerry Katona everyone else knows. He wasn't interested in the fame side of things. Of course he had a preconception of me when he first met me, but it changed. He had met me at my lowest, the mess I was. No false lashes or lip liner, nothing to hide what I really was. He fell in love with the person he saw starting to grow. I think he wanted to fix me as well, although he didn't realise how much I had already fixed myself in the gap between bootcamp and him getting back in touch.

It was as though, for the first time in my life, I was having an adult relationship. As though Kev taught me what a proper relationship should be like and how one adult should treat another. He made me feel special, and confident about me, and he would never put me down. It was such an amazing experience in comparison with what I had put up with at the hands of Mark.

But he didn't have me on a pedestal, either. If I did something wrong, he would bollock me, 'Oi, enough of that!' And because he was a fitness freak, he pushed me in the right direction: 'Next thing we are going to do is stop you smoking.'

Then it got to Christmas. Kev had his kids and was staying with his mum, so I wasn't going to see him until after, and I was at home with my kids. My first Christmas alone in a while without a man, and I was a bit worried about it – and feeling lonely. I love Christmas, and making it special for the kids, but sitting wrapping up the presents on my own on Christmas Eve, after they had gone to bed, just wasn't the same when I was alone. I was feeling upset as I was doing it, and wishing Kev and I could have been doing it together for our kids.

Then he rang me up. 'Have you seen the shooting stars outside?'

'No,' I said.

'Well, go and look out the window because they are everywhere tonight, there are loads!'

And I looked, and he was running down the drive towards my house, with three red Santa sacks in his hands, and when he got to the door he gave me a massive hug and a kiss, and said, 'I have to wake up with you on Christmas morning.'

We sat up the rest of the night, and he had brought presents for the kids and me, and we got everything ready, and put together a train set for Max. Oh, it was perfect! And we got to wake up together in the morning, and he went home early before his kids were up. It was one of the nicest, most romantic things anyone has ever done for me.

Just after Christmas, I got really poorly with some horrendous 'flu-type virus, and I also had two popped ribs from ice skating. I was so sick and ill, and I lost loads of weight, but for the two weeks I was suffering, he nursed me through it and took me to hospital when I needed an x-ray.

Then he got it, and I looked after him.

Then *Dancing on Ice* started on television, and I knew Kev was at home watching me. I used to give a salute when I was onscreen, which was my secret sign to Kev at home, a Royal Marines sign that he had taught me. It was a great feeling to know he was watching and I wanted to make him proud of me.

By Week Seven, when I was out of the show, we were as strong as ever. But Claire and Neville were not happy at all that I was dating him, because although he was separated from his wife, they weren't divorced, so they thought it looked bad.

I remember Neville telling me to stop and I was like: 'Who are you to tell me who I can and can't date? I'm sorry, but if I am at work on time and professional, my love life has absolutely nothing to do with you. When Kev looks at me, I feel like I'm the only girl in the world, as though no one else exists, and I am special, and you want me to give that up, 'cause you aren't happy about it? Screw you.'

And I carried on seeing him.

But then we were papped together, and I remember both Claire and Neville screaming down the phone at me. Neville told me: 'You are stupid, my son has more brains!' The way they were carrying on, you would think I had just done a big fat line of coke in front of the kids. The more they screamed, the more upset I got.

I came off the phone and Kev was in the kitchen cooking tea for the kids. I like to deal with things on my own, so when I walked in and he came up to me, I pushed him away, but he grabbed me and hugged me so tightly I couldn't escape, and then I broke down. But it worked, because he just held me, and I thought it would all be alright. Out of everyone I have ever been with, I really knew Kev could and would protect me.

But things started to get messy, and one night Kev ended up sleeping with his estranged wife Sarah. He called to tell me, and I couldn't breathe. He told me he didn't know why he did it.

I was in the middle of doing *Dancing on Ice*, and no one knew except my partner Dan. I love Dan, he is like a brother to me, and I trusted him with all my secrets. And I was crying on camera, saying, 'It is all too difficult, the pressure of the competition has got to me and I'm really struggling.'

Everyone thought my breakdown was to do with the show, but it wasn't, it was about Kev.

And I was dancing to the song 'Woman in Love' ('I'm just a woman in love, And I'd do anything…') and I was crying 'cause of the words and knowing he was watching. I was so hurt, but there was no question as to whether or not I would forgive him. I loved him too much to let him go.

Then he went away to Wales to a camp for his job. His mum kept ringing, saying she had never seen him this happy – I think the family were pleased to see him moving on. And his sister Paula called me up to say she had never seen Kev like that with anyone. 'He loves you,' she said. 'This is it for him'

And I replied, 'It is for me'. I really, truly believed that it was.

But then his wife Sarah sold a story, and Kev got really upset. He was like: 'You don't need this, I am no good for you.'

He was struggling to handle my job and the fact that I am famous. There is always this flurry at the start when a paper realises that I am in a relationship, and then it calms down, but he didn't give it time to do that.

And unknown to me, CAN phoned him up and asked him to stay away. I didn't know this at the time, but I found out later and was furious. They had no right. I felt I had done everything else they asked without question and it was going to be hard to put up with this.

He sat me down and said to me, 'I need to leave you for your own good. I am thinking maybe I should give things another go with Sarah for the sake of the kids, and you should carry on with your own life.'

I was devastated, but I thought he must clearly love her, and who am I to stand in the way of a marriage? I have been on the receiving end of that, and I would never want to be the one doing that to another woman. I have never been out with a married man, and never would, but Kev was very much separated when I started seeing him and a divorce seemed a formality as far as he was concerned.

So in April 2011 he came round with his kids once more, and they stayed over for a bit, and then he left. That was the last I saw of him. And I haven't spoken to him since, as I think it is better that way.

I would never want to come between a man and his kids in a million years. I have full respect for him for putting them over me – for goodness sake, it is what I have wanted both my kids' dads to do, so it is amazing and fair play to him for that. I just hope that there is someone else out there who can come close to being as good for me as Kev was.

Out of anyone I have ever been with, out of everyone I have ever been in love with (and I have been in love many times) I think the only real, true, pure love I have ever felt was for Kev. If I had to say my one, real, true love, it would be him. And that is still so hard to admit.

Everyone always thinks it must be Brian, but that was kiddy love. With Kev, it was adult love. As for it being Mark... you're joking, right?!

I have moved on from Kev now. That chapter of my life is closed, but I wish him lots of love and happiness, as he really was my saviour and I owe a lot to him.

The End of CAN

The day after Kev and I split for good, I snogged a guy called Dan Foden, from the TV show *Take Me Out*. My aim was purely to piss off Kev, but somehow it turned into a well-publicised, eight-week relationship.

But then we split up – or, to be precise, he dumped me in the papers, although it was the way my life was being run that he slagged off in the article rather than me! He said that he thought I was a lovely girl, but he didn't like my fake friends or the showbiz bubble I was living in. And looking back, I can't argue with him that that is how it was.

But Neville got me round to his office, and was really angry. CAN hated it when they had no control over an article in the newspapers or magazines.

Straight after my split with Dan, at the end of May 2011, I went off on a girls' holiday to Marbella with Danielle while the kids stayed at home with Cheryl. Claire set it up for me with the idea of going out there to let my hair down and, quite frankly, get pissed! I'd had a hard year getting my life back on track, and the kids weren't with me, and it was just intended as a real relaxing holiday. We spent the days around the pool and the evenings in bars and clubs, exactly what we had planned.

A really nice thing happened on the plane home. I was sitting there waiting to take off, when my phone bleeped with a message from Brian. He never sends me texts and this one was all chatty. He had just split from Delta the month before, after seven years. The evil bit of me that remembered the pain it had caused me when they got together was pleased. But at the same time I felt bad for them – it was a long relationship and the end of anything deserves sympathy. But it looked that now he was single again, Brian wanted to be in touch.

And the conversation went like this:

Brian: 'Hiya! How are my babies? I'm missing them like mad!'

Me: 'Really good, I'm just on my way home to them again. Our Molly just had her exams and she got 94 per cent. Dead proud of her.'

Brian: '94 per cent? Bloody hell. Did you shag a genius when we were together? 'Cause she certainly didn't get that from me or you!'

Me: 'Haha, you still make me laugh, Brian. No, I definitely think she got that from me.'

Brian: 'I'm going to be back over in England in a few weeks. I think it would be a really good idea if you me and the kids go watch a show and go out for dinner.'

Me: 'Brian, you know what, the kids would love that, and so would I. I won't say anything, but it would be really great for them.'

I was so happy, because that was exactly what I had been wanting all along. I thought that this was the progress I had always wanted.

But then that was it. End of contact, nothing more, and no visit in England. I only found out afterwards that a week or so later he met Vogue Williams, an Irish reality-TV star, and they are now married. In true Brian style, he got carried away in his new relationship, and couldn't think outside of that. I was only glad I hadn't told the kids about it, so I hadn't got their hopes up for nothing.

After my holiday, I was feeling a bit lost. Without *Dancing on Ice*, I had gone from working really hard every day to just filming for my reality show *The Next Chapter*, Series Three, so I threw my focus into that. And one of the things I did, which was filmed for that series, was have speech therapy. Although my speech had improved a lot since coming off the bipolar medication, I still felt like it wasn't clear enough.

It felt like it had been permanently affected because of the way I had come off my medication. This is why I don't recommend just stopping the medication, because I do believe the remains of my slurred speech are probably caused by the fact I did that. I don't know for a fact that lowering the dosage gradually would have made the difference, but it is what I believe. My words getting mixed and being a bit slurry was never something I had when I was younger. So yes, that was the downside of the way I came off my meds.

Although I could make myself out perfectly, and so could Mark and the kids, other people still said they couldn't always understand me exactly. As I wanted to keep doing TV, it seemed important for me to improve on it. So I had some sessions with this therapist, and it was actually quite interesting, as she did a proper breakdown of the way I speak.

When I lived in Ireland with Brian and was around his friends and family, I spoke a lot more correctly. I guess I worried they wouldn't understand me, so I slowed myself down and pronounced everything properly. Then I moved back to England and to Warrington, and everyone around there talks in a real lazy kind of way. We don't finish half our words, and leave bits out or say them in a kind of half way.

On top of that, she told me I had a lazy tongue anyway – I guess I would be a rubbish lesbian!

She taught me to really concentrate on certain ways of saying words, and to think about my breathing, as apparently I breathed in all the wrong places too. So now I am much more aware of how I speak and it is completely different, especially when I am onscreen. Not that I can't drop straight back into my old way of talking the minute I am around northerners again!

I also notice I change my voice when I talk to fans as well. It is like I put on an accent, which isn't the one I taught myself, but isn't my original Warrington accent, either. It is hard to describe on paper, but it's a kind of jolly northern way of speaking. All like: 'Hiya love, y'alright? Isn't everything bloody brilliant!' I don't know why I do it. If it is nerves, or habits, I'm not sure, but it is like a public character I am playing without even realising. It is like a kind of role I take on with the public. I do the same to the press without meaning, and I start being a bit crude with it. And while I can blame the way I took my medication for some of the changes in the way I spoke in terms of my accent, I can't blame that for my public persona!

I think that is more down to the fact that after I won *I'm A Celebrity… Get Me Out Of Here*, I tried too hard to make people laugh. I was the real me in the jungle, but after I came out I thought I had something to live up to, so I became this exaggerated version of myself. Then Brian left me and I tried even harder to be funny and likeable, as I didn't have his love, so I was craving love from elsewhere, anywhere, even from the public – love of any kind would have done! But that person is not really the way I am and I guess I went about looking for love in the wrong way.

More and more, it felt like I was moving in the right direction. But things had started getting strange at CAN. Claire and Neville were in the middle of their own relationship drama. They were splitting up and it all got so personal, I felt like my parents were getting divorced. I tried to keep out of it, but it was impossible. I just wanted to do my job and get paid, but it became almost like a case of: 'Well, which of your parents are you going to go and live with? Who are you siding with?'

It all got very complicated, and eventually, after trying a couple of different approaches, I decided I would have to move on from CAN Management while staying with Neville for the TV side. It was difficult, and sad, because I owed them so much and they had set up my new life down south, but it had to be done. I was never sacked or dropped, which were the rumours that were put out there at the time. Instead I chose to move on, but all sorts of stories were flying around about why I had left CAN Management. Like the story that Claire had sacked me for going wild when I was in Marbella. I'm sorry, but Claire set that holiday up and the point of it was to have a holiday and relax, I'm not going to apologise for the fact that that is exactly what I did! But then I had reporters outside my house going, 'Oh, Kerry, are you back on drugs?' just because they had seen me having fun with my mates.

That was a step too far. I was raging, and went straight to Max Clifford and said I want to do a drugs test to prove everyone wrong.

I had got back in touch with Max since moving down south, after I had watched him on television, discussing a footballer's affair. I remembered how great a relationship we had had at one point, and I realised I wanted it back. Although I don't think he did everything in the right way around *This Morning*, I knew I owed him a massive apology too for the way I had been behaving when I was with Mark and on the drugs. There were definitely times I must have been an awful client. So I got hold of his number, and rang him up, shaking. But I needn't have worried. As soon as he heard my voice, he said, 'Hello, poppet!' and I just burst into tears.

I went to his house for dinner and we had been friends again ever since. So without Claire around to do my PR, and once the drug accusations started flying around again, the first person I thought to turn to was Max.

He sorted out a hair test and, of course, it came back that I was clean as a whistle. Eighteen months on and I was still having to prove myself, to prove I was no longer 'troubled druggie Kerry'.

But I said at the time I am never doing this kind of test again. It is bollocks that every time I have fun I have to prove to doubters that I am not back on the cocaine. I am no longer going to feel I have to justify myself and prove them wrong.

The best thing was that Max and I decided to work together again. So I completely moved from CAN to him. I had tried to keep going with Neville for my TV work, but it became clear that it would be better to cut all ties and start fresh. And who better to start again with than Max?

One of the first things we decided I should do was go on *Celebrity Big Brother*. Now that the programme had moved from Channel 4 to Channel 5, they had been approaching me on and off for a while. It was so exciting, especially as I hadn't been allowed to do it before. It felt great to get a second chance.

It made me sad, though, that things with CAN – both Claire and Neville – ended like that. Because I am eternally grateful for what they did for me – without them taking me on, I could have ended up back on drugs, back with Mark, and then either dead or in a gutter somewhere with the kids having been taken off me. The fact they prevented that being a possibility, and got me back on the straight and narrow, is something for which I will forever be thankful to them. But after I was back on the right track, it seemed like the best choice that I took over control of my own life.

CBB

On 16 August 2010 I was picked up from my home in a car and taken off to go into hiding for two days before going into *Celebrity Big Brother*.

I just about had my head in order by the time I left, although I was so tearful as well. The night before, I had had a complete panic attack. Lovely Danielle had come to stay with me, to keep me company and encourage me, as she knew I was having doubts.

And I just spent the whole evening in tears. Since Mark and I had split, it was like I was married to my kids – I was with them all the time and they were my life. I kept thinking about the fact I was gone for three weeks, and about everything that could happen in that time. I knew that when you are on *Big Brother* you become more of a focus for stories, so what if something came out in the papers, and the kids found out about it at school, and I wasn't home to explain things to them and protect them?

I worried as well that the public would judge me for leaving them. I always face so much criticism in the press for my role as a mother, and even though 99 per cent of the time they are basing that on incorrect facts, I still worry about it. No one wants to be thought of as a bad mother.

Molly and Lilly were in Ireland with their grandparents, and Heidi and Max were with Mark. Even that had been a drama, with him throwing it in my face, as though I was off on holiday for three weeks and he was doing me a favour taking the kids. That drove me mad. It is a privilege, not a chore, to look after your kids, Mark!

You have to remember as well, that Brian always used to have a go at me when I went away for work – even though he was away working all the time. He was really traditional and thought I should be at home being a mum all the time, and not have a career. Which is all well and good, but without him there providing, it was impossible. I had to take what work I could. Mark would say the same. 'You can't leave the kids with a nanny while you go to work.'

I knew in my rational mind that I had no choice: to bring up my four children by the pair of them, I have to do it! And while neither of them could comment when they were no longer around at all, what they had said played round and around in my head. It preyed on my mind.

I had a massive panic attack, crying and struggling to breathe. But Danielle was great and kept talking me through it and reassuring me it was fine and that I was doing the right thing.

So I refocused my mind on the fact that doing this would pay off my bankruptcy, which would make a huge difference to me – and the kids. And I pulled myself together, finished packing, and was ready for the car in the morning.

I was taken to the Hilton Hotel in Elstree, and I was checked into a room along with a chaperone, who stayed with me 24 hours a day except for when I was sleeping. I wasn't allowed to leave the room.

All the other contestants were in the hotel too, but we weren't allowed any contact. At this point, I knew only two of the people who were going in: Amy Childs and Sally Bercow, the Speaker's wife, who was on Max's books at the same time.

The only time I left that room was for the photo shoot for my official *BB* photo – the one they use for voting – and for the official interviews pre-entry. To do that was like this exciting covert operation. I felt like I was on some TV drama – *CSI: Crime Scene Investigation*, or something! All the corridors were secured before I could leave, and I had to wear a big cloak with a hood, which didn't let any of me show. I could hardly see out, either, so there was very little chance I'd catch sight of another housemate. Even if I had, I wouldn't have been able to tell who it was.

Those couple of days just sitting in the hotel thinking about what was going to happen really built up the anticipation for me. By the time the big day came on 18 August, I was completely petrified! I was obviously worried about what the public was going to think about me, but I think I was mostly nervous about getting on with the other people in the house. You are stuck in there with them for 22 days – depending on how far through you get – so whether I got on well with them was crucial to whether I was going to have a good experience. I told producers I really wanted to be the first person in because I thought that would make things easier – I didn't fancy walking down the stairs into a room of people who might hate me!

On the night, I put on the dress I had chosen for my entry, a black silk dress with a long train behind. I thought I should go all-out dramatic and glam to make an entrance, but not a tacky one! I had short spiky hair at the time like a Bart Simpson haircut, and I was wearing bright red lipstick.

I walked down the catwalk to the house and stopped to talk to Brian Dowling. I tried to look confident, but I told him I was shaking like a leaf I was so nervous! I told him I had felt guilty leaving my kids, but added: 'I'm here to change my life and stand on my own two feet.' The response from the crowd was mainly positive, which was great, then I headed up the stairs and in. And I was happy when I got my wish – I was the first in the house!

The second person to come down the stairs was Tara Reid, an actress who is best known for *American Pie*. And my first thought was: 'Oh God, she's a loon!' I suppose I have a quite strong accent, so she might not have really got my name when I first said it, but come on, she called me 'Curry' for the first week! She really was completely cuckoo, that girl.

As for the other housemates, well, the two people I got on best with in the house were Paddy Doherty and Darryn Lyons. The three of us were really tight. I'm not a girly girl, I'm more one of the lads, and I prefer to hang out with them, so I clicked best with those two.

I remember when Paddy Doherty came into the house. I hadn't watched *My Big Fat Gypsy Wedding*, but I had seen it advertised, so I knew who he was. And I remember when he walked in: he came down the stairs with his casual but manly walk, scanned the room, and straightaway he looked at me and went, 'Thank God you are in here.' I didn't even know the guy! But I took it as a good thing. And even though I couldn't understand what he was saying for about a week, as his accent is so strong, we eventually hit it off and were inseparable.

As for Darryn, I remember just before he came in, Amy whispering to me, 'Wait until you see who is coming in next, wait till you see.' I started shitting myself. I was thinking, 'God, please don't let it be Mark Croft or Brian McFadden' 'cause I imagined that would be the kind of thing *Big Brother* would have loved to have done to me! And then it turned out it was Darryn. I was confused at first because I recognised him but I couldn't place him at first, and then I was like, 'Oh yeah, you are Mr Paparazzi'. I'd never met the guy before and we hit it off straightaway too.

I think Amy expected me to resent him being there, but I didn't. I might get annoyed at times when I feel paps are overly intrusive, trying to trip you up to get a photo of you looking daft, which might sell, or when I can't get off my driveway for the number of them waiting at the end if some disaster or another has happened in my life. But ultimately I know they have a job to do, they have helped make me who I am, and some of them are nice people and just earning a living, giving the public what they seem to want. I guess I have a bit of a love/hate relationship with them really!

I felt sorry for Pamela Hasselhoff, I think she was massively lost in life, like she was struggling to find her own identity. She was only really known for being David Hasselhoff's wife, and now that they were split she seemed lost without him. It was all 'David this' and 'David that'.

She also was very close to her children. I remember her kicking off one night when she couldn't talk to her 'babies'. The way she was going I presumed they were four and five – it turned out they were 21 and 18! There was me at the time with a three-, four-, eight-, and nine-year-old, and I was coping better than her!

Jedward are the housemates people ask me about the most, and I love them. I'm a very maternal person and I think I was the only member of the group they listened to. There was one day I bollocked them, when they had left things out for people to fall over. I remember telling them, 'You are a pair of jackasses! Get in there and get it cleaned up. You are 19, not 9!'

I'm really laid back – I've got four kids, so of course I can take a lot – but only until I think someone has pushed me too far, and then I explode, and I think Jedward saw that. After that, I only had to give them a look and they behaved. Whereas Paddy, the so-called hard man of the house, they didn't give a shit what he said to them!

I also really believe in Jedward, because as a mum, I believe in everything they do. They don't drink, they don't smoke, I think they are both still virgins – I don't know that for fact as I've never pried, that is just my feeling – and for people with that status and that commitment to their fans, I think fair play to them for being so moral.

They definitely have a bit of ADHD or whatever they want to call it these days, but they are so creative and they write their own songs, come up with their own dance routines, and design all their outfits. And I love that they are actually really sensitive and sentimental. It was Molly's birthday while they were in the house and they were the first people to come over and say to me that they wished her a Happy Birthday, which made me feel good. Above all, those boys are truly unique and entertaining beyond words, whether you're watching them on TV or being co-stars in their crazy world.

Later, when I did get to speak to Molly, I was a complete mess. I really missed her, and I was so relieved to hear her voice and that everything was okay. I was crying and gasping as I spoke to her, full-on hysteria!

I remember I could hardly get the words out. 'Happy birthday, baby. I love you!'

And she was so calm. 'Don't cry, Mum!' Hearing her voice, how loving and proud she sounded, but also how strong she was, gave me everything I needed to get back into the house with a determination to be happy, knowing I'd be hugging all of the kids before I knew it.

*

Something Darryn said on the last day was the most moving thing anyone said about me while we were in there. I don't think it was shown onscreen, but we all did speeches about each other, and he said, 'I've watched Kerry's career and personal life through pictures over the years and I thought I knew her, but I'll be the first to hold my hands up and say I've completely got this girl wrong.' That was so good to hear.

Darryn wasn't the only housemate who had to admit to changing his mind about me. Model Bobby Sabel had to as well, which I thought was funny, as I wasn't a fan of his. I thought he was really sly, and I know he was supposed to be in there as a bit of eye candy, but I don't think he was even good-looking.

On the sixth night we were in there, we were sat around having a drink and just chatting as a group. And Bobby stood up and walked off. At the time I was like: 'Did I say something wrong?' But I didn't think too much of it until I watched the show back after I left the house. Then I saw he had gone off on his own to the cameras and started having a rant, and calling me all these names, and proper slagging me off. He said, 'She said she can't find a guy because of her status. What status? She's a complete moron!' It was completely uncalled for, and clearly just playing to the viewers – who the hell has a rant out loud like that, standing on their own?!

But days later, when we had a *Wizard of Oz* task, and he was dressed as Dorothy, he went in the diary room and admitted he had got me completely wrong. He had judged me – as most people do – on what they read. And once he had actually taken the time to know me, he could see I was different. I don't bear any grudges on this stuff, though, never have.

I fully expected the public to kick me out at any point, but when it got to the final night of *CBB*, I was still in the house! There were seven of us left (if you count Jedward as one person, which the voting public did), and I was terrified and so afraid of going out to boos. It was scary to know I had to leave the house – it had become quite a comfy little bubble over those three weeks. I didn't think I had done anything bad, but then no one in the house ever does, until they get out and see the video evidence!

Despite *Dancing on Ice* and my reality shows, I still wasn't sure the public had really forgiven me for all my mistakes, and it really felt like this was the test. And that if I had got through this without being hated, everything would be alright.

Each time Brian Dowling came over the speaker in the house, my heart rate would double its speed as I waited to hear whose name he called next. Then, finally, it was down to just Paddy Doherty and me. We were sat on the sofa clinging on to each other. My heart was going so fast, I thought my mike was probably picking it up and everyone could hear!

Brian came on the speaker. 'For the last week the great British public have been voting for their winner and I have the result. I can now reveal the housemate with the most votes and the winner of this year's *CBB* is…' And I swear he waited for about five minutes, while Paddy sat there and I clung to his arm. I couldn't stop grinning, 'cause although I'd be lying if I said I didn't want to win, I was just so happy to have got this far. And if I was going to lose to anyone, Paddy was your man!

So it was a genuine scream of delight I gave when he won. Then it was out to meet the crowds. I was in a red, black and leopard print prom-type dress, and before I had time to think about it, Brian had me out of the house – to cheers, thank God!

It is hard to know why I got so far. If anything, I think I was one of the most normal people in there, which must have shocked viewers! Although I have issues, I didn't sit and dwell on them in there. I think I came across reasonable and sensible, which is how I am in reality – most of the time! Let's face it, there were that many lunatics in there, it kind of proved I wasn't as crazy as everyone thought.

But although the viewers who watched *CBB* changed their mind about me, I still struggle to change what the press say about me. To this day, every journalist seems to think I am this crazy, outrageous, messed-up, partying loon. Even now it is 'troubled reality-TV star' or 'former coke addict'. Is there any need to keep putting that in? It's like: 'Get over it, let's move on. I have!'

The biggest surprise to me out of my *Celebrity Big Brother* experience was the way I was perceived in the house in terms of romance. To me, I had split with Dan Foden not long before, so yes, I was single, but I wasn't going in for romance, and there certainly wasn't anyone in there who caught my eye in that respect. But in my eviction interview, Brian Dowling was like: 'Let's talk romance, Kerry.'

I said, 'Okaaaaay. Me?!'

'Yes, you, Kerry.'

I looked over to me mum in the audience, and she nodded and looked all smug, and I was really confused! Brian said he was talking about me and Lucien Laviscount. Now Lucien was a beautiful actor from *Coronation Street*, but he was 19. I'm sorry, but his balls haven't even dropped! Lucien was like a brother for me in the house, and I would have been devastated if he hadn't made the final, but that was it! He was a good-looking lad, don't get me wrong, and if he had been a few years older... but I'd never go near someone that young. Dan, at two years younger than me, was enough of an age gap for me! Lucien was closer in age to

Molly than to me! I mean, we got into bed and had a cuddle, but that was it. That was as mates. If I had done anything to Lucien, I really would have expected social services at my door. That is how wrong it would have seemed.

Watching the show back, I think it is clear I was trying to fix him up with Amy. But even for her I think he was too young and nothing would have happened there on either side. If I am honest, I think a lot of it for both of them was about air time. I don't mean that in a disrespectful way, but it was a storyline. And when you are in the house, you have to pick the best-looking of the boys, and Lucien was definitely that. And Amy was the best of the girls, so it kind of made sense. You make do with what you have and I think that is what happened.

But I guess the public didn't buy the potential for romance amongst them – because of the fact *OK!* magazine decided they wanted to shoot *me* with Lucien when we got out of the house! I didn't know anything about it when I first came out of the house, because obviously we had no contact with the outside world, and we were relying on our PRs to set anything up. But the night I came out, both Lucien and I were told we were doing a photo shoot the next morning. I think it was clear, despite *OK!* maybe wanting more, that me and Lucien are good friends and I am not interested in him as anything more. But the pictures did look more couply, and I suppose I went along with that. Let's face it, showbiz isn't always 100 per cent the same as reality, and there are some bits that are a bit like acting, especially shoots. That was one where I just went with it.

I loved the whole *Big Brother* experience. It did feel like it helped correct what the public thought of me a bit. With shows like that, you see people come out thinking they have been themselves, but then because of one action, or the way they have been edited, you see the horror on their face when they realise they are hated. But one of the first people I spoke to when I came out was one of the production crew, and she said to me, 'You did really well in there. Everyone who writes you off as crazy, or an ex-druggie, has had to have a rethink! You kind of reminded people of the Kerry in the jungle, the nice one.'

And that made me feel really positive, as though the real me was back.

Moving on with Life

Getting the old me back – the best bits of her anyway – has been fun and exciting. But some things have been harder than others! Since *Big Brother* I had been unhappy with my figure, and kept comparing it to my body in my Atomic Kitten days.

The biggest downside of being in *Big Brother* was what it did to me on the health front. I had been so good since bootcamp at the start of that year. I had been doing all my exercises and routines and kept my eating healthy, but I got in there and it was like I lost my exercise mojo.

Yes, there was a gym in the house, but for some reason I always felt weird about using it. So instead we just used to spend loads of time sitting around and smoking. I have never smoked so much as I did in there, because it was so boring it was the only thing to do!

Can you believe I put on a stone in the short time in the house?! Sitting around all day long had not been good for me. No matter whether I lost weight or not, it just seemed that after having four kids, I had developed like a pouch around my stomach, and no matter what I did with my diet and exercise, I couldn't get rid of it. It wasn't fat, so much as excess skin, from where it had stretched when I was pregnant and then not sprung back into place as much as I would have liked. Even when I was down to 8st 7lb, when I did *Dancing on Ice* back at the start of 2011, it was still there, hanging out.

Then I got offered a free mini tummy tuck. That is not the same as a full-blown tummy tuck – for that, they cut you and pull your skin up, and have to move your belly button. But the one I had was a mini one. Despite what people thought, it wasn't for weight loss, it was purely for skin. So what they did was cut over the top of my caesarean scar, pull the skin up and sew it back up.

I had it done with The Hospital Group and again, it didn't cost me anything. I would never ever in a million years pay for surgery 'cause I can't afford it. So it makes me laugh, all these stories about 'Kerry's £10k surgery spree' and stuff like that. Nope, it was a £0k spree! Afterwards I just had to promote the surgeon who did it, and mention him in a photo shoot. It was a deal basically, and that is how I got it for free. If you can afford it, do it. I'd advise surgery to anybody who thinks it would make them feel better, but I would never ever pay for it. I see it as a luxury, but not something I can afford if I had to pay for it.

At the same time, I had liposuction on my knees. I wanted my bum done too but the doctor wouldn't do it, as he said I didn't need it. But with me knees, they were kind of lumpy. What happens when you have lipo is that the fat doesn't grow back in the same place, but if you then put weight on, the fat will reappear in a different place – and it is a lot bumpier. So I was getting these weird lumps sticking out by my knees. For other people, though, it might have appeared elsewhere. In the same way that everyone is a different shape, so their fat reappears in different places. It was an easy enough procedure, though, and left just a little mark that faded over time.

But that is the truth about my weight – not all the constant ridiculous stream of stories about other surgery plans and weight crazes I'm on. The latest, as I write this, claims that I am going to have butt implants. My arse is big enough, thank you!

I'd love to know who these bloomin' close sources are who are always quoted. I'm sure it's that ketchup and mustard in my fridge. They talk about as much sense anyway!

Other things have been much more important than my weight, of course. After *CBB*, I turned my attention back to my kids. It is crazy how quickly they grow, and I'm always scared that I am missing out on time with them.

I think I worry as well that because all four of them don't have their dads around, I need to make up for it by being an extra-attentive parent. But so far I think their dad's absences haven't stopped them being all-round amazing and well-balanced children.

Sadly, Mark has not kept up the visitation he promised the kids, of a weekend every two weeks. In a way I am glad but the other bit of me has always been so keen for them to keep up some kind of relationship.

But they would come back so filthy and dirty, and I would have to bathe them and get their clothes cleaned. It's heart-breaking. But he is still their dad and they always seemed like they had fun and they still want to see him. I would never stop that, but he needs to do it in a stable way.

The last time he saw them was in February 2012, a few days before Heidi's birthday. I remember asking when he dropped them off where her birthday card and present were, and he said she would get them next time he saw her.

For weeks after, she would bring it up. We were driving in the car one day and she just suddenly said, 'I bet Dad has got me loads of presents. I bet the card is so big it wouldn't fit in the post, so he has to wait to see me.' Then she went quiet again, lost in her own thoughts. It was heart-breaking. I always say Heidi is a really old soul in a little person's body – she sees and understands everything well before her time. It's frightening how intelligent and perceptive she is at times. And it worries me, 'cause I think it makes her more open to being hurt by her dad's actions.

A month later, when he still hadn't seen them, I dropped them with a mutual friend up north and sent him a text telling him they were waiting there to see him. I added, 'Mark, you need to see your kids.'

He just replied that it wasn't his turn, and said, 'I feel sorry for them kids having you as a mother. Wait 'til I get you back in that court, I'm going to show you now.'

I replied, 'I'm not texting you to row, Mark. I'm letting you know the babies are there. Whether you have them or not is up to you. If you don't want them, then at least drop a card off for Heidi, as she thinks you've not got her anything for her birthday. I will not protect you again.'

He didn't see them, but instead went off to New York with his girlfriend on holiday.

Next thing I know he sold a story to the *Sunday Mirror* newspaper claiming I had stopped him seeing his kids. What a liar – and I have kept all my texts to prove it.

I had to block him on Twitter he was giving me so much abuse, but he writes things like: 'Can't wait to get you back in court, bring you back down to earth. Your fans should really know what you are about.'

It's pathetic and just shows the bullying nature that for some weird reason I failed to notice when I was with him but which is so obvious to me now. I just look back and think, 'Kerry, what the hell were you thinking?!'

I did think Mark was a good dad when he was with me, but looking back I wonder if I pushed him into being that person.

And now he is out of the marriage, it is easier for him to duck the responsibility.

Part of me hopes that one day he sees sense and comes back into their lives, not for a fleeting visit but as a permanent part. Because watching my beautiful Heidi and Max, I can't imagine what father would ever not want to be involved with them every step of the way. Part of me knows it's very unlikely he'll ever change his ways, at least not for many years to come.

Early in 2012, a more positive thing happened – my manager from Atomic Kitten days, Martin O'Shea, got in touch. We hadn't spoken properly in 11 years because after I left Atomic Kitten I isolated myself. I lost everybody from that time really, even the other two girls, Natasha Hamilton and Liz McClarnon, and I had been especially close to Liz.

He had got in touch about a possible TV project with another of his clients, Crissy Rock, and he invited me to come and see her at the Liverpool Philharmonic. Well, after wetting myself with laughter all the way through her show, Martin and I caught up on old times and really clicked. We chatted for ages and it was like no time had passed. We had always been close and he had always looked after me in the Kittens – I admit at times it must have been an absolute nightmare! He had first approached me when I left CAN and we had met for a chat. Max told him he wasn't needed and that was that.

Now, in the January, we talked about where I was headed and what I really wanted to do next. He was still managing the Kittens as well as loads of other people. He also had a successful TV production company and lots of ideas for me and thought maybe I wasn't doing everything that I could be.

I told him about some other ideas I had and which I was getting excited about. It was great, because he got excited too, and that made me more excited! So I decided that I wanted Martin to be my manager and Max to still be my PR, which was how it used to be with James Grant. Ultimately, Max does PR and the management is kind of a side issue. But Max wasn't happy about that, and sadly we parted on pretty bad terms. In fact, he was furious. Which is a shame, because apart from the period after *This Morning* when I felt let down by him, I have always thought a lot of Max and would really like to still have him in my life. Being honest I didn't feel good about the conversation, or leaving things like that.

Another idea Martin and me discussed was to do with an Atomic Kitten reunion. He asked how I would feel about getting back together with the girls if the opportunity arose, and it kind of felt like the right time. I was excited about it, but it was also a terrifying idea. And there was also the question of Jenny Frost, who had replaced me when I left the group. How would she feel? Would we do it the four of us?

I hoped we would do it as a foursome. We're all grown up now, so I thought it would be fun, like a new chapter for the band. But it is all still up in the air – it may happen or may not, but fingers crossed! I know I'd do it at the drop of a hat, though, because being up on a stage, watching my girls watching me belt out those hits with my bandmates, well, that would just be indescribable.

I've really had the bug for music again in the last 6 months and have my own single, 'Feeling Love', which is about learning to love and accept who you are. I've learnt that the hard way but can finally say I'm Feeling Love – for who and what I am, a mother first and foremost.

I showcased it at a charity gig for the Cystic Fibrosis Trust in Glasgow, alongside a few of the old Atomic Kitten classics. I got a really good response. I was so scared before I went on stage that day, as it has been a long ol' time, but then I loved it. And the crowd's standing ovation didn't half give me a boost!

Then I performed at Gay Pride in Birmingham, which was really good. I sang live and the crowd loved it. More importantly, Molly and Lilly were there and I got them up on stage with me. You have to remember this is the first time they have ever seen me perform. They had never seen me up on stage before that, so to have them there watching, and then coming on stage and looking so happy and proud of me, was just really cool.

I have been working on other music too, including with Al Kapone, an American rapper who put down a rap for me on one of my songs, which was very cool. It was as part of a TV show I have done with David Gest, called *David's Fair Kerry*, which is due on TV next year. David produced the pilot and we spent ten days in Memphis, which was absolutely amazing. We met a great group of people, all legendary musicians in their own time, and were accepted as part of their community instantly. It was great fun. At the end of the shoot David and I cruised around the city in a Victorian pony and trap hurling fun and abuse at each other – partly for the cameras but partly because it was the end of our trip and we needed to let off a little steam at each other... David is another truly unique character and I love him dearly, mad as he is.

Bootcamp and the Speakmans have remained a constant in my life since my recovery. I regularly go and see Nik and Eva when I have something that I am trying to work through in my mind, and I consider them friends now as much as therapists. I credit them with saving my life, I really do.

As for GI Jane, I have been back there loads of times, probably for about 10 visits – so much so, I think I am part of the furniture!

I just go whenever I think I need to – sometimes for a week, sometimes just a couple of days.

The owner Sharon has become a genuine friend, and says I have really helped with the reputation of the camp – apparently lots of people go there because of having seen how much it has helped me. That is great. It makes me really proud to think other people have been helped by seeing what I've experienced. And on some level it makes it worthwhile. I like to think I've been through everything I have for a reason. Not just so that people keep going, 'Oh, poor Kerry.' No. I want people to see that I have been through this and come out the other side. It's now my turn to help change other people's lives and give them some kind of hope and inspiration. Think about it, if I have been through all the shit I have been through in my life – and you only have to read my two books to see what I have gone through – and I am not only still here but have got back on the straight and narrow, anyone can do it. The most important thing is to surround yourself with good people.

Ever since I had left bootcamp, I had been thinking about how I could get involved in doing something similar, but moving it on a level. Bootcamp had been amazing for me – without that, I would never have broken up with a bad husband or come off drugs. And as for weight, I know people may think I am a hypocrite for having had surgery, but my genuine opinion is that you can have all the surgery in the world and you won't lose weight, get fitter or tone up the way you can through exercise. And, more crucially, you won't get the mental benefits that come with it.

Rehab itself… I feel well placed to comment on it, as I have been enough times! And my problem with it is that it is expensive. This means it's often just for the select few, and I did often find the doctors and psychotherapists to be condescending.

As for the meds, well, this is something I have obviously worked through a lot in my own mind. I went into rehab the first time on no meds, and I came out rattling. Looking back, I feel that is almost a failure – that it is what they felt the need to do, and that I accepted it. Because, as I have learned myself, there are so many alternatives.

So Sharon and I started discussing options and how we could work together. And we have decided to set up what we are calling Project Reborn. The thinking being that I felt like I had been born again after bootcamp. Like I had a new lease of life. And, hopefully, we can make others feel the same.

It will be like a longer bootcamp, where people combine exercise with therapy. The power of exercise is so amazing, it can lift you from anything.

In the long run, we'd love to help people who can't afford rehab, either. I was lucky that I had the money to receive treatment in my down times. Because without that… well, I'm pretty damn sure you wouldn't be reading this book, as my story would have ended long ago.

Sadly, it is the same for thousands of others. They can't afford rehab, so they waste away their lives, or end up dying. So ideally we want to take in non-paying customers at some point too.

This is still all in the pipeline, though. It may well have moved on or changed a bit by the time you read this, but that is the plan for now. Hopefully we will have a TV show to go alongside the development of it, showing how life can work in a place like this. You know me, I love to get a camera crew involved!

One thing I was especially proud of in 2012 was getting a job presenting – on the very show where one of my biggest downfalls had happened!

I was invited back by *This Morning* to present a weekly slot about *Dancing on Ice* with Jeff Brazier, and I couldn't have been prouder. It was one of the things for me that truly proves the complete turnaround I have had in my life. Three years after my disastrous stint on the *This Morning* sofa, I was working for them.

And if I needed proof that I was doing a good job, they were nominated in March for a TRIC Award (from the Television Radio Industry Club) and the producers invited me to go along to the ceremony in the Grosvenor House Hotel and to be on the *This Morning* table. Not only that, but the show won the award for Best Daytime Programme – and they got me up onstage to accept it with them! I was flabbergasted. Who would have imagined that would be possible a few years back? Just being on the table was an enough of an award for me!

It goes to show that when people go through the stuff I've been through – whether it's drugs, bankruptcy, divorce – or you make some kind of a mistake in your life that feels at the time like it can't be repaired, well, actually, it can be. When you are at your lowest, the only way is up! You've just got to be true about who you are, true to yourself, and surround yourself with good people. And if I ever need reminded of that, I can just get out that video of me going 'bleugh, slur, bleugh' on *This Morning*. I feel sorry for that girl, but she is not me, I've moved on.

EPILOGUE

The Future

In August 2012, I moved into a new home. I wanted a new start for the kids and myself, in a new home with no memories apart from those we are about to create now, and I am aiming for them to all be happy ones.

It is a beautiful old country farmhouse set in the middle of nowhere in Surrey. We have roses growing up the walls, a swimming pool, a house next door for the nanny Cheryl to live in, and plenty of fields, which we are planning to fill with our own mini farm – micro pigs, micro goats… you name a micro animal, we have been to look at it!

I am so happy Cheryl is still with us. She and I really feel like a team – she is like the wife, staying home running the house most of the time, and I am like the husband, out earning money, but being home as much as I can. I couldn't do it without her – with Mark no longer around, and no family I can rely on to look after them, it would be impossible.

Sometimes I feel guilty when I go to work and am not with them, but then I have to earn money for us. And all my time that I am not in work, I am with the kids. Being a parent is the hardest job in the world, but also the most rewarding. Sometimes I want to scream at them all to 'shut up!' and they can be very trying – what kid isn't?

But other times, when I get in from a day's work, to find them all curled up on the sofa waiting for me, it is all worth it. Lilly will say, 'It's movie night, Mum, hurry up!' And Heidi will have decided what film we are watching: 'It's *How to Train Your Dragon* tonight, Mum – and no crying this time, 'cause you know it's a happy ending!'

And Max will climb into my lap and we'll all curl up together.

Or other nights, Molly will announce, 'Let's do some acting! Mum, tell me and Lilly where we are, and who we are.'

And I make up a situation: 'One of you is in a restaurant, and wants to complain to the other who is the waitress.' And before I know it, there is a full-blown play unfolding before me – these girls really have imaginations, I can tell you! And Heidi and Max sit back and watch too, not quite confident enough yet to join in. I can't help but sit back and feel proud and think how amazing our little family is.

Mum is a really important part of it too. She stuck to her decision to give up cocaine, which has made me more happy than anything she has done in a long time. I'm sure she has had the odd slip along the way – she says not – and I hope that's right. Despite all my doubts about her, thinking she was too deep in it to ever give it up, she proved me wrong. She has done so well. I am so, so proud of her for that.

I do worry about her health too, though. She still smokes about 30 cigarettes a day and drinks way too much. She is forever on the vodka still – her liver is screwed, but what can you do? It is her body and her decision about what she does with it. She's no different with or without a drink though, so I hope she can cut that out in time also.

At the end of the day, she's my mum and I idolise her. I love her to bits, I really do. I would say we are still mates rather than mother and daughter. That will never change. But she is a lot better than she used to be, a hundred times better. She has changed so much compared with the mum she used to be. Our relationship is much more healthy and adult now. We have both been through so much, and both come out the other side stronger for it.

I have spent a lot of time thinking over the past seven years, and wondering what I should have done differently, and if I could have prevented it all happening. But I've decided that I need to accept it, and I think I have come to terms with everything that has happened. Everything that has happened to me has made me who I am today and I'm ready for whatever comes next, stronger and wiser for it.

And if there is one bit of philosophy I am going to remember, it is something Nik and Eva taught me. If you lie down with dogs, you get up with fleas. And it doesn't matter how many times you treat those fleas, if you go back to those same dogs, you will get the fleas again. If my four years with Mark have taught me anything, it's that!

Instead I want to surround myself with strong positive people, who can be a bit of a safety net, although I hope I am strong enough now to never need them for that.

Financially I spent a long time wanting to get back at David McHugh, and expose him for the crook I believe him to be, but it was purely the fact I didn't have money to take him to court or to pursue an investigation that stopped me. But actually his true colours came out, and karma did the job for me. Because it turned out I hadn't been the only person to have trouble with him.

David's offices were raided around the time I was splitting with Mark. The police told me they had found lots of boxes in the ceiling panels, with dozens of cheque books in my name, as well as lots of companies related to me, which I didn't even know existed. 'Kerry Katona enterprises', 'Katona Ltd', 'KK Amusements', all that kind of thing. It was insane. No wonder I didn't have a clue where my money was!

But it seemed like what happened with me was minor in comparison with other stuff. In 2011, David was jailed for 3 years and 8 months, after apparently being part of an international multi-billion-pound fraud conspiracy since early 2008, which had taken money off other investors for fake projects. Hmm, that sounds familiar! Apparently he has been convicted of 40 offences since 2000. So yep, good choice of accountant, Mark…

And although he has never been prosecuted for my financial dealings, I feel like at least that proved what I have said about him all along. If only I had trusted my instincts.

As far as men go, I have never been so mentally bruised and damaged by someone as I was by Mark Croft. How a man can treat his wife and the mother of his kids the way he treated me, I will never understand. But if there is one thing I have proved to myself, it is that I can bounce back from anything. And, luckily, I think I am still the same girl I once was underneath it all. Mark wasn't able to break me.

For now, I plan to do without a man for a while. My good friend Danielle is newly single as well, and we are intending to enjoy the single life together. Although, I hold my hands up, I know I always say that, and then end up falling for 'the one!'. But this time I really am going to try. And I do think it will be different, as I feel stronger by myself.

Of course it would be nice if I could find someone one day. I still have the romantic idea of finding my soul mate and growing old with them, and if that can happen, then great.

But for now I feel happier with myself, and more confident. I don't need a man to complete me anymore, I am happy it just being the kids and me.

As for drugs, I know in my heart I will never go near them again. I've been there, done that – way too much! – and I know how damaging the consequences are.

And that is one of the reasons I have done this book and made it as open and as honest as I have been. Not just to warn others off them, but in particular my children. One day when they are older, I hope they read this book, and learn from it, and I pray they do not make the same mistakes that I have. My biggest hope is that I can keep them on the straight and narrow and provide them with the best possible future.

I know I go on about it, but I couldn't be more proud of my children. They really are my greatest achievement in life and give me my real reason for living. And I feel really positive about my future as well, and just want to keep working on improving myself.

I have learned a *hell* of a lot over the last few years, and feel like I am only getting stronger. I have gone from Queen of The Jungle to some of the deepest and darkest depths possible. But I have climbed back up again, and despite it all, I'm still standing, and that's what really counts.

Useful contacts

The Priory
Priory Lane
Roehampton
London
SW15 5JJ
020 8876 8261

GI Jane Bootcamp
0208 301 4353
e-mail:info@gijanebootcamp.co.uk
www.gijanebootcamp.co.uk

Nik and Eva Speakman
e-mail: info@speakman.tv
www.speakman.tv

Photo credits

I was still a kid myself at this stage but the rot was already setting in my brain © Glenn Copus/Evening Standard/Rex Features

Lilly was the image of me at this age. Her accent is now the opposite of mine © Mark Campbell/Rex Features

Coleen Nolan and I remain great mates today © Mark Campbell/Rex Features

Still upsets me now seeing this. Realisation that my life was falling apart was starting to dawn on me © Mark Campbell/Rex Features

Getting to grips with what the ice really meant © Ken McKay/Rex Features

On my way... © Ken McKay/ITV/Rex Features

Dancing on Ice was a big step up in me realising I could turn my life around, with the likes of Dan helping me beyond words © Ken McKay/ITV/Rex Features

Happy with life and look where I was headed... hello *Big Brother* © David Fisher/Rex Features

So happy I got as far as I did. I had so much fun in the *Big Brother* house © Rex Features

At Birmingham Pride – my first proper gig in 10 years © McPix Ltd/Rex Features

Molly as fearless and cool as ever © McPix Ltd/Rex Features

Helping the Dreams Come True gang – very inspirational people © McPix Ltd/Rex Features

Happy times with the amazing *This Morning* team. It's crazy how things have come full circle, but I am so happy to be where I am today © Ken McKay/Rex Features